"Vegan baking comes of age with this collection of baked delights. Colleen Patrick-Goudreau has put together a comprehensive tome that is sure to be useful to baking novices as well as those of us who've been wielding the whisk for years."
—Isa Moskowitz, author of *Veganomicon*, *Vegan Cupcakes Take Over the World*, and others

"Finally! A contemporary dessert book with all the traditional favorites—that happen to be vegan!"
—Tanya Petrovna, chief executive officer, Native Foods Restaurant Group

"I just love this book! I can't wait to give it to all my friends—both the vegans and nonvegans alike—who will learn and will undergo an instant conversion experience!"
—Jeffrey Masson, author of *When Elephants Weep* and *Altruistic Armadillos, Zenlike Zebras*

"Whether you want to prepare an occasional vegan meal, or make vegan eating a major part of your lifestyle, *The Joy of Vegan Baking* will take you the next step forward."
—John Robbins, author of *Healthy At 100*, *The Food Revolution*, and *Diet For A New America*

"Thanks for nothing, Colleen. Now, I want to quit my job and spend a year exploring each and every incredible recipe in this book."
—Matt Ball, co-founder of Vegan Outreach

"*Eating dessert first* is not a mantra of which mothers would approve, and it's usually risky for those who avoid cream, eggs, and butter. Until now. *The Joy of Vegan Baking* corrects both of these non-edible edicts so that everyone, no matter where she falls along the dietary spectrum, can enjoy traditional baked goods without compromise. Colleen Patrick-Goudreau blends the perfect mix of stories, photos, and recipes with amazing grace and taste. Her words will open your heart; her recipes will fill your tummy."
—*VegNews* Magazine

Revised
and Updated
Edition

The Joy of Vegan Baking

MORE THAN 150 TRADITIONAL TREATS & SINFUL SWEETS

COLLEEN PATRICK-GOUDREAU

FAIR WINDS

Brimming with creative inspiration, how-to projects, and useful information to enrich your everyday life, Quarto Knows is a favorite destination for those pursuing their interests and passions. Visit our site and dig deeper with our books into your area of interest: Quarto Creates, Quarto Cooks, Quarto Homes, Quarto Lives, Quarto Drives, Quarto Explores, Quarto Gifts, or Quarto Kids.

Text © 2007, 2017 Colleen Patrick-Goudreau

First published in 2007 by Fair Winds Press,
an imprint of The Quarto Group,
100 Cummings Center, Suite 265-D,
Beverly, MA 01915, USA.
T (978) 282-9590 F (978) 283-2742
www.QuartoKnows.com

Fair Winds Press titles are also available at discount for retail, wholesale, promotional, and bulk purchase. For details, contact the Special Sales Manager by email at specialsales@quarto.com or by mail at The Quarto Group, Attn: Special Sales Manager, 401 Second Avenue North, Suite 310, Minneapolis, MN 55401, USA.

21 20 19 18 17   2 3 4 5

ISBN: 978-1-59233-763-7

Originally found under the following Library of Congress Cataloging-in-Publication Data
Patrick-Goudreau, Colleen.
The joy of vegan baking : traditional treats and sinful sweets / Colleen Patrick-Goudreau.
p. cm.
Includes index.
ISBN 1-59233-280-3
1. Vegan cookery. I. Title.
TX837.P337 2008
641.5'636--dc22
2007016559

Cover and book design by Rita Sowins / Sowins Design
Photography by Glenn Scott Photography
Food and Prop Styling by Natasha St. Hailare Taylor
Cover photo and images appearing on pages 14–15, 40–41, 84, 85, 94, 95, 134, 135, 244–245, 258, 259, 302–303, and 304 by Michelle Cehn Photography

Printed and bound in China

THIS BOOK IS DEDICATED TO EACH AND EVERY PERSON WILLING TO CHALLENGE THE PRECONCEPTIONS AND ABANDON THE MISCONCEPTIONS OF WHAT "VEGAN BAKING" REALLY MEANS.

"DON'T DO NOTHING BECAUSE YOU CAN'T DO EVERYTHING. DO SOMETHING—ANYTHING!"

—COLLEEN PATRICK-GOUDREAU

CONTENTS

INTRODUCTION
The Whys and Wherefores of Choosing Vegan 9
A Journey to Compassionate Living 9
Why Vegan? 17

CHAPTER ONE
The How-to's and What-nots of Vegan Baking 19
Better Than Eggs 19
Better Than Cow's Milk 27
Better than Buttermilk, Condensed Milk, and 30
    Evaporated Milk
Better Than Butter 31
How to Read a Recipe 34

CHAPTER TWO
Rise and Shine: Muffins, Biscuits, and Scones 39

CHAPTER THREE
Cozy Comforts: Sweet and Savory Quick Breads 57

CHAPTER FOUR
Cause for Celebration: Cakes and Cupcakes 75

CHAPTER FIVE
Timeless Temptations: Pies and Tarts 101

CHAPTER SIX
Familiar Favorites: Cookies, Brownies, and Bars 117

CHAPTER SEVEN
Bearing Fruit: Crumbles, Cobblers, Crisps, ... 141
    and Whole Fruit Desserts

CHAPTER EIGHT
Decadent Delicacies and Elegant Eats: Strudel, Crêpes,   161
Blintzes, and Pastries

CHAPTER NINE
Ancient Wonders: Yeast Breads and Rolls   175

CHAPTER TEN
Creamy Concoctions: Mousses and Puddings   191

CHAPTER ELEVEN
Sweet Somethings: Confections and Candy   203

CHAPTER TWELVE
Frozen Treats: Sorbets, Shakes, and Smoothies   213

CHAPTER THIRTEEN
Fundamental Foundations: Crusts for Pies and Tarts   221

CHAPTER FOURTEEN
Restorative Refreshments: Hot and Cold Beverages   229

CHAPTER FIFTEEN
Over the Top: Frostings, Sauces, Syrups, and Spreads   241

LAST BUT NOT LEAST: THE APPENDICES
Appendix I: Stocking Your Vegan Pantry   260
Baking Staples: A Guide to Ingredients   260
Essential Kitchen Tools   267
Resources and Recommendations   270
Appendix II: Making Sense of It All   273
Glossary of Terms   273
Cake Pan Substitutes   276
Common Ingredients: Yields and Equivalents   280
Baking Soda and Baking Powder: What's the Difference?   282
Suggested Reading   284
Suggested Viewing   286

FINDING YOUR WAY: THE INDICES
Index I: General   287
Index II: Seasonal   297
Index III: Celebrations and Occasions   299
ACKNOWLEDGMENTS   300
ABOUT THE AUTHOR   304

INTRODUCTION: THE WHYS AND WHEREFORES OF CHOOSING VEGAN

A Journey to Compassionate Living

The foods we choose, the meals we plan, and the way we construct our plates are all habits. They're cultural, personal, familial, and social habits, but they're all habits. Deeply ingrained, these habits are tied to our most basic needs and earliest memories. As children, we received applause for finishing our dinner and admonishments for not cleaning our plates. Food was used as both reward and punishment, and the eating habits and patterns with which we grew up still inform our adult choices.

Despite how little people cook these days, the kitchen remains the center—the heart—of the home. No matter how small, it is the room that everyone gravitates to, and it is there that we celebrate family traditions and create new ones around what we eat. Simple images and recollections arouse pleasurable emotions for most of us: picking fruit from a tree, gathering vegetables from a home garden, cooling a homemade pie on a windowsill, or using a recipe that has been passed down from previous generations. And yet despite our strong attachment to food, most of us know very little about the processes by which it winds up on our plates. The rest of us say we don't want to know.

SELECTIVE COMPASSION

Born in a suburban New Jersey town, I grew up during the 1970s eating everything from roast beef and hamburgers to cupcakes and ice cream—and lots of
it! My father owned several ice cream stores, and we had a separate freezer for
the tubs he would bring home. From a child's perspective, it was a pretty fantastic way to grow up. Looking back, I realize that much of my bliss was due to my
ignorance about what I was actually eating.

I didn't know that my steak was from the same cattle I admired at the
petting zoo; that pork, veal, and lamb chops were from the backs of baby pigs,
calves, and sheep, whose adorable faces were depicted on all of my childhood
clothing; or that the ice cream, on which I so voraciously feasted, was made
with the eggs of hens, whose maternal instincts, lauded in all the books read to
me, were denied so I could eat their eggs. I had no idea. And nobody told me.
Even when I asked.

In fact, my parents, like many in our society, created in me a contradictory
attitude toward animals. On the one hand, I grew up in an environment that
used the images of baby animals to create feelings of peace, joy, and security.
On the other hand, I was fed these very same animals. My bedroom was not
unlike that of any other child. Animals were everywhere—hanging over my crib,
stuffed on my bed, painted on my walls, and printed and sewn on almost every
piece of fabric I wore. Even more striking is the fact that animals—in books, on
television, and at school—were used to teach me my most basic skills: how to
count, spell, read, and talk. Through the use of myths and fables, animals even
taught me such values as respect and kindness.

Like most children, I had a natural instinct to act compassionately toward
animals. I cried when Bambi's mother was shot, I wept when Dumbo was sep-
arated from his mother, I helped baby birds back into their nests, I adored my
dog, and I took in stray animals. The adults around me, as well as my parents—
like all parents who seek to encourage compassion in their children—were
supportive of my actions and praised my responses. Kindness toward animals

is usually a good indication of a child's ability to empathize with others. It's a virtue we admire.

But when I asked about what I was eating—about where my hot dogs came from, for instance—the adults around me either evaded the question entirely or deceived me completely, creating specious arguments and misleading justifications for eating animals, their milk, and their eggs. The adults around me spent so much time disguising, rationalizing, romanticizing, and ritualizing eating animals that, as a child, I was totally unaware that I was saving one bird while eating another. By the time I was four or five, my innate childhood compassion and empathy for animals was dulled, and I learned that animals were arbitrarily categorized in our society: those worthy of our compassion and those undeserving of it because they happen to be of a particular species. Puppies, good. Calves, food.

AN AWAKENING

I was nineteen years old when I read John Robbins' book *Diet for a New America*, which looks at how our animal-based diet affects the animals, our health, and the Earth. It was the first time I had ever seen the images of "food animals," regarded merely as machines and valued only for what they could produce. I saw hens in cages with the tips of their beaks seared off, female "breeding" pigs confined in crates the size of their own overgrown bodies, turkeys packed in windowless sheds, calves chained to wooden boxes. I remember staring at those photos in utter shock. How could I not have known about this? How could this even happen? I knew I didn't want to be part of it, so I stopped eating land animals that very day.

People didn't quite react the same way they did as when I was a child. Helping fallen baby birds and taking in stray animals were considered admirable childhood pursuits, but when that very same compassion followed me into adulthood and extended to pigs, cattle, chickens, and other animals killed for human consumption, it was met with hostility and suspicion. Despite the fact that my motivation to become vegetarian sprang from the very source that compelled me to intervene in animals' lives when I was a child, praise and encouragement were replaced with defensiveness and anger. Although I was surprised, confused, and even a little hurt, I wasn't deterred.

I read every book I could get my hands on. The Internet was in its infancy, so I relied on library resources, literature from nonprofit groups, and the few videos that were available. My eyes were open, but I wasn't fully awake. I began reaching out to others, informing them about what I learned, but I was still disconnected. I was eating sea animals, and I was consuming chickens' eggs and cow's milk. I justified my actions by declaring that I was buying "free-range" eggs and "organic" milk, as if these marketing terms absolved me from my responsibility. But I stopped consuming fish when I realized my reasons for eating them were as arbitrary as my reasons for eating land animals.

My true awakening was yet to come, and it's the one that expanded every aspect of my life and subsequently led to the cookbook you're holding in your hands. I read a book called *Slaughterhouse: The Shocking Story of Greed, Neglect, and Inhumane Treatment Inside the U.S. Meat Industry* by investigative journalist Gail Eisnitz. In the few excruciatingly painful days it took me to read this book, I literally woke up. I woke up to the truth about our treatment of animals and realized that no matter how they were raised and what they were raised for (their flesh, eggs, or milk), they all wind up in the same horrible place: the slaughterhouse. I had been deceived into believing that somehow the chickens' eggs and cow's milk I had been consuming were from animals who were protected from harm and even spared death. I was very wrong. The process of breeding, transporting, and killing young and innocent lives is ugly and violent—whether on a small farm or in a large factory-type operation—and I wanted nothing to do with it.

A VOCATION

My outreach increased, and I found that most people had the same reaction I did. Their first question was always "How can this happen?" But it was their subsequent questions that led me to begin teaching cooking classes. "Where do I shop?" "What do I eat?" "How do I cook?" "Will I get enough protein?" "Where will I get my calcium?" "Will I get enough iron?" I realized that a huge gap needed to be filled, one that would provide resources, answers, and empowerment to people who desperately wanted to make a change but just didn't have the tools to do so. In response, I began teaching vegan cooking classes and conducting workshops.

When I look back, I realize that I always loved being in the kitchen and around food. One of my favorite pastimes was playing "supermarket." My playroom was full of empty food boxes and containers that my mother would save for me. I would set them up all around the room and invite everyone to come and shop! I even had a little shopping cart, a cash register, and fake money. As I grew up, I derived pleasure from shopping in a real grocery store, because I loved nurturing people with food. Despite this, I had no interest in building a career around cooking—my first passions had always been writing and reading—so, I pursued a bachelor's and a master's degree, both in English literature.

It may seem odd that someone who taught cooking classes, produces cooking videos, and has written three cookbooks has had no formal training in the culinary arts, but I think the fact that I'm self-taught is even more beneficial for those who follow my recipes. If I can do it, so can they. (Incidentally, neither Martha Stewart nor *Joy of Cooking* author Irma Rombauer had formal culinary training.) I've learned much in the many years I've been teaching, and I have much more to learn, but one thing I know for sure is that people are learning, they're becoming empowered, vegan cuisine is being demystified, new advocates for the animals emerge every day, and more and more people are aligning their behavior with their principles.

I feel privileged to combine my skills and passion and am honored to witness the many transformations I see people experience. I never set out to "convert" anyone, and yet over the two decades I've been doing this work, I've guided thousands of people through the transition. My intention has always been to raise awareness and offer a different perspective to allow people to find their own answers. With every book I write, every lecture I give, every recipe I share, and every podcast episode I record, I'm responsible only for speaking my truth and sowing the seeds that others may one day reap. I strive to have no attachment to what people do with the information I provide. Their journey is their own, though I am grateful to be a messenger along the way. That's all any of us are.

THE POWER OF KNOWING

I've heard people say that eating vegan is "limiting" and "restrictive," and I couldn't disagree more. In fact, I find that it's quite the opposite. Your awareness is expanded. You try foods and cuisines you never even noticed before. The compassion you knew as a child is restored—and fully manifested. But even more than that, I find that living in such a way that we cut ourselves off from the truth, from *our* truth, is what's truly limiting. People tend to avoid knowing about how the animals suffer not just because it's too painful for them but also because they know deep down inside that once they find out this information, they're going to *want* to make a change, and it's *change* they're afraid of: afraid of not knowing what it will look like and how it will change their lives. So instead, we choose fear. We create boundaries to our compassion. We choose ignorance over knowledge. We choose complacency over empowerment. To my mind, *that's* restrictive, *that's* limiting.

Every time we say "I don't want to know," we limit our potential for growth, change, and making possible everything we want to be and everything we want this world to be. What could be more limiting than cutting ourselves off from our own compassion, our own values? Quite the contrary, being vegan is about knowing, exploring, evolving, participating, and taking responsibility. Being vegan is about removing barriers and embracing what it means to be human—experiencing sorrow as well as joy. To my mind, *that's* expansive. *That's* abundance.

It was only when I was willing to know—willing to look—at how I contributed to the suffering of animals that I woke up. When I was a child, I acted compassionately without any thought—as if I didn't know any better than to respond to those who needed my help. It just came naturally. Now that I'm an adult, I act compassionately *with* thought, and I regret only that the innocent kindness of a child is valued more than the informed kindness of an adult. Though the process of desensitization was full and complete by the time I was a young adult, I'm grateful it was not irreversible, and I fully embrace what I hope will be my legacy: unabashed, unfettered, unconditional compassion.

Why Vegan?

Derived from the beginning and end of the word "vegetarian," the word "vegan" (VEE-gun) was coined in 1944 by British activist Donald Watson (1910–2005), founder of the first vegan organization, who was frustrated that the word "vegetarian" had come to include dairy products and eggs. He defined "veganism" as a "philosophy and way of living which seeks to exclude—as far as is possible and practical—all forms of exploitation of and cruelty to animals for food, clothing, or any other purpose."

Watson's definition is a profound statement in a world where the pursuit of pleasure is considered a right rather than a privilege. Despite assumptions and misconceptions about veganism, it's not about asceticism or martyrdom. It's not about deprivation and sacrifice. It's not about being perfect, and it's not about being pure. Though vegans try to avoid all animal products, it is virtually impossible to avoid every hidden, animal-derived ingredient, particularly because many show up in such common items as books (glue), car tires (rubber), organic produce (fertilizing manure), and even our water (bones are sometimes used as filters in treatment plants). Being vegan is a *means* to prevent suffering rather than an end in itself. The goal is to prevent cruelty to animals, not to become a 100 percent certified vegan. There is no such thing—the world is just too imperfect for that. But there is much we can do, and being vegan is an easy and effective step to creating the world we all envision.

Individually and collectively, we all say we want to make a difference in the world, find meaning in our lives, and create meaning in the lives of others. We want to make a positive contribution to the world and leave it a better place than we found it. Many people say these things, but they don't realize that to make a difference, they may have to do something *different*. They don't realize the power they have to make this happen, and some don't even try. I learned long ago that it's not that we can make a difference in the world, it's that we do make a difference in the world—every day, with every choice we make. Every action we take, every product we buy, every dollar we spend, everything we do has an effect on something or someone else. *There are no neutral actions.* I think this idea is both frightening and empowering for many. It's frightening because it means we're responsible and have a tremendous amount of power. It's empowering because it means we're responsible and have a tremendous amount of power. *We* get to choose not whether we want to make a difference but whether we want to make a *positive* difference or a negative difference.

I'm vegan for a very simple reason: I don't want to contribute to violence against animals—any animal, including humans—and the slaughter industry is inherently violent for everyone involved. There is no greater feeling than knowing that my behavior is aligned with my values. Regardless of why we decide to "choose vegan," we can take solace in the fact that our choices have a profound impact—on human rights, workers' rights, human health, wildlife preservation, world hunger, and our own health. Like the waves created by a stone thrown into water, the ripples extend beyond our control, beyond our intentions. Eating vegan is a powerful, compassionate, and healthful way to live. And as you'll discover with the recipes provided herein, it's most definitely a delicious way to live.

THE JOY OF VEGAN BAKING

CHAPTER ONE

THE HOW-TO'S AND WHAT-NOTS OF VEGAN BAKING

One of the reasons people are incredulous when they think of "vegan baking" is because they can't imagine that delicious baked goods are possible without butter, eggs, and dairy. It is more accurate to say that baked goods rely on fat, moisture, and leavening—all of which exist outside of animal products. The options for obtaining these qualities may be unfamiliar at first, but they are indeed endless and quite a bit healthier than their conventional counterparts.

Better Than Eggs

Did you know that about 70 percent of the calories in eggs are from fat, and a large portion of that fat is saturated? Eggs are also loaded with cholesterol—about 213 milligrams for an average-sized egg.

Chickens' eggs have a long history in baked goods, but they are certainly not indispensable. Baking without eggs has been done for centuries, for religious, health, and ethical reasons. During the great wars of the twentieth century—when "luxury foods" (i.e., animal products) were scarce—people perfected the art of eggless baking.

One of the joys of egg-free baking is being able to lick the bowl without the fear of being exposed to salmonella! The Centers for Disease Control and Prevention estimates that 48 million Americans get sick from foodborne illnesses each year, resulting in 4,000 annual deaths. Every year, there are more than a million salmonella-related cases of food poisoning, and 400 of them are fatal. Eggs with salmonella pose a threat to one out of every 50 people each year, and since bacteria are most likely to be in the whites of the egg, it is a myth to think that it's a safe "alternative" to the cholesterol- and fat-laden yolk.

DESSERT CRÊPE,
PAGE 166. CHOCOLATE
ALMOND SPREAD,
PAGE 257.

As with any new cuisine you're trying for the first time, there is a learning curve. Most of us were taught that chickens' eggs were essential for baking, and such strongly ingrained habits can be hard to change. It may feel like you're learning to bake all over again, but I assure you, once you begin practicing these new techniques, new habits will replace the old ones, and you'll never look back again. Baking without eggs will become as natural to you as laying eggs is to chickens.

GENERAL SUGGESTIONS FOR REPLACING EGGS

Chickens' eggs perform various functions in baked goods, from binding and leavening to adding moisture and richness, all of which can be replicated as well—if not better—with healthful, plant-based ingredients. Some recipes do well with just vinegar and baking soda, others are better with tofu, and still others really shine with the use of a commercial egg replacer. A new discovery called "aquafaba" offers yet another option. When I include a replacement at all, I tend to default to "flax eggs" (see below), but my suggestion is to follow the recipes as I have written them.

Below is an overview of which ingredients work best when, in what quantities, and where you can find them.

What? Vinegar and Baking Soda

Why? The chemical in baking soda is bicarbonate of soda ($NaHCO_3$). When combined with an acidic ingredient, such as vinegar, cocoa, or citrus, baking soda releases carbon dioxide that forms into bubbles in the food. When heated, these bubbles expand and help to rise or lighten the final product.

How? A ratio I find that works well is 1 teaspoon of baking soda along with 1 tablespoon (15 ml) of vinegar. Apple cider vinegar and white distilled vinegar are the two I use most frequently.

When? I find this combination works best in cakes, cupcakes, and quick breads.

Where? Most grocery stores carry vinegar and baking soda.

What? Ground Flaxseed

Perhaps you haven't eaten flax, but most likely you've worn it! Flax has been used to produce linen for more than 5,000 years. A beautiful and versatile plant, flax is also used to make dye, paper, medicines, and soap.

Why? Flaxseed is the most concentrated source of essential omega-3 fatty acids, so it should be a staple in your diet even if you're not using it for baking! Always buy whole flaxseed (golden or brown) and grind it yourself using a coffee grinder for best results. Once you grind it, store it in a glass container in the fridge or freezer. Consume 2 teaspoons a day by adding it to a fruit smoothie, oatmeal, cereal, soup, salad, or just eating it on its own.

How? For each egg you replace, whisk 1 tablespoon (15 g) of ground flaxseed with 3 tablespoons (45 ml) of water in a blender or food processor until the mixture is thick and creamy.

When? Because flaxseed has a nutty flavor, it works best in baked goods that are grainier and nuttier, such as waffles, pancakes, bran muffins, breads, and oatmeal cookies.

Where? You can often buy flaxseed in the bulk section of natural/health food stores. Ask your local grocer to carry it if they don't already.

COLLEEN'S TIP: *Though you may find ground flaxseed or "flax meal" in your grocery store, I recommend buying the whole seeds and grinding them yourself. I realize this adds an extra step, but it's better in terms of freshness and flavor and for ensuring that you absorb the healthful omega-3 fatty acids, which may not be as available in the finely ground meal.*

What? Ripe Banana

Did you know that bananas are among the most widely consumed food in the world? Most banana farmers receive a low price for their produce, so look for the "fair trade" label when purchasing this tropical fruit.

Why? Packed with potassium and magnesium, bananas provide a great energy boost when you need it, so eat them as a snack, put them on your cereal, or add them to your morning smoothie for a great way to start the day.

How? Although mashed bananas are great binding ingredients in baked goods, they aren't necessarily a measure-for-measure replacement. In general, consider half a mashed or pureed banana as a replacement for one or two eggs.

When? Bananas are fantastic "egg replacers" in baking, particularly in breads, muffins, cakes, and pancakes. I don't use bananas, however, when I don't want the banana flavor, so consider this factor when deciding.

Where? Although I advocate shopping seasonally and locally as much as possible, it's hard to follow this rule when it comes to buying bananas, unless you live in the tropics. Be sure to look for those labeled "fair trade" and "organic."

What? Applesauce

Choose organic applesauce, as apples are among the most commonly sprayed fruits.

Why? Because apples are just plain good! Full of fiber and vitamin C, apples are as versatile as they are delicious.

In baking, applesauce not only acts as a binding agent, but it's also a good substitute for eggs or oil when you want to reduce fat and calories.

How? ¼ cup (60 g) of unsweetened applesauce equals one egg. Anywhere from ¾ cup (80 g) to 1 cup (185 g) of applesauce equals 1 cup of butter (225 g) or oil (235 ml). Rather than replace all the eggs or oil in a recipe with applesauce, try replacing just half.

When? Unsweetened applesauce provides the binding and moisture you need in baked goods. It works best when you want the results to be moist, such as in cakes, quick breads, and brownies.

Where? From your local farmer, of course! If you're not going to make your own applesauce, choose organic with no added sugars.

NO-BAKE CHOCOLATE
PUDDING TART, PAGE 114.
RASPBERRY SAUCE
(COULIS), PAGE 248.
BROWNIE CRUST, PAGE 227.

What? Silken Tofu

Tofu is made by soaking, boiling, and straining fresh soybeans and adding a coagulating agent to produce the desired texture. Silken tofu, often used to make puddings, mousses, and pie fillings, is the softest and creamiest type and is often sold in aseptic or vacuum-packed boxes. You'll find them on the shelves not in the refrigerators in the grocery store—usually in the Asian foods section. You may store it unrefrigerated for many months until you open it. Don't be confused, because silken tofu comes in soft, firm, and extra-firm varieties, all of which are pretty similar to one another. Recipes will often specify which to use.

Why? Soybeans, like all beans, are rich in protein and fiber. Like all plant foods, soybeans—and soy-based foods such as tofu, tempeh, and miso—contain no cholesterol and very little, if any, saturated fat. Calcium and iron contents vary according to the brand, and organic soy is the way to go.

How? Whip ¼ cup (55 g) in a blender or food processor until smooth and creamy, leaving no chunks. You may need to turn off the food processor and scrape down the sides. This equals one egg.

When? I find the silken tofu "egg" works best when you want rich, dense, and moist cakes and brownies.

Where? Many grocery stores carry silken tofu these days, but you'll definitely find it in a natural food store. If your local grocer doesn't carry it, request it. Look for vacuum-packed silken tofu on the shelves, or the silken tofu in the refrigerated section. The former tends to be slightly creamier than the latter.

What? Commercial Egg Replacer Powder

There are at least two commercial "egg replacers" available, both of which are essentially made from potato starch that acts as eggs in baked goods. Ener-G Egg Replacer and Bob's Red Mill Egg Replacer are fabulous products that last forever in your pantry, providing a convenient and economical alternative to perishable chickens' eggs. For instance, one 16-ounce (455-g) box of Ener-G Egg Replacer makes the equivalent of 112 eggs!

Why? The benefit of a commercial egg replacer is that it can sit on the shelf for a long time, so I always have it around. I use it more often than any other egg replacer, but it doesn't add any nutritional value, per se, as in the case of tofu, flaxseed, or bananas.

How? Follow the instructions on the box. In the case of Ener-G Egg Replacer, mix 1½ teaspoons of the egg replacer powder with 2 tablespoons (30 ml) of water to produce one egg. The ratio for Bob's Red Mill is like that of flaxseed: 1 tablespoon (6 g) of powder mixed with 3 tablespoons (45 ml) of water. I find the results are best for both when you whip the mixture in a food processor or blender to make it thick and creamy. (Note: The recipes in the book that call for commercial egg replacer specify Ener-G Egg Replacer.)

When? Whereas I tend to use silken tofu or no "eggs" at all when making cakes and muffins, I find commercial egg replacer works best in cookies.

Where? You can find these brands at most health food stores and in some larger supermarkets, but also consider asking your local grocer to carry it.

What? Vegan Egg

Created by Follow Your Heart (the brand that created Vegenaise), the revolutionary Vegan Egg can be used the same way you used to use chicken's eggs: as scrambles, omelets, and quiches—and also in baked goods. Here are tips from followyourheart.com, where you can also find where to buy near you:

If your recipe calls for:
* 1 egg—use 1 pre-mixed VeganEgg with no adjustment
* 2 eggs—4 level tablespoons of VeganEgg powder and ¾ cup cold water (175 ml)
* 3–4 eggs—reduce the amount of water you'd need by about ½ per VeganEgg. So you'd need about ¼ cup (60 ml) water per egg

What? Aquafaba

In December 2014, French chef Joël Roessel, discovered that the liquid from canned beans such as chickpeas has a chemical composition that mimics the functional properties of egg whites. Hence, aquafaba ("water from beans," coined by Goose Wholt) was born. It is taking the vegan world by storm and used to make everything from whipped cream, buttercream frosting, nougat, marshmallows, fudge, cakes, waffles, cookies, mayo, butter, and even meringue. Yes, meringue. Everything you need to know is at www.aquafaba.com, the official Aquafaba website, to which I credit this helpful information:

Generally 3 tablespoons of aquafaba (the liquid left over from a drained can of beans or from the cooking liquid from homemade beans) replace one chicken's egg, but this really depends on whether your aquafaba is close to the right consistency. It should be a bit slimy, but not too thick, and not too runny. Ideally it should be the same consistency as egg whites. If you are using aquafaba from a can of beans and it seems very watery, you can reduce it on the stove by 25 or 33 percent to get a slightly thicker consistency. Thicker is generally better, but you don't want it to end up goopy or solid, so don't reduce too much.

Other Ways to Replace Eggs

Chickens' eggs are often called upon to act as a thickener in sauces, gravies, custards, desserts, and beverages. Pastries and breads also use an "egg wash" to glaze their tops. Here are ways to get the same effect without the use of eggs.

For Thickening:

✳ **Kudzu:** This is a high-quality starch made from the root of the kudzu plant that grows wild in the mountains of Japan and in the southern region of the United States. When added to water and heated, kudzu powder becomes clear and thickens whatever you add it to. Though it is more expensive than other thickeners, such as arrowroot and cornstarch, I prefer it for its effectiveness and lack of flavor. I find that arrowroot can sometimes have a chalky aftertaste if not mixed properly. To prepare kudzu, dissolve 1 tablespoon (7 g) in 2 tablespoons (30 ml) of cool liquid, mix well, then stir slowly into whatever sauce you are cooking. Once it begins to heat, you will notice the liquid start to thicken. Continue stirring and let it cook for at least 5 minutes.

* **Agar:** Derived from the Malay word "agar-agar," which means "jelly," agar comes from a type of seaweed that is odorless and tasteless. It becomes gelatinous when dissolved in hot water and cooled. It's ideal when you want a vegetarian gelatin, and it is used often in jellies, ice cream, and Japanese desserts.
* **Arrowroot:** This is a fine, easy-to-digest starch from the rhizomes of the West Indian arrowroot plant. Because it's so fine, it dissolves well and is a great thickener.
* **Cornstarch:** Cornstarch (also known as cornflour) is ground from the endosperm, or white heart, of the corn kernel. Whereas wheat flour works equally well as a binder and thickener in puddings and sauces, cornstarch is especially useful when you want to avoid gluten, as some people cannot digest wheat protein. In pies, flour tends to work best with apples, and cornstarch works really well with berries.
* **Flour:** Flour works well as a thickener, though it should always be whisked with water first before adding it to a sauce to avoid clumping.
* **Nut and Seed Butters:** Depending on the dessert you are making, nut butters, such as those made from cashews, almonds, peanuts, and sesame seeds, produce a creamy effect.

For Glazing:

Eggs are often used as a glaze for certain desserts, most often flour-based foods such as pastries or breads. Instead of an egg wash, simply use oil, nondairy milk, or nondairy butter. Another method that works well is to thin ¼ cup (60 ml) of light corn syrup with very hot water and brush the mixture onto the pie or pastry crust once you remove the baked item from the oven. Sprinkle a little granulated sugar on top, if desired, and return the pie or pastry to the oven for 2 to 3 minutes to let the glaze dry and set.

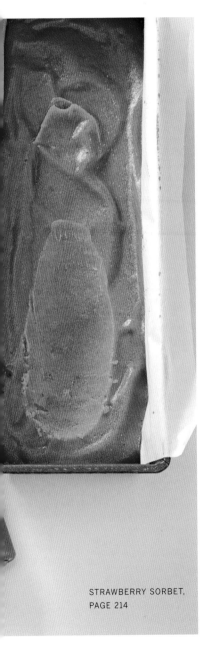

STRAWBERRY SORBET,
PAGE 214

Better Than Cow's Milk

When people think of milk the first thing they think of is cow's milk. Through clever and expensive advertising campaigns, we have been taught that humans have a nutritional requirement for the milk of another animal, despite the fact that even the offspring of that animal stops drinking his or her mother's milk once he or she is weaned. Mammalian milk is the fluid that a female produces when she is lactating. It is indeed "nature's perfect food," designed perfectly for each mammal to provide nourishment for her own young. (See page 104 for more on cow's milk as a substitute for human milk.)

Although the dairy industry has made attempts to essentially own the word "milk" and calls anything that isn't from an animal an "alternative," the word also refers to the liquid extracted from various plants, whether they are nuts, grains, seeds, or fruits. Many of these milks have been around for thousands of years in different parts of the world. Keep your eye out for the many new plant-based milks and creamers coming on the market all the time.

Although plants formed the foundation of the early human diet before animal foods began to replace them (particularly when animals were domesticated about 10,000 years ago), the milk from these plants are hardly "alternatives." Rather, they stand on their own as delicious and much healthier choices for human consumption—and for baking.

The many options include almond milk, oat milk, hazelnut milk, peanut milk, coconut milk, cashew milk, rice milk, and soymilk. Most of these are available commercially (see Appendix I, "Resources and Recommendations" on page 270), and all of them can be made in your own kitchen. (Recipes for some are in this book.)

BAKED APPLES,
PAGE 148

ALMOND MILK—FOOD OF THE ANCIENTS

Botanically speaking, the almond tree is part of the plum family and is native to North Africa, West Asia, and the Mediterranean. Prized for its high protein content and ability to keep better than milk from animals, almond milk has no cholesterol and no lactose and is high in fiber, protein, vitamin E, and monounsaturated fats. And it's absolutely delicious, especially the vanilla- and chocolate-flavored varieties. (See page 234 for the recipe.)

RICE MILK

Commercial brands of rice milk are available in such flavors as chocolate, vanilla, and plain, most of which are made from brown rice. Rice milk is thinner than the other nondairy milks, so try choosing a creamier milk when baking. Oat, soy, and almond milks are all good options.

OAT AND HAZELNUT MILKS

Although you can use any nut or grain to make milk at home, oat and hazelnut milks are also available commercially, and they're both very good. In my cooking classes, I used to conduct taste tests of various milks, and people were always pleasantly surprised by the taste and texture of these two milks in particular.

CASHEW MILK

The indigenous tribes of the rainforest have used the cashew tree and its nuts and fruit for centuries, and it is a common cultivated plant in their gardens. In addition to being delicious, cashew fruit is a rich source of vitamins, minerals, and other essential nutrients. I have not seen any commercial brands, but it is incredibly easy to make from scratch (see page 234).

SOYMILK

Soymilk is perhaps the most popular nondairy milk and the one most people assume you drink when you want to wean yourself off of cow's milk. It originated in China, a region where the soybean was native and used as food long before the existence of written records. Soymilk is reputed to have been discovered and developed during the Han dynasty in China about 164 B.C. It can be made at home with a little more effort than it takes to make almond milk, but an array of commercial brands in different flavors is also available.

COCONUT MILK

The milk of young coconuts, often referred to as coconut water or coconut juice, is delicious and drunk just like a beverage. Culinary coconut milk sold in a can, however, typically refers to the thick, sweet, milky white substance derived from the meat of a mature coconut. Common in many tropical cuisines, most notably those in Southeast Asia, it forms the basis of most Thai curries. However, coconut milk is also now sold as a beverage where all plant milks are sold.

WHEN TO USE WHAT IN BAKING

Any of the nondairy milks are great for any baking recipe. Just keep in mind that they all have different flavors and levels of thickness. For instance, soy, oat, and almond milks tend to be thicker than rice milk, and there are low-fat and unsweetened soymilks and low-fat almond and hazelnut milks, which also make them much thinner and less rich. Culinary coconut milk is very rich, but you can find "lite" versions, as well.

Better Than Buttermilk, Condensed Milk, and Evaporated Milk

Once vegan baking is demystified, you can take any recipe and easily "veganize" it, which is a very satisfying endeavor, I might add. Though the addition of cow's milk is unnecessary and easy to replace with any nondairy milk, there may be times when a recipe calls for buttermilk, condensed milk, or evaporated milk. Here are suggestions for what to do in such scenarios.

BUTTERMILK—PUCKER UP

Most of the modern, commercially available "buttermilk" is cow's milk to which souring agents have been added, but any baker will tell you how to do this yourself. For every cup (235 ml) of nondairy milk, just add 1 tablespoon (15 ml) of lemon juice or vinegar, and allow the soured milk to stand for 10 minutes before adding to recipes. Voilà—you have "buttermilk."

CONDENSED MILK—SUGARY SWEET

Condensed milk is cow's milk from which water has been removed and to which sugar has been added, yielding a thick, sweet product that can last on the shelf for years. It contains something like 50 to 60 percent added sugar, so one way to make a substitute is by adding sugar or another sweetener to soymilk, silken tofu, or a combination of the two, depending on the texture you want. Try this recipe:

* 4 ounces silken tofu (115 g)
* ¼ cup (60 ml) soymilk
* ¼ cup (50 g) granulated sugar or ¼ cup (85 g) pure maple syrup

   Blend all the ingredients in a blender until very smooth. Adjust to your taste by adding more sweetener. For a thinner consistency, add more soymilk; for thicker results, use a bit more tofu.

MILLED CIDER, PAGE 236

EVAPORATED MILK—NOT SO SWEET

Evaporated cow's milk is related to condensed milk in that about 60 percent of the water is removed, but it undergoes a more complex process and is not sweetened. I don't use too many recipes that call for this, but if you come across one, just try using an unsweetened nondairy milk and adding a thickener such as arrowroot, kudzu root, or cornstarch.

Better Than Butter

I'll admit it: fat tastes good. It adds substance, flavor, and texture to food, and it is an essential dietary requirement. Certain vitamins (A, D, E, and K) are fat-soluble, meaning they can only be digested, absorbed, and transported in conjunction with fats, which also play a vital role in maintaining healthy skin and hair, insulating body organs against shock, maintaining body temperature, and promoting healthy cell function.

However, there is a big difference between animal fats and vegetable fats, and even within the latter category, some are better than others. Do we need fat? Yes. Do we need animal fat? No. Is it better to eat fats in their whole state? Yes. Do we need to consume vegetable oils? No. Do I use vegetable oils for recipes in this book? Yes.

The foundation of the diet I advocate is based on plant-based whole foods, and by whole foods I mean foods in their whole state. Nuts and seeds are examples of whole foods, but oils from nuts and seeds are not. Once oil is extracted from those foods, you're moving away from the food in its whole state. Rice is a whole food, Rice Krispies are not.

But as I say in "Defending Desserts" (page 56), I don't have a problem with eating desserts as a treat—not as the foundation of my diet. Where fat is used in the recipes, it is in the form of oil and nondairy butter. The oil I recommend using is canola because it has a mild flavor ideal for desserts and because it is high in monounsaturated fats, but coconut oil can be substituted especially in recipes where you prefer, or at least don't mind, the coconut flavor.

When it comes to nondairy butter, my favorite is: Earth Balance. Made from a blend of vegetable oils through a process that does not include hydrogenation (which is what creates trans fats), Earth Balance is able to be solid at room temperature. The flavor is fantastic, and you can use Earth Balance just as you would dairy-based butter—in every way. As of this writing, Earth Balance comes in its original "buttery spread," organic, sticks, and shortening. The company does not, at this writing, make unsalted.

True, there are nondairy margarines on the market, and some are better than others, but I like Earth Balance best, and I always buy organic. If you cannot find this brand in your area, ask your grocer to carry it or experiment with other nondairy margarines until you find one you like.

UNSALTED BUTTER—UNNECESSARY

You can easily replace unsalted butter with salted butter measure for measure, though you may or may not need to reduce or eliminate the salt in the overall recipe. I've adjusted the recipes in this cookbook to account for the fact that I'm recommending salted (nondairy) butter, but if you'd like to reduce the salt even more, feel free to do so.

MEASURING BUTTER—A GUIDE

Recipe authors have made measuring butter more complex than it needs to be. One recipe may ask for a ½ cup. Another may call for 8 tablespoons. Still another may recommend one stick. And yet, they're all the same.

Nondairy butters, such as Earth Balance, often come in sticks, like dairy-based butter, and are packaged in 1-pound boxes, with four individually wrapped quarters. Each pound equals 2 cups of butter. Each ¼-pound stick equals 8 tablespoons or ½ cup (112 g).

In other words:
1 stick = ½ cup = 8 tablespoons (112 g)

Cups	Sticks	Pounds	Tablespoons	Grams
¼	½	⅛	4	55 g
½	1	¼	8	112 g
⅓	½ + 1⅓ tablespoons	n/a	5⅓	75 g
⅔	1 + 2⅔ tablespoons	n/a	10⅔	150 g
¾	1½	⅜	12	170 g
1	2	½	16	225 g
2	4	1	32	450 g

NOT USING STICKS? TRY THIS TRICK

On the wrapper of nondairy butter sticks, there are markings for each tablespoon increment. To measure nondairy butter that doesn't have a wrapper, try this trick: partially fill a measuring cup with water, then add the butter until it reaches the amount you need. For example, fill a cup with ½ cup (120 ml) of water. If you need ½ cup (112 g) of butter, then add the butter to the water until the water line reaches 1 cup.

TAKING BACK THE WORD

The word "butter," unqualified, almost always refers to that which is made from the milk of an animal. Any spread considered a "butter substitute" tends to be called "margarine," despite the fact that some margarines use animal as well as vegetable fats. I prefer to use the term "nondairy butter" instead of margarine. Our choice of words reflects our perceptions, and I prefer to use language that most accurately describes what something is. Too often "vegan food" is assigned labels that suggest it is of an inferior status, and I think that hinders our experience and enjoyment as well as misleads and misinforms us.

BANANA CHOCOLATE
CHIP MUFFINS, PAGE 42

A BUTTER BY ANY OTHER NAME

As with the word "milk," the word "butter" refers to products made from pureed nuts or peanuts, such as peanut butter, almond butter, and cashew butter. It's also used in the names of fruit spreads, such as apple butter. Other fats naturally solid at room temperature are also known as "butters"—examples include cocoa butter and shea butter. Cocoa butter is the edible natural fat of the cacao bean, used for making chocolate and cocoa, and shea butter is the natural fat extracted from the fruit of the shea tree, often used in skin moisturizers but also used as a substitute for cocoa butter.

How to Read a Recipe

Reading a recipe may seem like a pretty straightforward task—something you wouldn't need a manual for, but I thought it would be helpful to include a few suggestions for making the process as enjoyable and successful as possible.

CHOOSING A RECIPE FROM THIS COOKBOOK

A number of factors go into choosing what to make, so I've created a number of indices (see pages 287–299) to help you choose recipes according to certain criteria:

* **Based on the primary and secondary ingredients in the recipe.** This is the main index of the book and is the most direct and common way to find a recipe. If you want blueberry muffins, for example, you'll look under "B" for blueberry and find what you need. If you're in the mood for cinnamon, however, you may not know that Rice Pudding or Apple Cake features this spice; this index will help you locate desserts based on less-obvious ingredients or flavors.
* **The main index also includes entries based on the type of dessert.** While you would find blueberry muffins under "B" for blueberry, you'll also find the recipe under muffins.
* **Based on the season.** This index includes recipes based on season-specific ingredients (e.g., strawberry pie in the summer and pomegranate sauce in the fall) as well as those recipes associated with particular seasons (hot chocolate in the winter and sorbet in the spring).
* **Based on a holiday or occasion.** Whether you're throwing a children's birthday party, hosting an elegant tea party, or making desserts for the holidays, you can find what you're looking for in this special index.

Timing Recipes

When choosing a recipe, always consider the timing. There is the preparation of individual ingredients and the preparation of the entire recipe. In this cookbook, those recipes that require advance preparation, such as bread dough that has to rise or cookie dough that has to be refrigerated, are flagged for easy reference.

If you're timing a specific recipe to coincide with a meal, such as the drop biscuits on page 52, you will want to make sure that your biscuits come out of the oven just as you are serving the main course.

Reading a Recipe

It may seem obvious, but many people simply skim through a recipe, proving fatal to the recipe process and/or the final outcome.
* **Take the time to read carefully through the ingredients and directions,** and check your cupboard for any ingredients you may already have. Put those out on the counter.
* **Carefully write out the ingredients you need.** You may even consider bringing the recipe—or the entire cookbook, if possible—with you to the store. It's an awful feeling to get home and realize you've forgotten something.

Shopping for Ingredients

Because certain ingredients may not have hit the mainstream grocery stores yet, I regret that you may need to go to more than one store to find what you need. Here are some ways of getting around this:

✳ **Check out VeganEssentials.com**, which carries most of the vegan products you love—especially helpful for those items you can't find in your local store.

Ten Tips for Perfect Baking

1. FRESH IS BEST

In my cooking classes, I used to always ask my students to raise their hands if they had spices in their cupboard or on a spice rack. Most did. Then I asked them to raise their hands if those little jars had dust all over them. Most did. Even dried herbs, dried spices, baking powder, and yeast have a shelf life, so if you haven't used something in a year, it's best to toss it. Buying in bulk can save you time and money in the long run; bulk goods usually cost less pound for pound and will obviously last longer than smaller sizes so you make fewer trips to the grocery store.

2. PRECISE IS NICE

Whereas cooking allows for flexibility, baking is more scientific and calls for accurate measurements. Use the proper measuring spoons and cups, don't pack dry ingredients into the measuring cups, and always read the liquid amount at eye level.

3. RESIST THE WRIST

Overmixing your batter causes it to become gummy or tough because the protein/gluten in your flour gets overdeveloped. Follow the directions in each recipe and think about the outcome you want: Gluten in pie crust = bad. Gluten in yeast breads = good. Overdeveloped gluten in cakes and cookies = not so good. Lumps tend to work themselves out in the baking process, but if you tend to obsess over lumps, then sift your dry ingredients first.

4. HASTEN YOUR BAKIN'

Once your batter is mixed, put it in a preheated oven immediately, because the leavening process begins as soon as the wet ingredients are combined with the dry. See more about baking soda and baking powder in the appendix.

5. SCAN YOUR PANS

Dark pans absorb more heat and may speed up the baking process, so I always check my baked goods about 10 minutes before the directions suggest. Lighter pans reflect the heat and may need the

* **Bulk up.** When shopping for humane ingredients (e.g., egg replacer instead of eggs), I highly encourage you to stock up! Ingredients such as flaxseed, flour, sugar, and egg replacer powder have a long shelf life (the equivalent of 112 eggs is in just one case of Ener-G Egg Replacer!), so it will help you to always have these items on hand. Vacuum-packed, nondairy milks and silken tofu, and not having to worry about the expiration date of chicken's eggs, are just a few more

full baking time (or even a little longer), but I still set the timer early just to be sure.

6. EVEN STEVEN

For even cooking, place your baked goods, particularly cakes, cookies, muffins, and other quick breads, in the center of the oven where the heat circulates most evenly.

7. BE PREPARED

Read your recipe carefully first, pull out all the necessary ingredients from your cupboards, and place them on the counter. Measure everything out. Take into account nondairy butter that may need to be at room temperature and the oven that will need to be preheated.

8. CEASE THE GREASE

Parchment paper is a wonderful way to eliminate extra fat and calories and makes cleanup a breeze. Though you can buy it at most stores, I prefer the unbleached parchment paper, found in natural food stores and through my website. Parchment paper, unlike waxed paper, is specially designed for use in the oven, so it doesn't burn. You just lay a sheet down on your cookie pan, and drop your dough directly onto the parchment. No oil, no grease, no mess.

9. LOVIN' YOUR OVEN

Because every oven is different, it's important to know yours—intimately. If your oven's temperature is off by even a few degrees, you could have

fatal results. If you're uncertain of your oven's temperature relative to what the dial says, invest in an oven thermometer. At least be aware that the temperature and baking time called for in the following recipes (or any recipe!) may not match your oven.

10. THE BEST TEST

To test for doneness in cakes and quick breads, insert a toothpick into the center. The toothpick should come out clean and dry or have only a few crumbs clinging to it. Yeast breads, rolls, and loaves should be golden brown on the top, sides, and bottom, and sound hollow when tapped.

reasons to bake without animal products, especially because they allow for spontaneous baking.

✳ **Befriend your grocer.** I realize the prevalence of large supermarket chains means greater convenience to the consumer, but at what cost? Small, locally owned grocery stores are becoming extinct, and it's taking a toll on everyone from the merchants to the customers. Local stores ensure choice and diversity and help maintain community character, and you'll have much better luck asking your local grocer to carry an unfamiliar product than asking your large, cookie-cutter supermarket. Because you often deal directly with the owner, you'll get a fast response while building an invaluable relationship.

✳ **Befriend your neighbors.** Remember hearing about those days when people would actually ask to borrow a cup of sugar from their neighbor? If you didn't know your neighbors before, you'll certainly get to know them this way. Don't be shy—most will be happy to oblige, especially if they get to sample your sweet creation. Seriously, knowing our neighbors is beneficial for several reasons, so don't hesitate to ask if you need something. You can always return the favor later.

Preparing Your Ingredients

Organizing everything ahead of time makes for a stress- and mistake-free process. Trying to chop and measure everything as you're going along will only distract you and create an opportunity for you to make a mistake.

✳ **Go through the recipe,** grab what you need from the cupboard or refrigerator, and set everything on the counter.

✳ **Preheat your oven,** pull out the pans you need, and grease them, if called for.

✳ **Get out your measuring spoons and cups,** and measure out your ingredients into individual bowls.

✳ **Take care of any peeling, chopping, slicing, or pureeing** first before attempting to assemble the entire recipe.

Once you have all your ingredients prepared, glance at the recipe again. Make sure you haven't forgotten anything. Now you can begin to put it all together. Buon appetito!

CHAPTER TWO

RISE AND SHINE: MUFFINS, BISCUITS & SCONES

The goodies in this chapter can be eaten any time of the day, but they are a healthful way to start the morning, particularly those with the most wholesome ingredients. Though all are delicious, muffins, biscuits, and scones do have some differences between them. A muffin is generally a small, cake-like quick bread that can be made with a variety of flours and often contains additions, such as nuts, fruit, or chocolate chips. In the United States, biscuits refer to small, tender quick breads, which rely on leaveners such as baking powder and baking soda. Another quick bread, scones are thought to have originated in Scotland and are similar to biscuits in terms of ingredients.

THE RECIPES

Banana Chocolate Chip Muffins ... 42
Blueberry Lemon Muffins ... 43
Apple Pecan Muffins ... 44
Bran Muffins with Raisins ... 46
Corn Muffins ... 47
Ginger Muffins ... 48
Hearty Spiced Cocoa Muffins ... 49
Jam-filled Oat Bran Muffins ... 51
Drop Biscuits ... 52
Chocolate Chip Scones ... 53
Classic Currant Scones ... 54
Gingerbread Scones ... 56

TIPS FOR MAKING MUFFINS, BISCUITS, & SCONES

FOR MUFFINS:

* Grease muffin tins with canola oil or a nonstick spray.
* Use paper liners in muffin cups for easy cleanup. No need to spray with oil.
* If muffin cups are filled more than three-quarters full, the muffins will have flat tops.
* If some muffin cups remain empty during baking, fill them with 2 to 3 tablespoons (30 to 45 ml) of water so the muffins bake evenly.

* If baked muffins stick to the bottom of the muffin cup, place the hot muffin pan on a wet towel for 2 minutes and try again.

FOR BISCUITS & SCONES:

* Don't overmix the dough. Overmixing will cause the biscuits and scones to be tough.
* Know that your biscuit and scone dough tends to be wet and sticky, not smooth like yeast-based dough.

* Make sure your leaveners (baking powder and baking soda) are fresh. They each have a shelf life of 6 months. Use old baking powder as an abrasive cleanser.
* To make flaky biscuits and scones, leave some of the butter pieces as large as peas instead of incorporating them fully into the batter/dough.
* For soft-sided biscuits, bake them with the edges touching. For crusty-sided biscuits, bake them ¼ to ½ inch (6 to 12 mm) apart on the baking sheet.

BANANA CHOCOLATE CHIP MUFFINS

YIELD: 12 MUFFINS OR ONE 9-INCH (23-CM) CAKE

This is a very versatile recipe that can be made in the form of muffins, bread, or a cake. You can make it more appropriate for breakfast by reducing some of the sugar and not adding chocolate chips. Walnuts are a great addition, but these muffins are also divine without any additions at all. This recipe has been adapted from my favorite cookbook, *The Peaceful Palate.*

INGREDIENTS

2 cups (250 g) unbleached all-purpose flour

1½ teaspoons baking soda

½ teaspoon salt

1 cup (200 g) granulated sugar

⅓ cup (80 ml) canola oil

4 ripe bananas, mashed

¼ cup (60 ml) water

1 teaspoon vanilla extract

1 cup (175 g) nondairy semisweet chocolate chips

1 cup (150 g) walnuts (optional)

Preheat the oven to 350°F (180°C, or gas mark 4). Lightly grease your muffin tins.

In a medium-size bowl, mix the flour, baking soda, and salt together.

In a large bowl, beat the sugar and oil together, then add the mashed bananas. Stir in the water and vanilla and mix thoroughly. Add the flour mixture, along with the chocolate chips, and stir to mix.

Fill each muffin tin halfway with the batter. Bake for 20 to 30 minutes, until they are golden brown and a toothpick inserted into the center comes out clean.

COLLEEN'S TIP: *The baking time specified is for muffins. If you are baking this as a bread or cake, you may need to bake for 40 to 45 minutes. Check for doneness by inserting a toothpick into the center and looking to see whether it comes out clean.*

BLUEBERRY LEMON MUFFINS

YIELD: 12 MUFFINS

Citrus flavors complement blueberries well, so feel free to switch out the lemon here for orange zest and/or extract. You can also add a little cinnamon or nutmeg. Enjoy these muffins for breakfast or as a quick snack.

INGREDIENTS

2 cups (250 g) unbleached all-purpose flour
1½ teaspoons baking soda
½ teaspoon salt
Zest of 2 lemons
⅓ to 1 cup (150 to 200 g) granulated sugar
1 cup (235 ml) nondairy milk
⅓ cup (80 ml) canola oil
1 teaspoon lemon extract
1 tablespoon (15 ml) white distilled vinegar
1½ cups (218 g) fresh blueberries, picked over to remove stems

Preheat the oven to 400°F (200°C, or gas mark 6). Lightly grease your muffin tins.

In a medium-size bowl, combine the flour, baking soda, salt, and lemon zest. (Use a lemon zester or a "microplane," which is available in any kitchen supply store.)

In a large bowl, combine the sugar, milk, oil, lemon extract, and vinegar. Mix well. Add the flour mixture, stirring until the ingredients are just blended. Gently fold in the berries using a rubber spatula.

Fill greased or nonstick muffin tins about two-thirds full. Bake until the muffins are lightly browned and a wooden skewer inserted into the center comes out clean, about 20 minutes. While the muffins are baking, lick the bowl clean. No eggs means no salmonella!

Remove from the oven and let sit for 5 minutes. Remove the muffins from the tins and cool on a wire rack.

COLLEEN'S TIP: *Choose berries that are round and firm and are blue-black in color. Discard any shriveled or moldy berries. Store in the refrigerator for up to 6 days, but do not wash until ready to use. If you won't be using them as quickly as you thought, throw them on your cereal or toss them in your morning smoothie. They also freeze very well.*

DID YOU KNOW? *While most commercial berries are very high in insecticide residues, blueberries are among the lowest of any fruit. When organic blueberries are unavailable, conventionally raised ones are an acceptable alternative.*

APPLE PECAN MUFFINS

YIELD: 12 MUFFINS

These muffins are prized not only for their flavor but also for their rustic appearance. So easy to prepare, they are very healthful and contain lots of dietary fiber.

INGREDIENTS

1½ cups (190 g) unbleached all-purpose flour
½ cup (63 g) whole wheat flour
1 tablespoon (4.6 g) baking powder
1 teaspoon cinnamon
½ teaspoon salt
2 tablespoons (30 g) ground flaxseed or
   3 teaspoons Ener-G Egg Replacer (equivalent of 2 eggs)

6 tablespoons (90 ml) water (4 tablespoons or 60 ml if you use Ener-G)
½ cup (125 g) unsweetened applesauce
⅓ cup (80 ml) canola oil
½ cup (100 g) granulated sugar
1 teaspoon vanilla extract
1½ cups (225 g) peeled and chopped raw apples
½ to 1 cup (60 to 125 g) chopped pecans

Preheat the oven to 350°F (180°C, or gas mark 4). Lightly grease your muffin tins.

In a medium-size bowl, combine the flours, baking powder, cinnamon, and salt.

In a food processor or blender, whip the flaxseed and water together, until it reaches a thick and creamy consistency.

In a separate bowl, combine the applesauce, oil, sugar, vanilla, and flax mixture. Beat with an electric hand mixer or wire whisk until creamy smooth. Add to the flour mixture, stirring until well blended. Do not overmix. Fold in the apples and nuts.

The batter will be thick rather than smooth and wet, but it's okay. If you feel it's too stiff, you may add 1 or 2 tablespoons (15 or 30 ml) of water.

Fill the greased muffin tins about three-quarters full. Bake until a wooden skewer inserted into the center comes out clean, about 20 minutes.

Cool in tins for 5 minutes, then transfer to a wire rack.

DID YOU KNOW? *Flaxseed is the most concentrated source of essential omega-3 fatty acids, so it should be a staple in your diet even if you're not using it for baking! Always buy whole flaxseed (golden or brown) and grind it yourself, using a coffee grinder for best results. Once you grind it, put it in a glass container and store in the freezer. Consume 2 to 3 teaspoons a day by adding to a fruit smoothie, oatmeal, cereal, soup, or salad, or just eat flaxseed on its own.*

BRAN MUFFINS WITH RAISINS

YIELD: 24 MUFFINS

Who said healthful can't be flavorful? These muffins are moist, sweet, and dark and will keep you regular all day, which is a good thing. Store uneaten muffins in a sealed plastic bag in the fridge or—to keep them even longer—in the freezer.

INGREDIENTS

6 teaspoons Ener-G Egg Replacer or 4 table-spoons (60 g) ground flaxseed (equivalent of 4 eggs)

½ cup (120 ml) water

2½ cups (250 g) wheat bran

1½ cups (188 g) whole wheat flour

¾ cup (170 g) firmly packed brown sugar

2½ teaspoons baking soda

1 teaspoon salt

1 cup (235 ml) nondairy milk

⅓ cup (80 ml) canola oil

1 cup (145 g) raisins

Preheat the oven to 400°F (200°C, or gas mark 6). Lightly grease your muffin tins.

In a food processor or using an electric hand mixer, whip the flaxseed and water together, until it's thick, creamy, and gooey. This can all be done by hand, but a food processor works really well.

In a large bowl, combine the bran, flour, brown sugar, baking soda, and salt. Set aside. In another bowl, whisk together the "flax eggs," milk, and oil until smooth. Stir in the raisins. Add to the combined dry ingredients and stir just until blended. Do not overmix.

Spoon into the prepared muffin tins, filling each cup about two-thirds full. Bake until a toothpick inserted into the center of a muffin comes out clean, about 15 minutes. Cool in the tins for 5 minutes, then remove and cool on a wire rack.

SERVING SUGGESTIONS & VARIATIONS

You can use either light or dark brown sugar in this recipe.

DID YOU KNOW? *Bran is the hard outer layer of cereal grains, including maize, wheat, rice, barley, millet, oat, rye, and quinoa, among others. Along with germ, it is an integral part of whole grains and is often produced as a by-product of milling in the production of refined grains. When bran is removed from grains, they lose a portion of their nutritional value, particularly dietary fiber, protein, fat, vitamins, and dietary minerals.*

CORN MUFFINS

YIELD: 12 MUFFINS

Between the cornmeal and the whole corn kernels, these gorgeous yellow gems scream flavor and texture. They're sweet but not too sweet and are perfect for breakfast or as a snack.

INGREDIENTS

½ cup (70 g) coarse yellow cornmeal (may also be called polenta)

1 teaspoon salt, divided

1 cup (235 ml) nondairy milk

1½ tablespoons (25 g) ground flaxseed (equivalent of 1 egg)

2 tablespoons (30 ml) water

2 cups (250 g) unbleached all-purpose or whole wheat pastry flour

3 tablespoons (39 g) granulated sugar

2 teaspoons baking powder

½ teaspoon baking soda

⅓ cup (75 g) non-hydrogenated nondairy butter, melted and cooled

1½ cups (233 g) or 1 (15-ounce or 420-g) can whole corn kernels

½ to 1 cup (73 to 145 g) blueberries (optional)

Preheat the oven to 375°F (190°C, or gas mark 5). Lightly grease your muffin tins.

Soak the cornmeal and ½ teaspoon of the salt in the milk for about 15 minutes while you prepare your other ingredients.

Meanwhile, whip the ground flaxseed and water together in a small bowl or food processor, until thick and creamy.

In a medium-size bowl, combine the flour, sugar, baking powder, baking soda, and the remaining ½ teaspoon salt.

In a small bowl, stir together the nondairy milk (along with the cornmeal), melted butter, and "flax egg" until combined. Add to the dry ingredients, and stir just until blended. Add the whole corn kernels and blueberries (if adding), and stir to combine. Do not overmix.

Spoon into the prepared muffin tins, filling each cup about three-quarters full. Bake until a toothpick inserted into the center of a muffin comes out clean, about 25 minutes. Cool in the tins for 5 minutes, then remove to cool on a wire rack.

WHAT'S THE DIFFERENCE?

* Cornmeal is dried corn kernels ground to a fine, medium, or coarse texture.
* Corn flour is finely ground cornmeal.
* Polenta, a staple of northern Italy, is a mush made from cornmeal.
* Hominy is dried white or yellow corn kernels from which the hull and germ have been removed.
* Grits is a common dish in the southern United States. Similar to polenta, grits are usually made from coarsely ground hominy as opposed to cornmeal.

GINGER MUFFINS

YIELD: 12 MUFFINS

These are delicately flavored little muffins that make a satisfying breakfast treat or anytime-of-the-day snack. Serve warm with jam or nondairy butter.

INGREDIENTS

2 tablespoons (30 g) ground flaxseed
    (equivalent of 2 eggs)
6 tablespoons (90 ml) water
¼ cup (24 g) finely minced fresh ginger
1 cup (200 g) granulated sugar, divided
2 tablespoons (12 g) grated lemon zest

2 cups (250 g) unbleached all-purpose flour
¾ teaspoon salt
1 teaspoon baking soda
½ cup (112 g) non-hydrogenated, nondairy butter
1 cup (235 ml) nondairy milk
Juice from 1 lemon

SERVING SUGGESTIONS & VARIATIONS

If you prefer a muffin without flax flecks, feel free to use a commercial egg replacer (see "Better Than Eggs" on page 19) or try ¼ cup (115 g) silken tofu instead.

Preheat the oven to 375°F (190°C, or gas mark 5). Grease your muffin tins.

In a food processor or in a bowl using an electric hand mixer, whip the flaxseed and water together, until it reaches a thick and creamy consistency.

In a small saucepan, combine the ginger and ½ cup (100 g) sugar and cook over medium heat, stirring until the sugar melts and is thoroughly combined with the ginger, which will start to release its juices. This takes only a few minutes. Set aside to cool, then add the lemon zest.

In a medium-size bowl, stir together the flour, salt, and baking soda. Set aside.

In a large bowl, beat the nondairy butter until smooth. Add the remaining ½ cup (100 g) sugar and beat until blended. Add the flax mixture and stir well. Add the milk and lemon juice and mix well. Add the combined dry ingredients and ginger/sugar mixture, and stir just until blended.

Spoon into the tins, about half full. Bake until a toothpick inserted into the center of a muffin comes out clean, 15 to 20 minutes. Cool in the tins for 1 minute, then remove to cool on a wire rack.

COLLEEN'S TIP: *The easiest way to mince fresh ginger is in the food processor. Peeling is optional, but you can use a sharp knife and carefully cut away the thin skin, taking care not to cut away too much of the ginger flesh. A trick many chefs use to peel ginger is to scrape away the skin with the edge of a spoon.*

WHAT'S THE DIFFERENCE? *Ground and fresh ginger have quite different tastes, and ground ginger is a poor substitute for fresh ginger. However, fresh ginger can be substituted for ground ginger at the ratio of ⅛ teaspoon ground ginger to 1 tablespoon (8 g) fresh grated ginger.*

HEARTY SPICED COCOA MUFFINS

YIELD: 12 MUFFINS

I used to make a version of this recipe long before I was vegan, and it was incredibly satisfying to make it again—but even better! The spices in these special muffins make them perfect for the winter holidays. These are muffins, not cupcakes, but you can make them sweeter by adding more sugar.

INGREDIENTS

1¾ cups (219 g) unbleached all-purpose flour

¾ cup (150 g) granulated sugar

6 tablespoons (50 g) unsweetened cocoa powder

2 teaspoons baking powder

½ teaspoon baking soda

2 teaspoons ground cinnamon

¼ teaspoon ground cloves

¼ teaspoon cayenne pepper (optional)

1 teaspoon salt

2 tablespoons (30 g) ground flaxseed (equivalent of 2 eggs)

4 tablespoons (60 ml) water

1 cup (235 ml) nondairy milk

½ cup (112 g) non-hydrogenated, nondairy butter, melted, or canola oil

½ cup (88 g) nondairy semisweet chocolate chips (optional)

½ cup (50 g) finely chopped pecan or walnuts (optional)

Preheat the oven to 400°F (200°C, or gas mark 6). Lightly grease your muffin tins.

Sift the flour, sugar, cocoa powder, baking powder, baking soda, cinnamon, cloves, cayenne (if using), and salt together in a large bowl.

In a food processor or in a bowl using an electric hand mixer, whip the flaxseeds and water together until creamy and thick, about 1 minute.

In a separate bowl, combine the "flax eggs," milk, and melted butter. Add the liquid to the dry ingredients, stirring just enough to combine. Fold in the chocolate chips and/or nuts.

Spoon the mixture into the muffin pans, filling them three-quarters full. Bake until a wooden skewer inserted into the center comes out clean, about 15 minutes.

Let sit for 5 minutes, and then remove to cool on a wire rack.

JAM-FILLED OAT BRAN MUFFINS

YIELD: 16 MUFFINS

These are special little muffins with a surprise inside! Of course, any muffin can easily be filled with little treats, and I chose strawberry jam for these healthful, hearty muffins that don't taste like "health food."

INGREDIENTS

2 tablespoons (30 g) ground flaxseed (equivalent of 2 eggs)

6 tablespoons (90 ml) water

2 cups (200 g) oat bran

1 cup (125 g) unbleached all-purpose or whole wheat pastry flour

½ cup (115 g) firmly packed light or dark brown sugar

4 teaspoons (6 g) baking powder

1 teaspoon ground cinnamon

½ teaspoon salt

1¼ cups (295 ml) nondairy milk (try oat milk!)

⅓ cup (80 ml) canola oil

1 cup (150 g) chopped walnuts (optional)

½ cup (160 g) strawberry (or any fruit) jam, preferably fruit-sweetened

Preheat the oven to 425°F (220°C, or gas mark 7). Lightly grease your muffin tins.

In a food processor or in a bowl using an electric hand mixer, whip the flaxseed and water together, until you have a thick and creamy consistency. This can all be done by hand, but a food processor/hand mixer does a better job in 1 to 2 minutes. It also makes it creamier than can be done by hand.

In a large bowl, combine the oat bran, flour, brown sugar, baking powder, cinnamon, and salt. Set aside. In a small bowl, whisk together the flaxseed mixture, milk, and oil. Stir in the walnuts, if using. Add to the dry ingredients, and mix just until blended.

Fill the prepared muffin cups less than half full with batter. Place a dab of jam or preserves in the center of each cup. Add more batter to fill the cups two-thirds full, concealing the jam. Bake for 15 to 20 minutes, depending on your oven. Cool in the tins for 3 minutes, then remove to cool on a wire rack.

DID YOU KNOW?

* *Americans consume about only 12 grams of fiber a day. Vegans consume, on average, 40 to 50 grams of fiber per day. The high-fiber intake of vegans is believed to be at least partly responsible for the numerous health benefits of all-plant diets.*
* *Fiber is found only in plant foods—not in animal products.*

WHAT'S THE DIFFERENCE?

* *Wheat bran, an example of insoluble fiber, is helpful for keeping the intestines working properly.*
* *Oat bran, an example of soluble fiber, has been shown to reduce the risk of coronary heart disease when part of an overall diet that is low in or free of saturated fat and cholesterol.*

DROP BISCUITS

YIELD: 10 TO 12 BISCUITS

Traditionally served as a side dish with a meal, these are perfect for making biscuits and gravy (make them a tad larger for this purpose), a hearty breakfast dish. These simple biscuits are especially delicious served with nondairy butter and jam or preserves. There's no need for a commercial "biscuit mix"; the preparation is only 5 minutes.

INGREDIENTS

1²⁄₃ cups (208 g) unbleached all-purpose flour
1 tablespoon (4.6 g) baking powder
½ teaspoon salt
²⁄₃ cup (157 ml) nondairy milk
⅓ cup (80 ml) canola oil or melted non-hydrogenated nondairy butter

Preheat the oven to 475°F (240°C, or gas mark 9). Lightly grease a baking/cookie sheet.

In a large bowl, mix together the flour, baking powder, and salt until combined. Add the milk and oil and stir just until the dry ingredients are moistened. It will be very sticky and thick, not smooth like cake batter. Use one teaspoon to form walnut-sized scoops of batter and another spoon to scrape the batter onto a cookie sheet, spacing the biscuits about 1½ inches (3.8 cm) apart.

Bake until the bottoms are golden brown, about 8 minutes. Serve hot.

SERVING SUGGESTIONS & VARIATIONS
Add any of the following for more flavorful biscuits:

* Melted nondairy butter (instead of canola oil) for a buttery flavor
* Sundried tomatoes: 5 to 6 tablespoons (34 to 41 g) finely chopped
* Chives: ¼ cup (12 g) snipped fresh
* Rosemary: 1 teaspoon minced fresh or ½ teaspoon dried and crumbled
* Chili peppers: ¼ to ⅓ cup (30 to 40 g) canned, drained and diced
* Watercress: 1 cup (30 g) chopped leaves
* Whole wheat flour: split the all-purpose flour with whole wheat flour
* Raisins or currants: ¼ cup (36 g)
* Sunflower or pumpkin seeds: ½ cup (68 g)

CHOCOLATE CHIP SCONES

YIELD: 8 TO 10 SCONES

In the United States, scones tend to feature sweeter fillings, such as cranberries, blueberries, nuts, or even chocolate chips, as in my recipe here.

INGREDIENTS

1½ tablespoon (25 g) ground flaxseed (equivalent of 1 egg)
2 tablespoons (30 ml) water
2½ cups (315 g) unbleached all-purpose flour
⅓ cup (67 g) granulated sugar
4 teaspoons (6 g) baking powder
½ teaspoon salt
¾ cup (170 g) non-hydrogenated nondairy butter, cold
1 cup (175 g) nondairy semisweet chocolate chips
½ cup (120 ml) nondairy milk
Extra milk or water as needed
2 to 3 tablespoons (30 to 45 ml) nondairy milk for brushing tops
Cinnamon and sugar for sprinkling on top

Preheat the oven to 425°F (220°C, or gas mark 7). Lightly oil a cookie or baking sheet, or line with parchment paper.

In a food processor or by hand, whip together the ground flaxseed and water until thick and creamy. Set aside.

In a large bowl, combine the flour, sugar, baking powder, and salt. Add the butter to the dry ingredients and cut it into small pieces with two knives or with a pastry blender. You're not creating a paste; you want a coarse crumbly batter that resembles bread crumbs. (To make flaky scones, leave some of the butter pieces as large as peas.) Stir in the chocolate chips.

Add the milk and "flax eggs," and keep the mixing to a minimum to avoid developing the gluten in the flour (which produces tough scones). Mix with a wooden spoon, fork, or your fingers just until the dry ingredients are moistened or nearly moistened. The dough will not be completely smooth like bread dough.

Gather the dough into a ball (you may need to add just one more teaspoon of nondairy milk or water, but you will be able to form it into a ball), and place on a lightly floured surface. Pat or roll the dough out to a ½-inch-thick (1.3-cm) round, and cut into 8 or 10 pieces—triangles are a traditional shape. Place them ½ inch (1.3 cm) apart on the baking sheet, brush with nondairy milk, and sprinkle with some cinnamon and sugar.

Bake until the tops are golden brown, 12 to 15 minutes. Let cool on a rack or serve warm.

CLASSIC CURRANT SCONES

YIELD: 8 TO 10 SCONES

In Great Britain, it's traditional for scones to include raisins, currants, or dates. Enjoy these for breakfast or a mid-afternoon snack with some black tea!

INGREDIENTS

1½ tablespoons (25 g) ground flaxseed (equivalent of 1 egg)

2 tablespoons (30 ml) water

2½ cups (313 g) unbleached all-purpose flour

⅓ cup (67 g) granulated sugar

4 teaspoons (6 g) baking powder

½ teaspoon salt

¾ cup (169 g) non-hydrogenated, nondairy butter, cold

1 cup currants (145 g) or raisins

½ cup (120 ml) nondairy milk

Extra milk or water as needed

2 to 3 tablespoons (30 to 45 ml) nondairy milk for brushing tops

Cinnamon and sugar for sprinkling on top

Preheat the oven to 425°F (220°C, or gas mark 7). Lightly oil a cookie/baking sheet, or line with parchment paper.

In a food processor or by hand, whip the ground flaxseed and water together until thick and creamy. Set aside.

In a large bowl, combine the flour, sugar, baking powder, and salt. Add the butter to the dry ingredients and cut it into small pieces with two knives or with a pastry blender. You're not creating a paste; you want a coarse crumbly batter that resembles bread crumbs. (To make flaky scones, leave some of the butter pieces as large as peas.) Stir in the currants.

Add the milk and "flax eggs," and keep the mixing to a minimum to avoid developing the gluten in the flour (which produces tough scones). Mix with a wooden spoon, fork, or your fingers just until the dry ingredients are moistened or nearly moistened. The dough will not be completely smooth like bread dough.

Gather the dough into a ball (you may need to add just one more teaspoon of nondairy milk or water, but you will be able to form it into a ball), and place on a lightly floured surface. (You may want to lightly flour your hands, as well.) Pat or roll the dough out to a ½-inch-thick (1.3-cm) round, and cut into 8 or 10 pieces—triangles are a traditional shape. Place them ½ inch (1.3 cm) apart on the baking sheet, brush the tops with nondairy milk, and sprinkle with some cinnamon and sugar.

Bake until the tops are golden brown, 12 to 15 minutes. Let cool on a rack or serve warm.

SERVING SUGGESTIONS & VARIATIONS

* Add ½ to 1 cup (62 to 125 g) chopped almonds or hazelnuts.
* Add ½ teaspoon almond extract.
* Add ½ cup (60 g) dried cranberries and zest from 2 lemons or oranges.
* Add 1 cup (145 g) fresh blueberries in place of the currants.

GINGERBREAD SCONES

YIELD: 8 TO 10 SCONES

These are perfect for a chilly autumn morning or a winter tea party with close friends.

INGREDIENTS—DOUGH

1¾ cups (220 g) unbleached all-purpose flour

¾ cup (60 g) rolled oats

⅓ cup (75 g) firmly packed light brown sugar

2 teaspoons ground ginger

1½ teaspoons ground cinnamon

⅛ teaspoon ground cloves

¼ teaspoon salt

2 teaspoons baking powder

½ teaspoon baking soda

½ cup (112 g) non-hydrogenated, nondairy butter, cold

⅓ cup (48 g) raisins or currants

⅓ cup (40 g) dried cranberries or cherries (optional)

½ cup (120 ml) nondairy milk

1 tablespoon (15 ml) white distilled vinegar

2½ tablespoons (106 g) unsulphured molasses

1 teaspoon vanilla extract

Nondairy milk for brushing tops

Rolled oats for sprinkling on top

INGREDIENTS—MAPLE GLAZE (OPTIONAL)

⅓ cup (33 g) powdered (confectioners') sugar, sifted

1 to 2 tablespoons (20 to 40 g) pure maple syrup

1 to 2 teaspoons nondairy milk

Preheat the oven to 400°F (200°C, or gas mark 6). Lightly oil a cookie/baking sheet or line with parchment paper.

To make the dough, in a large bowl, whisk together the flour, oats, brown sugar, ginger, cinnamon, cloves, salt, baking powder, and baking soda. Add the butter to the dry ingredients and cut into small pieces with two knives or with a pastry blender. You're not creating a paste; you want a coarse crumbly dough that resembles bread crumbs. Stir in the raisins, currants, dried cranberries, and/or cherries, if using.

In a separate bowl mix together the milk, vinegar, molasses, and vanilla to create "buttermilk." Let this mixture stand for 5 to 10 minutes, then add it to the flour mixture. Mix just until the dough comes together; do not overmix. The dough will not be completely smooth like bread dough. If it's a little too wet, add a little more flour; if it's too dry, add a little more milk.

Gather the dough into a ball and place on a lightly floured surface. Pat the dough out to a ½-inch-thick (1.3-cm) round, and cut into 8 or 10 pieces. Place them ½ inch (1.3 cm) apart on the baking sheet, brush with some nondairy milk, and sprinkle the tops with some rolled oats.

Bake for 15 to 20 minutes, or until golden brown and a toothpick inserted into the center comes out clean. Transfer to a wire rack to cool.

To make the glaze, mix together the glaze ingredients, adding more sugar or milk until it's thin enough to drizzle. Use a spoon to drizzle the glaze over the cooled scones and let dry.

CHAPTER THREE

COZY COMFORTS:
SWEET AND SAVORY QUICK BREADS

A quick bread refers to any flour-based bread or muffin that is leavened by baking soda and/or baking powder as opposed to yeast. Though it may seem odd to group pancakes and waffles here, by definition, they do fall into this category.

TIPS FOR MAKING QUICK BREADS

* Mix the wet and dry ingredients only until combined and the flour is just incorporated. Overmixing will create a tough batter and an equally tough finished product.

* Allow the bread to cool in the pan for 10 to 15 minutes before transferring to a wire rack to cool completely before cutting.

* Check for doneness at the minimum baking time, then every 2 minutes thereafter.

* If using chopped nuts or fruits, or grated carrots or zucchini, make sure they are prepared before starting the batter. You want to put the batter into the oven right away once it's mixed.

* If your quick bread rises unevenly, try baking it in the center of your oven, where the heat is most evenly distributed. Also, double-check the baking time and adjust your oven temperature if it tends to be off by a number of degrees.

* If your quick bread has a dense, heavy, tough texture, the batter may have been overmixed.

* To store quick breads: Cool completely, then wrap individual loaves in plastic wrap. Freeze for up to 2 months or refrigerate for up to 10 days. Store the bread at room temperature for up to 4 days, as long as it's not too humid.

THE RECIPES

Cornbread ... 59

Mediterranean Olive Bread ... 62

Zucchini Bread ... 64

Cranberry Nut Bread ... 65

Irish Soda Bread ... 66

Brown Bread ... 67

Pumpkin Spice Bread ... 69

Fig Date Bread ... 70

Pancakes ... 71

Waffles I ... 72

Waffles II ... 74

CORNBREAD

YIELD: 9 SERVINGS

When I make recipes such as this one, I wonder why instant mixes even exist. This recipe takes no time at all to prepare and is out of the oven in 30 minutes—hot, moist, and delicious. I particularly like the addition of whole corn kernels, but you can eliminate them if you want.

INGREDIENTS

1½ cups (355 ml) nondairy milk

1½ tablespoons (23 ml) distilled white or apple cider vinegar

1 cup (140 g) cornmeal (it may be sold as cornmeal, coarse cornmeal, or polenta)

1 cup (125 g) unbleached all-purpose flour

3 tablespoons (39 g) granulated sugar

½ teaspoon salt

1 teaspoon baking powder

1 teaspoon baking soda

2 tablespoons (30 ml) canola oil

½ to 1 cup (80 to 155 g) whole corn kernels (optional)

Preheat the oven to 425°F (220°C, or gas mark 7). Lightly oil a 9 × 9-inch (23 × 23-cm) baking dish.

In a small bowl, combine the milk and vinegar, and set aside.

Mix the cornmeal, flour, sugar, salt, baking powder, and baking soda in a large bowl. Add the milk and vinegar mixture as well as the oil. If adding the corn kernels, now is the time to do so. Stir until just blended. Spread the batter evenly in the prepared baking dish. Bake until the top is golden brown, 25 to 30 minutes. You may serve it at room temperature, but it's most delectable hot out of the oven.

SERVING SUGGESTIONS & VARIATIONS

* Serve it as breakfast, with various soups, or with spicy dishes such as chili. It's wonderful with a little nondairy butter, particularly when it's hot.
* Add fresh or frozen blueberries.

COLLEEN'S TIP: *Because genetically modified varieties now make up a significant proportion of the total harvest of corn (though most of it is fed to animals raised for human consumption), choose organic.*

FOOD LORE: *We have the Native Americans to thank for this simple dish that is appropriate as a meal, snack, or dessert. Because different varieties of corn grew throughout North America, the cornbread of early days differed by region. Blue corn was popular in the Southwest, yellow corn was favored in the northern regions, and white corn was preferred throughout the South. Early cornbread was made from a simple mixture of water, salt, and cornmeal and resembled a flat cake that traveled well on long trips. Because of some of the natural components in the corn, there was never a need to use yeast to get the bread to rise, so this American staple was "vegan" long before the word was even created!*

Defending Desserts

Let's face it. We have a love-hate relationship with desserts. We labor over our loved ones' birthday cakes and cherish the recipes that have been passed down to us from our ancestors. At the same time, we make excuses for eating our favorite "guilty pleasures" and justify why we deserve whatever sweet we're craving. We admit we "can't live without chocolate" and are "addicted to sugar," and we obsess over favorite indulgences. Whereas dessert was once considered a luxury, it is now perceived almost as a birthright, and daily consumption of some form of sugary snack is common among the young and old. In fact, the average American consumes an astounding 5 pounds of sugar each week, much of which is from the high-fructose corn syrup prevalent in so many packaged, processed, frozen, and commercial products and in soft drinks.

THE EVOLUTION OF DESSERT

The word "dessert" derives from the Old French word *desservir*, which means "to clear the table" or "remove the dishes," and the custom of eating fruits and nuts after a meal goes back several hundred years. Dessert as a standard part of a Western diet, however, is a relatively recent development. Before the nineteenth-century rise of the middle class and the mechanization of the sugar industry, sweets were a rare holiday treat or a privilege of the upper class. As sugar became cheaper and more readily available, the development and popularity of desserts spread accordingly. Instead of reserving them for special occasions, we began to indulge every day—sometimes several times a day. It is taking its toll on our health, our waistlines, our pocketbooks, and even on the Earth.

In the latter part of the last century, a number of diet fads greatly influenced the public's eating habits, aided by the multibillion-dollar food industry. The commercial desserts industry, not wanting to lose its health- and weight-conscious customers, began manufacturing low-fat cookies, low-calorie cakes, and sugar-free doughnuts, touting them all as guilt-free food. Artificial sweeteners, such as aspartame, stevia, saccharin, and Splenda, were praised as health foods and heralded as the solution to the rise in obesity. With abandon, people indulged more than ever, and dreams of weight loss turned into the reality of weight gain.

GOING HOMEMADE

So why am I telling you this? It probably seems contradictory coming from someone who wrote a desserts cookbook, but I will be the first to tell you that we have no nutritional requirement for sugar. While I do advocate a whole foods plant-based diet, I'm not proposing that we all have to live an ascetic lifestyle, devoid of gustatory pleasures. What I do propose is that we treat desserts for what they are: treats!

The answer is not in "fat-free," "low-fat," "low-calorie," or "sugar-free" store-bought commercial products whose ingredients lists confound even the most sophisticated consumer. One of the problems

with packaged desserts posing as health food is that people think they can indulge even more, completely forgetting the fact that these foods still contain empty calories and will increase your waistline as much as if they were "full fat." Preparing your own baked goods ensures that you know exactly what goes into them, enables you to adjust the sweetness to your own liking, and guarantees that you're not consuming preservatives meant only to prolong the shelf life of processed foods.

Invariably, there is always someone who asks whether they could use maple syrup instead of sugar, carob instead of chocolate, prunes instead of oil, etc. I like to remind them that when we're making chocolate cake—no matter what I do to it, it's not going to turn into broccoli. There's a time for broccoli and there's a time for chocolate cake. If you want broccoli, have broccoli; if you want chocolate cake, have chocolate cake. If you want a sugar-free, wheat-free, oil-free, salt-free chocolate cake, have broccoli.

THE JOY OF SAVORING

It's important that we recognize that by the time we reach for dessert, we're doing so for the sake of the pleasure it will bring to us—not because we're trying to fulfill any nutritional need. When I treat myself to cheesecake, I recognize it for what it is: a treat for celebrating a special occasion. It is for this reason that I am perfectly comfortable using plain old sugar for most of the desserts I make. (See "A Word about Sweeteners" on page 173.) I use this because I want my vegan recipes to compete with what most people consider the "standards," but also because I also didn't set out to write a health food cookbook—I set out to write a book on vegan desserts, which just happen to be healthier insofar as they are free of cholesterol, saturated fat, lactose, and animal protein.

That doesn't mean that all the recipes in this book are rich and decadent. My intention was to provide a wide spectrum of baked goods, from breads and biscuits to pies and beverages, and though it's not an exhaustive collection, I think there is a good variety from which to choose.

TAKING A STEP BACK

There really is nothing like baking your own bread, creating your own cookies, and mulling your own cider. Infinitely less expensive and definitely healthier, homemade goodies are also—paradoxically—very simple. They are a celebration of the simplistic. They hearken back to a time when families gathered around the hearth because it was the source of heat and sustenance. Homemade goodies all have their own unique personalities, particularly when they are imperfectly shaped and dappled with flaws. And most importantly, they're infused with the generosity and love of the baker.

I relish the thought that my creations may become part of your own repertoire of favorite recipes and may have the high honor of marking your special occasions and celebrations.

MEDITERRANEAN OLIVE BREAD

YIELD: 1 STANDARD-SIZE LOAF

To get the look of true artisan bread, you can use a round pan instead of a loaf pan. A lovely breakfast or snack bread, it's also perfect for serving with Mediterranean dishes, particularly soup.

INGREDIENTS

3 tablespoons (45 g) ground flaxseed (equivalent of 3 eggs)
½ cup (120 ml) water
1½ cups (188 g) unbleached all-purpose flour
¾ cup (94 g) whole wheat flour
2½ teaspoons baking powder
1 teaspoon each chopped fresh rosemary and basil, or ¾ teaspoon each dried
½ teaspoon salt
1 cup (235 ml) nondairy milk
¼ cup (60 ml) olive oil
⅓ cup (50 g) finely chopped walnuts
⅓ cup (33 g) chopped pitted black olives
⅓ cup (33 g) chopped sundried tomatoes

Preheat the oven to 350°F (180°C, or gas mark 4), and lightly grease an 8-inch (20-cm) or 9-inch (23-cm) loaf pan.

In a food processor, whip the flaxseed and water together until thick and creamy.

In a large bowl, thoroughly combine the flours, baking powder, rosemary, and salt. In a separate bowl, combine the flaxseed mixture, milk, and olive oil.

Add the wet mixture to the dry and fold until about three-quarters of the dry ingredients are moistened. Add the walnuts, olives, and tomatoes, and fold just until the pieces are distributed and the dry ingredients are moistened; the batter will be stiff and a little sticky. Scrape the batter into the loaf pan and spread evenly. Bake until a toothpick inserted into the center comes out clean, about 40 minutes. Let cool in the pan on a rack for 5 to 10 minutes before unmolding to cool completely on the rack.

ZUCCHINI BREAD

YIELD: 2 STANDARD LOAVES, 4 MINI LOAVES, OR 24 MUFFINS

If 2 cups of sugar seems like a lot, please keep in mind this recipe makes 2 loaves of bread, but you can certainly cut down on the sugar. This classic zucchini bread is perfect for a chilly summer evening, when summer squash is still in season but autumn is right around the corner.

INGREDIENTS

3 tablespoons (45 g) ground flaxseed
  (equivalent of 3 eggs)
½ cup (120 ml) water
1 cup (235 ml) canola oil (or ½ cup [120 ml] oil
  and ½ cup [125 g] unsweetened applesauce)
1 tablespoon (15 ml) white distilled vinegar
2 cups (400 g) granulated sugar
2 cups (240 g) grated zucchini (peeling optional)
2 teaspoons vanilla extract

3 cups (375 g) unbleached all-purpose or whole
  wheat pastry flour
2 teaspoons ground cinnamon
½ teaspoon nutmeg
1 teaspoon baking soda
¼ teaspoon baking powder
1 teaspoon salt
½ cup (75 g) chopped walnuts (optional)
½ cup (75 g) raisins (optional)

Preheat the oven to 325°F (170°C, or gas mark 3). Lightly grease two 8 × 4 × 2-inch (20 × 10 × 5-cm) loaf pans, 4 mini loaf pans, or 2 muffin tins.

In a food processor or in a bowl using an electric hand mixer, combine the flaxseed and the water. Whip until it's thick and creamy, about 2 minutes. Add the oil, vinegar, and sugar, and combine. Stir in the zucchini and vanilla. If using a food processor, transfer the oil/vinegar/sugar mixture to a large bowl before stirring in the zucchini and vanilla.

In a separate bowl, sift together the flour, cinnamon, nutmeg, baking soda, baking powder, and salt. Add the nuts and raisins, if using, to the sifted ingredients. Stir this dry mixture into the wet mixture until just combined. Do not overmix. Divide the batter into the prepared pans, and bake for 60 to 70 minutes for standard loaves, 40 to 45 minutes for mini loaves, or 30 to 35 minutes for muffins. Check for doneness by inserting a toothpick into the center.

COLLEEN'S TIPS:

∗ *The fastest and easiest way to grate zucchini is by using the grating blade on your food processor, but it can easily be done by hand.*
∗ *Freezing grated zucchini is a great way to make use of this versatile veggie. First, steam in small quantities for 1 to 2 minutes until translucent. Drain well, pack into containers, cool by placing the containers in cold water, seal, and freeze. If watery when thawed, drain the liquid before using the zucchini.*
∗ *Good things always come in small packages! Use mini loaf pans to make great gifts for friends, neighbors, and co-workers.*

CRANBERRY NUT BREAD

YIELD: 1 STANDARD-SIZE LOAF

While this is a perfect fall/winter/holiday treat, it can be made any time of the year, particularly if you freeze fresh cranberries when they're in season. Though you can certainly serve this bread right away, it's even better a day or two later when the flavors have had time to mingle.

INGREDIENTS

1 tablespoon (15 g) ground flaxseed (equivalent of 1 egg)

3 tablespoons (45 ml) water

¼ cup (55 g) non-hydrogenated, nondairy butter, melted and cooled

1 teaspoon vanilla extract

1 cup (235 ml) orange juice

1 cup (235 ml) nondairy milk

4 cups (500 g) unbleached all-purpose flour

1 cup (200 g) granulated sugar

4 teaspoons baking powder

½ teaspoon salt

2 teaspoons orange or lemon zest

1½ cups (95 g) whole cranberries, fresh or frozen

½ cup (40 g) candied fruit or mixed peel, chopped

1 cup (125 g) coarsely chopped toasted almonds, walnuts, hazelnuts, or pecans

Preheat the oven to 350°F (180°C, or gas mark 4). Lightly grease an 8 × 4 × 2-inch (20 × 10 × 5-cm) or a 9 × 5 × 3-inch (23 × 13 × 7.5-cm) loaf pan.

In the small bowl of your food processor or by hand, whip together the flaxseed and water until thoroughly combined and thick, about 1 minute. Add the melted butter, vanilla, orange juice, and milk, and blend until combined. Set aside.

In a large bowl, stir together the flour, sugar, baking powder, salt, and zest. Stir the wet ingredients into the dry ingredients, and mix in the fruit and nuts. Pour into the prepared pan and bake for 60 to 70 minutes, or until a thin wooden skewer inserted into the center of the bread comes out clean. Leave to cool in the loaf pan for 30 minutes before turning it over to cool on a wire rack.

SERVING SUGGESTIONS & VARIATIONS

∗ You may also use dried cranberries, though the tartness of the fresh cranberries, which definitely mellows when they're cooked, contrasts nicely with the sweetness of the candied fruit.

∗ This bread freezes really well. To serve after freezing, bring to room temperature or heat in the microwave.

COLLEEN'S TIPS:

∗ *To toast almonds, spread on a baking sheet and place in a 350°F (180°C, or gas mark 4) oven for 5 to 10 minutes until lightly brown. Watch carefully to prevent burning. Cool before using.*

∗ *You may use your electric stand mixer to combine all the ingredients, but I recommend folding in your cranberries by hand lest you crush them with the mixer blade.*

IRISH SODA BREAD

YIELD: 1 ROUND LOAF

One of the things I love about traditional recipes such as this one is that they rarely need to be "veganized," because they just happen to be vegan already. Soda bread is called such because it relies on baking soda (bicarbonate of soda) as the leavening agent. The lactic acid in buttermilk is what activates the carbon dioxide, but adding vinegar, which is acidic, to nondairy milk creates the same effect.

INGREDIENTS

2 cups (470 ml) nondairy milk
2 teaspoons white distilled vinegar
4 cups (500 g) unbleached all-purpose flour
1 teaspoon baking soda
1 teaspoon salt
¼ cup (55 g) non-hydrogenated, nondairy butter, melted

Preheat the oven to 425°F (220°C, or gas mark 7). Lightly grease a round 9- or 10-inch (23- or 25-cm) cake pan.

In a small bowl, combine the milk and vinegar. Let stand for 5 to 10 minutes. Essentially, by adding an acidic agent, you just created "buttermilk."

In a large bowl, mix together the flour, baking soda, and salt. Add the milk and vinegar mixture and nondairy butter, and combine until you have a sticky dough. Knead the dough in the bowl or on a floured surface for 10 to 12 strokes.

Place the dough in the prepared pan, and cut a cross in the top. Bake for 40 to 45 minutes, or until the bottom has a hollow sound when thumped. Cool slightly before serving.

Soda bread can dry out quickly and is typically good for 2 to 3 days; it is best served warm or toasted with nondairy butter.

SERVING SUGGESTIONS & VARIATIONS

* Add 1½ cups (218 g) raisins.
* Add 1 cup (150 g) various nuts.

FOOD LORE: *Soda bread is a type of quick bread that dates to approximately 1840, when bicarbonate of soda was introduced to Ireland and replaced yeast as the leavening agent. The bread eventually became a staple of the Irish diet and is still used as an accompaniment to a meal.*

There are several theories as to the significance of the cross in soda bread. Some believe that the cross was placed in the bread to ward off evil, but it is more likely that the cross is used to help with the cooking of the bread or to serve as a guideline for even slices.

BROWN BREAD

This is a variation of Irish soda bread and strictly traditional brown bread, which was steamed in cans. Purists would never add raisins, but they do add a lot of flavor to this relatively simple bread.

INGREDIENTS

2 cups (470 ml) nondairy milk
2 teaspoons white distilled vinegar
3 cups (375 g) whole wheat flour
1 cup (125 g) unbleached all-purpose flour
1½ teaspoons baking soda
1 teaspoon of salt
⅓ cup (27 g) rolled oats (optional)
½ to 1 cup (75 to 145 g) golden raisins (optional)
2 tablespoons (28 g) non-hydrogenated, nondairy butter

Preheat the oven to 425°F (220°C, or gas mark 7). Lightly grease a round 9- or 10-inch (23- or 25-cm) cake pan.

In a small bowl, combine the milk and vinegar. Let stand for 5 minutes. Essentially, by adding an acidic agent, you just created "buttermilk."

In a large bowl, mix together the flours, baking soda, salt, oats (if using), and raisins (if using). Add the butter, and rub in with your fingertips until the mixture resembles coarse bread crumbs. Stir in the milk and vinegar mixture and combine until you have a sticky dough. Knead the dough in the bowl or on a floured surface for about 10 strokes. Don't over-knead, or it will become too tough.

Place the dough in the prepared pan, and cut a cross in the top. Bake for 30 to 40 minutes, or until the bottom has a hollow sound when thumped. Cool slightly before serving.

Brown bread can dry out quickly and is typically good for 2 to 3 days; it is best served warm or toasted with nondairy butter and jam.

FOOD LORE: *Various forms of soda bread are popular throughout Ireland. The bread is either brown or white (with the former known colloquially as "brown bread"). The two major types are the loaf and the farl. The loaf form takes a more rounded shape, and the farl, a more flattened type of bread, is absolutely unique to Northern Ireland. It is cooked on a griddle, allowing it to take a flatter shape.*

PUMPKIN SPICE BREAD

YIELD: 2 STANDARD-SIZE LOAVES OR 4 MINI LOAVES

This delicious, fat-free fragrant bread is perfect as dessert or a side dish for a winter holiday meal. Full or mini loaves make great gifts for coworkers, neighbors, and mail carriers. (Trust me! Our mail is never late!) This recipe was adapted from *La Dolce Vegan*.

INGREDIENTS

3 tablespoons (45 g) ground flaxseed
  (equivalent of 3 eggs)
½ cup (120 ml) water
2 cups (400 g) granulated sugar
1½ cups (370 g) unsweetened applesauce
1 (14-ounce or 392-g) can pumpkin puree
3 cups (375 g) unbleached all-purpose flour

1 teaspoon ground cloves
1 teaspoon ground cinnamon
1 teaspoon nutmeg
1 teaspoon baking soda
½ teaspoon baking powder
½ teaspoon salt

Preheat the oven to 350°F (180°C, or gas mark 4). Lightly oil two 8-inch (20-cm) loaf pans or four 6 × 3 × 2-inch (15 × 7.5 × 5-cm) mini-loaf pans.

In a food processor or in a bowl using an electric hand mixer, whip the flaxseed and water together until thick and creamy.

In a large bowl, stir together the sugar, applesauce, pumpkin puree, and flaxseed mixture.

In a medium-size bowl, stir together the flour, cloves, cinnamon, nutmeg, baking soda, baking powder, and salt. Thoroughly combine the dry ingredients, then add them to the wet. Stir until just combined.

Spoon the batter into 2 standard-size loaf pans or 4 mini-loaf pans. Bake for 55 to 60 minutes, or until a toothpick or knife inserted into the center comes out clean. If using mini-loaf pans, you will want to check for doneness after 30 minutes. Let the breads cool for at least 20 minutes before removing from the loaf pans. This is important, as the bread is still baking and needs time to coalesce in the hot pan.

SERVING SUGGESTIONS & VARIATIONS

* Use ½ cup (120 ml) canola oil and ½ cup (125 g) applesauce.
* Add 1 cup (175 g) nondairy semisweet chocolate chips and/or 1 cup (150 g) walnuts. These would be folded in after the wet and dry ingredients are combined.

DID YOU KNOW? *The World Health Organization recommends a daily intake of 27 to 40 grams of fiber for most adults. The USDA recommends 25 grams per day, and most studies have shown that optimal intake for cancer prevention is at least 30 to 35 grams per day.*

FIG DATE BREAD

YIELD: 1 STANDARD-SIZE LOAF

In a nutshell, I adore this bread. It's moist, hearty, healthful, and beautiful. In the fall, I make it with fresh figs, but because they add to the moisture content, I just cut back a bit on the amount. Look for farm-fresh dates at the farmers' market for the best varieties. Medjool and Barhee are my favorites.

INGREDIENTS

2 tablespoons (30 g) ground flaxseed (equivalent of 2 eggs)

6 tablespoons (90 ml) water

1 cup (175 g) pitted dates, chopped

1 cup (175 g) dried figs (or ½ cup [140 g] fresh), coarsely chopped

¼ cup (55 g) non-hydrogenated, nondairy butter or canola oil

1½ teaspoons baking soda

1 cup (235 ml) boiling water

½ cup (100 g) granulated sugar

1 cup (175 g) walnuts, chopped

¾ cup (94 g) unbleached all-purpose flour

¾ cup (94 g) whole wheat flour

½ teaspoon baking powder

½ teaspoon salt

Preheat the oven to 350°F (180°C, or gas mark 4). Grease an 8 × 4 × 2-inch (20 × 10 x 5-cm) or a 9 × 5 × 3-inch (23 × 13 × 7.5-cm) loaf pan.

In a food processor or in a bowl using an electric hand mixer, whip the flaxseed and water together until it reaches a thick and creamy consistency.

In a large bowl, combine the dates, figs, butter, and baking soda. Add the boiling water, stir well, and let it stand for 15 minutes to thicken up. After 15 minutes, stir in the sugar, walnuts, and flaxseed mixture.

In a medium-size bowl, combine the flours, baking powder, and salt. Add to the date mixture, and stir just until combined.

Spread evenly in the prepared pan. Bake until a thin wooden skewer inserted into the center comes out clean (a toothpick may not be long enough), 55 to 60 minutes. Cool in the pan for at least 30 minutes, then turn out onto a wire rack to cool completely.

DID YOU KNOW? *Figs have higher quantities of fiber than any other dried or fresh fruit. They are also high in potassium.*

COLLEEN'S TIP: *Fresh figs are one of the most perishable fruits and should be eaten within a day or two of purchase. Look for figs that have a deep color and are plump and tender, but not mushy. They should have a mildly sweet fragrance and not smell sour. Keep ripe figs in the refrigerator for up to 2 days. Under-ripe figs can be kept on a plate at room temperature, away from direct sunlight. Well-wrapped dried figs will stay fresh for several months and can be either kept in a cool, dark place or stored in the refrigerator.*

PANCAKES

YIELD: 8 TO 10 PANCAKES

These pancakes are fluffy, flavorful, and so easy to make. They can be made with no oil or butter or just a little bit. And a good nonstick pan enables you to cook them without any oil at all.

INGREDIENTS

1 cup (125 g) unbleached all-purpose flour (or use ½ cup [65 g]
    all-purpose and ½ cup [65 g] whole wheat flour)
1 tablespoon (4.6 g) baking powder
¼ teaspoon salt
1 cup (235 ml) nondairy milk
2 tablespoons (30 ml) canola oil or non-hydrogenated, nondairy butter, melted
3 tablespoons (45 ml) liquid sweetener, such as pure maple syrup, apple juice concentrate,
    or orange juice
Additional oil or butter for cooking (optional)

Combine the flour, baking powder, and salt in a bowl. In a separate bowl, combine the milk, oil, and sweetener.

Add the milk mixture to the flour mixture and mix just until moistened; a few lumps are okay. (Don't overmix, or the pancakes will be tough.)

Heat a nonstick griddle or sauté pan over a medium-high flame. (You may add some oil to the griddle/sauté pan and heat until hot, but with a nonstick pan, you don't even need it.)

Pour the batter onto the griddle to form circles about 4 inches (10 cm) in diameter. Cook the pancakes for a couple of minutes on one side until bubbles appear on the surface. Slide a spatula under the pancake and flip it over. Cook the pancakes on the other side for another 2 minutes or so. Continue until golden brown on each side, about 4 minutes in all.

SERVING SUGGESTIONS & VARIATIONS

* Add a handful of fresh blueberries, chopped peaches or apples, raisins, walnuts, pecans, or nondairy chocolate chips to your pancake batter. A dash of cinnamon in the batter is nice, too.
* Serve with pure maple syrup or a fresh fruit puree.
* Top with berries.
* Serve with tempeh bacon and tofu scramble. (See recipes in *The Vegan Table*)
* Try the Brown Sugar Syrup (page 27) if you're out of maple syrup.
* Top with Sautéed Bananas (page 150) or Bananas Foster (page 151).

WAFFLES I

YIELD: 4 TO 6 WAFFLES

The ground flaxseed is perfect in this American favorite—not only as the "egg replacer" but also for their flavor and nutrition. Here is a case when the specks of flaxseed add character to the final product. This recipe is based on a typical, traditional waffle recipe. See page 74 for a lighter version that contains no added oil/butter.

INGREDIENTS

3 tablespoons (45 g) ground flaxseed (equivalent of 3 eggs)

½ cup (120 ml) water

6 tablespoons (85 g) non-hydrogenated, nondairy butter, melted

1½ cups (355 ml) nondairy milk

1¾ cups (220 g) unbleached all-purpose flour

1 tablespoon (4.6 g) baking powder

1 tablespoon (25 g) granulated sugar

Pinch of salt

Preheat your waffle iron. In a food processor or blender, whip the flaxseed and water together until it reaches a thick and creamy consistency, about 2 minutes. Add the butter and non-dairy milk, and whip for another minute.

In a large bowl, combine the flour, baking powder, sugar, and salt. Create a well in the center of your dry ingredients, and pour in the milk mixture. Stir until just combined. If you'd like to add any optional ingredients (see below), fold them in now.

Spoon ½ cup (120 ml) batter (or the amount recommended for your waffle iron) onto the hot iron. Spread the batter to just within ¼ inch of the edge of the grids using the back of your spoon or spatula. Close the lid and bake until the waffle is golden brown. Serve immediately or keep warm in a single layer on a rack in a 200°F (93°C, or gas mark ¼) oven while you finish cooking the rest.

SERVING SUGGESTIONS & VARIATIONS

Add any of the following to your batter:

* ½ cup (90 g) nondairy semisweet chocolate chips
* ½ cup (75 g) raisins
* ½ cup (65 g) finely chopped walnuts or pecans, toasted
* 1 small ripe banana, thinly sliced

DID YOU KNOW? *The word "waffle" is derived from the Dutch word wafel, which means "honeycomb." The waffle iron was patented in 1869.*

COLLEEN'S TIP: *If you use less butter, you may have trouble with the waffles sticking to your iron. I find that 6 tablespoons (85 g) is perfect, but you can add more if that's your preference.*

WAFFLES II

This delicious, oil-free recipe is from my friend Laura Barney, who counts this as one of her favorites. She recommends freezing them so you— and the kids—can have healthful waffles anytime.

INGREDIENTS

2 cups (470 ml) water

2 tablespoons (50 g) sugar or concentrated apple juice

1 cup (80 g) quick-cooking oats

¼ cup (35 g) cornmeal

4 tablespoons (60 g) ground flaxseed (equivalent of 4 eggs)

¼ cup (40 g) raw cashews or walnuts

2 tablespoons (16 g) cornstarch

¾ teaspoon salt

1 teaspoon cinnamon (optional)

Preheat your waffle iron. Blend all the ingredients in a blender for 1 minute. Let sit for 10 to 15 minutes so all the ingredients have some time to incorporate into one another and thicken up.

   Spoon ½ cup (120 ml) batter (or the amount recommended for your waffle iron) onto the hot iron. Spread the batter to just within ¼ inch of the edge of the grids using the back of your spoon or spatula. Close the lid and bake until the waffle is golden brown. Serve immediately or keep warm in a single layer on a rack in a 200°F (93°C, or gas mark ¼) oven while you finish cooking the rest.

SERVING SUGGESTIONS & VARIATIONS

Serve with pure maple syrup, Brown Sugar Syrup (page 257), sifted confectioners' sugar, fresh fruit, jam, or preserves.

FOOD LORE: *Waffles have their roots in Western Europe and go far back as the ninth and tenth centuries. A waffle iron, which consisted of two metal plates connected by a hinge, was placed over a fire and manually flipped to cook both sides of the waffles, which would have been made from a mixture of barley and oats.*

CHAPTER FOUR

CAUSE FOR CELEBRATION: CAKES AND CUPCAKES

Whether you want a treat to mark a special occasion, serve at a brunch, or impress coworkers, any of these delightful desserts will do.

TIPS FOR BAKING THE PERFECT CAKE

TO SIFT OR NOT TO SIFT
All-purpose flour usually doesn't need to be sifted—simply stir it lightly with a spoon before measuring.

KEEP IT SHUT
Do not open the oven during the first half of the baking time. Cold air will interfere with the cake's rising.

FRESHEN UP
Use fresh ingredients and organic when possible.

NO NEED TO CHILL
Have all ingredients at room temperature for best results.

LAST BUT NOT LEAST
Always add nuts, raisins, chips, and fruits to the batter last. This will avoid color bleeding as well as overmixing.

FIRE IT UP
Always preheat the oven first. Plan for 10 to 15 minutes before it's at the desired temperature.

PASS MUSTER
Test your cakes for doneness while they're still in the oven. Cakes are done when the sides shrink slightly away from the pan and a toothpick inserted into center comes out clean.

CLEAN CUT
For perfect slices, briefly run a sharp knife through an open flame or under hot water before cutting. Wipe the blade and reheat between cuts.

COOL IT
Cool cakes in the pan for 10 to 15 minutes before loosening the edge and turning them out onto a wire rack to cool.

CHILL OUT
Chill the cake for about a half hour before filling and frosting. The cake will be much easier to work with. Similarly, when applying multiple layers of frosting, refrigerate between applications.

For cheesecake tips, see page 98.

THE RECIPES

Chocolate Cake ... 77
Apple Cake ... 78
German Apple Cake ... 80
   (Versunkener Apfelkuchen)
Carrot Cake ... 82
Blueberry Cake ... 83
Light Lemon Bundt Cake ... 86
Blueberry Orange Bundt Cake ... 89
Cinnamon Coffee Cake ... 90
Vanilla Cupcakes ... 91
Chocolate Cream Cheese Cupcakes ... 92
Strawberry Cupcakes ... 93
Chocolate Peanut Butter Cupcakes ... 96
Chocolate Cheesecake ... 97
Lemon Cheesecake ... 98
Pumpkin Cheesecake ... 100

CHOCOLATE CAKE

YIELD: ONE 9-INCH (23-CM) CAKE OR 8 CUPCAKES

This chocolate cake might be the easiest cake in the world to prepare, and it's incredibly versatile, lending itself to a layer cake, a Bundt cake, or (shown at left) cupcakes. (Double the recipe for a layer cake or a Bundt cake.) I want to give credit to Jennifer Raymond, for it was in her cookbook, *The Peaceful Palate*, that I first saw this recipe. Add ¼ teaspoon of cayenne pepper or chili powder for a "Mexican Chocolate Cake."

INGREDIENTS

1½ cups (188 g) unbleached all-purpose flour

¾ cup (150 g) granulated sugar

½ teaspoon salt

1 teaspoon baking soda

¼ cup (30 g) unsweetened cocoa powder

1½ teaspoons vanilla extract

⅓ cup (80 ml) canola or coconut oil

1 tablespoon (15 ml) white distilled vinegar

1 cup (235 ml) cold water

1 recipe Chocolate Frosting or Buttercream Frosting (page 247)

Preheat the oven to 350°F (180°C, or gas mark 4). Lightly oil a Bundt pan, 9-inch (23-cm) spring-form pan, or muffin tins.

Combine the flour, sugar, salt, baking soda, and cocoa powder in a bowl until thoroughly combined. Create a well in the center of the dry ingredients, and add the vanilla, oil, vinegar, and water. Mix until just combined. Pour into your prepared pan, and bake in the preheated oven for 30 minutes, until a toothpick inserted into center comes out clean. If making cupcakes, check for doneness after 15 minutes.

Cool on a wire rack. To remove the cake from the pan, run a sharp knife around the inside of the pan to loosen the cake. Cool completely before frosting. You may also dust with sifted confectioners' sugar and top with fresh raspberries.

WHAT'S THE DIFFERENCE?

* **Cacao:** *The tropical evergreen tree and its dried and partially fermented beans that are processed to make chocolate, cocoa powder, and cocoa butter.*
* **Cocoa Butter:** *The ivory-colored, naturally occurring fat in cacao beans.*
* **Chocolate:** *The general term for the products of the seeds of the cacao tree, used for making beverages or confectionery.*
* **Cocoa Powder (Unsweetened Cocoa):** *Made when chocolate liquor is pressed to remove most of its cocoa butter.*
* **Bittersweet, Dark, and Semisweet Chocolates:** *Made when the chocolate liquor, pressed from the cacao bean, is combined with cocoa butter, sugar, vanilla, and lecithin. Some brands add dairy, so read the ingredients.*
* **Baking Chocolate:** *Pure, unsweetened chocolate liquor, pressed from the cacao bean during processing. Also called unsweetened and/or bitter chocolate.*

APPLE CAKE

This is a hearty, moist cake reminiscent of traditional winter holiday fruit cake in terms of its denseness. Only here, we pour Brown Sugar Syrup (page 257) over it instead of soaking it in rum or brandy.

INGREDIENTS

3 cups (375 g) unbleached all-purpose flour
1 teaspoon baking soda
¼ teaspoon salt
1 teaspoon cinnamon
3 tablespoons (45 g) ground flaxseed (equivalent of 3 eggs)
½ cup (120 ml) water
1½ cups (300 g) granulated sugar
1¼ cups (300 ml) canola oil
2 teaspoons vanilla extract
3 cups (450 g) peeled and chopped apples
1 recipe Brown Sugar Syrup (page 257), optional

Preheat the oven to 350°F (180°C, or gas mark 4). Lightly oil a Bundt pan, tube pan, or 9- or 10-inch (23- or 25-cm) springform pan.

Sift together the flour, baking soda, salt, and cinnamon. Set aside. In a food processor or blender, whip the flaxseed and water together until it becomes creamy and thick, about 1 minute. Add the sugar, oil, and vanilla, and beat for 2 minutes. Stir the dry ingredients into the wet. Fold in the apples. You will have a pretty thick batter.

Pour the batter into the pan, and bake for 1 hour and 15 minutes. Pour the syrup over the cake as soon as it comes out of the oven, if using. Let the cake cool, loosen the sides, invert onto a plate, then invert onto another plate, with the syrup topping side up.

SERVING SUGGESTIONS & VARIATIONS

If you want the cake to more closely resemble a traditional fruit cake, feel free to add raisins, dried apricots, chopped dates, walnuts, and a combination of wintry spices (cloves, cinnamon, allspice, nutmeg, etc.) If this is the kind of cake you're aiming for, you can't really add too many extras.

Troubleshooting Cakes

Please also refer to "Tips for Baking the Perfect Cake" on page 75. The guide below is meant to help you identify problems, which is the first step in solving them.

IF YOUR CAKE HAS A CRACKED SURFACE AND/OR HOLES AND TUNNELS:

* the batter may have been overmixed.
* you may have used too much flour.
* you may have used too little baking powder or baking soda.
* the oven may have been too hot.

IF YOUR CAKE SINKS IN THE CENTER:

* the batter may have been overmixed.
* there may be too much fat, sugar, or leavening.
* there may not have been enough liquid in your batter.
* the oven temperature may have been too low.

IF YOUR CAKE DIDN'T RISE:

* the batter may have not have been mixed thoroughly and evenly.
* there may be too much or too little fat.
* the baking powder you used is old.
* there wasn't enough leavening (baking powder, baking soda, etc.).

IF THE TOP CRUST OF YOUR CAKE IS TOO DARK OR TOO HARD:

* the cake was baked too long.
* the oven temperature was wrong.
* there was too much sugar, baking powder, or baking soda.

BLUEBERRY ORANGE BUNDT CAKE, PAGE 89

IF YOUR CAKE HAS A COARSE GRAIN OR IS DRY:

* the oven temperature was too low.
* you may have used too much baking powder or baking soda.
* there was not enough liquid in the batter.

IF YOUR CAKE IS FALLING APART:

* you used too much baking powder, baking soda, sugar, or fat.
* the batter was improperly (not thoroughly) mixed.
* the oven temperature was too low.

GERMAN APPLE CAKE (VERSUNKENER APFELKUCHEN)

YIELD: 8 TO 10 SLICES

From my friend Bylle Manss, this wonderful recipe is a variation of a very typical German cake. The original version, which includes raw apples and no topping, is called "Apfelkuchen, sehr fein," which translates loosely to "Apple cake, very delectable." This version is also "very delectable" but at the same time not overly sweet.

INGREDIENTS—CAKE

3 apples, peeled and cut into slices

½ cup (112 g) non-hydrogenated, nondairy butter

½ cup (100 g) granulated sugar

½ cup (125 g) unsweetened applesauce

2 tablespoons (30 ml) nondairy milk

1½ cups (188 g) unbleached all-purpose flour

2½ teaspoons baking powder

INGREDIENTS—TOPPING

¼ cup (60 g) firmly packed light or dark brown sugar

½ teaspoon cinnamon

½ teaspoon ground ginger

Preheat the oven to 350°F (180°C, or gas mark 4). Lightly grease a 9-inch (23-cm) springform pan. To make the cake, cook the apples in a little bit of water on the stove or in the microwave until they're just a little soft but not mushy. (I put them in the microwave for no longer than 1½ minutes.) Set aside.

With an electric hand mixer or by hand using a wooden spoon, cream together the butter and sugar. Add the applesauce and milk. Finally, add the flour and baking powder, and stir until just combined.

Add the batter to the prepared pan, and arrange the apple slices in a circle on top of the cake.

To make the topping, mix together the brown sugar, cinnamon, and ginger, and sprinkle over the apples, covering the top of the cake. Bake for 30 to 40 minutes, or until a toothpick inserted into the center comes out clean. Let cool for 15 minutes before unmolding from the cake pan.

SERVING SUGGESTIONS & VARIATIONS

To make this cake completely fat-free, use 1 cup (245 g) applesauce and eliminate the nondairy butter.

COLLEEN'S TIP: *See "Apples and Their Uses" on page 157 to decide which apples to use for this dessert.*

CARROT CAKE

YIELD: ONE 9-INCH (23-CM) CAKE

Resembling quick bread more than cake, this simple but delicious recipe may be made as a loaf, as a sheet cake, or in cupcake form. A grating blade on your food processor is the quickest way to prepare the carrots.

INGREDIENTS

3 tablespoons (45 g) ground flaxseed
   (equivalent of 3 eggs)
½ cup (120 ml) water
⅔ cup (155 ml) canola oil
1½ cups (180 g) finely grated peeled carrots
1 cup (150 g) chopped walnuts
1 cup (145 g) raisins
1⅓ cups (165 g) unbleached all-purpose flour
1 cup (200 g) granulated sugar

1½ teaspoons baking soda
1 teaspoon baking powder
1 teaspoon ground cinnamon
½ teaspoon ground cloves
½ teaspoon freshly grated or ground nutmeg
½ teaspoon ground allspice
½ teaspoon salt
1 recipe Cream Cheese Frosting (page 246)

Preheat the oven to 350°F (180°C, or gas mark 4). Lightly grease a 9 × 9-inch (23 × 23-cm) square cake pan.

In a food processor or blender, whip together the ground flaxseed and water until it's thick and creamy, about 2 minutes. Add the oil and blend until combined. Transfer this flaxseed and oil mixture to a large bowl, and add the carrots, walnuts, and raisins. Stir to combine.

In a separate bowl, thoroughly combine the flour, sugar, baking soda, baking powder, cinnamon, cloves, nutmeg, allspice, and salt. Add the wet mixture to this dry mixture, and stir with a rubber spatula until thoroughly combined, but do not overmix.

Scrape the batter into the pan and spread evenly. Bake until a toothpick inserted into the center comes out clean, about 30 minutes. Let cool in the pan for at least 15 minutes. Slide a thin knife around the cake to detach it from the pan. Invert the cake, and let cool.

Once cool, frost with Cream Cheese Frosting.

FOOD LORE: *Carrots have been used in cakes in Europe since the Middle Ages, when other sweeteners were hard to find or just too expensive. Carrots and beets contain more sugar than other vegetables and are ideal for using in sweet desserts.*

BLUEBERRY CAKE

YIELD: 8 TO 10 SERVINGS

Consider this a variation of the Cinnamon Coffee Cake (page 90)—with a bit more of a streusel topping. It's perfect for brunch and features antioxidant-rich blueberries.

INGREDIENTS—CAKE

1 tablespoon (15 g) ground flaxseed (equivalent of 1 egg)

3 tablespoons (45 ml) water

1 cup (125 g) unbleached all-purpose flour

1 teaspoon baking powder

⅛ teaspoon salt

¼ cup (55 g) non-hydrogenated, nondairy butter, at room temperature

½ cup (100 g) granulated sugar

½ teaspoon vanilla extract

⅓ cup (80 ml) nondairy milk

2 cups (290 g) fresh or frozen blueberries

INGREDIENTS—STREUSEL TOPPING

⅓ cup (40 g) unbleached all-purpose flour

⅓ cup (65 g) granulated sugar

½ teaspoon ground cinnamon

⅓ cup (75 g) cold non-hydrogenated, nondairy butter, cut into pieces

Preheat the oven to 350°F (180°C, or gas mark 4). Lightly grease a 9 × 9-inch (23× 23-cm) square cake pan or 9-inch springform pan. Set aside.

To make the cake, in the small bowl of a food processor or by hand, whip together the egg replacer and water until thick and creamy, about 1 minute. Set aside. In a separate bowl, whisk together the flour, baking powder, and salt. Set aside.

In a large bowl, cream together (by hand or using an electric hand mixer) the butter and sugar until light and fluffy, 1 or 2 minutes. Add the egg replacer mixture and vanilla and beat until incorporated. Add the flour mixture and nondairy milk, and beat only until combined. Spread the batter into the bottom of the prepared pan, smoothing the top with an offset spatula. Evenly arrange the blueberries on top of the cake batter.

To make the streusel topping, in a large bowl, mix together the flour, sugar, and cinnamon. Cut in the butter with a pastry blender or fork until it resembles coarse bread crumbs. Sprinkle the streusel topping over the blueberries, and bake for 40 to 50 minutes, or until a toothpick inserted into the center of the cake comes out clean. Remove from the oven and place on a wire rack to cool slightly. Serve warm or at room temperature.

DID YOU KNOW? *The compounds in blueberries can help prevent heart disease, urinary tract infections, and certain forms of cancer, as well as improve vision that is deteriorating from a disease called macular degeneration. Recent studies even show that blueberries can play a role in boosting memory and slowing the aging process.*

LIGHT LEMON BUNDT CAKE

YIELD: 1 BUNDT CAKE

"If it ain't broke, don't fix it," they say, and that's how I feel about this delicious cake from The Millennium Cookbook. I wanted to honor this fabulous Oakland restaurant by sharing one of my favorite recipes—only slightly modified—from their first cookbook.

INGREDIENTS

2 cups (250 g) unbleached all-purpose flour

1 teaspoon baking powder

½ teaspoon baking soda

⅛ teaspoon salt

Zest of 2 lemons, minced

4 tablespoons (60 g) ground flaxseed (equivalent of 4 eggs)

¾ cup (180 ml) water

⅓ cup (45 ml) fresh lemon juice

¾ cup (250 g) pure maple syrup

½ cup (120 ml) canola oil

½ cup (120 ml) nondairy milk

1 tablespoon (15 ml) lemon extract

1 ½ teaspoons vanilla extract

1 recipe Lemon Sauce (page 248)

Preheat the oven to 350°F (180°C, or gas mark 4). Lightly oil a Bundt pan.

Into a large bowl, sift the flour, baking powder, baking soda, salt, and lemon zest until well combined.

In a food processor or in a bowl using an electric hand mixer, combine the ground flaxseed and water and blend well for about 2 minutes. Add the lemon juice, maple syrup, canola oil, milk, and lemon and vanilla extracts, and blend again for another minute.

Pour the wet ingredients into the dry ingredients and whisk until combined. Pour the batter into the prepared pan and bake for 35 to 45 minutes, or until the cake is golden brown and pulls away from the edges of the pan. Let cool completely before unmolding. Serve with Lemon Sauce.

Cake Decorating Ideas

You don't have to be a professional pastry chef to add some pizzazz to your cakes. Just think in terms of color, contrast, season, and occasion—and you're good to go. Here are a few ideas to guide you along the way.

FLAUNT THE FLORA

Fresh edible flowers are gorgeous, inexpensive, and oh-so-easy cake decorations. You can start with a frosted cake or even just a plain cake (dust lightly with confectioners' sugar), then pile on such flowers as sweet violets, lavender, nasturtium, honeysuckle, rose petals, borage, bachelor's buttons, johnny-jump-ups, and calendula. Just make sure they're pesticide-free!

FLOURISH WITH FRUIT

Fresh fruit is another way to add color and elegance. Sprinkle berries with confectioners' sugar and add a few fresh mint leaves. Whole strawberries, kiwis, grapes, and orange wedges are all ideal for the top of a cake.

KEEP IT SIMPLE

Confectioners' sugar or cocoa powder lightly dusted over the tops of cakes makes a nice finishing touch. Create old-fashioned patterns by placing lace paper doilies on the top of the cake before dusting.

CHOCK FULL O' CHOCOLATE

Chocolate curls and leaves are another easy way to jazz up a cake. Chocolate curls can be made easily by shaving off pieces from a chocolate block using a vegetable peeler. To make chocolate leaves, care-

CARROT CAKE, PAGE 82. CREAM CHEESE FROSTING, PAGE 246.

fully brush melted chocolate onto the underside of a clean leaf, cool until the chocolate has fully hardened, then gently peel off the natural leaf from the chocolate one. Add contrast by making both white and dark chocolate leaves.

BLUEBERRY ORANGE BUNDT CAKE

YIELD: 1 BUNDT CAKE OR 12 MUFFINS

This is a lovely cake that cries out to be served at a tea party. You can also pour this batter into muffin tins.

INGREDIENTS

1 cup (145 g) blueberries, fresh or frozen
¼ cup (115 g) silken tofu (soft or firm)
½ cup (120 ml) water
¾ cup (175 ml) fresh orange juice
½ cup (120 ml) canola or coconut oil
1 teaspoon lemon or orange extract
2½ cups (315 g) unbleached all-purpose or whole wheat pastry flour
1 cup (200 g) granulated sugar
1½ teaspoons baking soda
½ teaspoon salt
Zest from 2 oranges (optional)

Preheat the oven to 350°F (180°C, or gas mark 4). Lightly oil a Bundt pan or muffin tins.

If using frozen blueberries, allow them to thaw slightly, about 15 minutes at room temperature.

In a blender, combine the tofu, water, orange juice, oil, and extract. Blend until smooth. In a separate bowl, combine the flour, sugar, baking soda, salt, and orange zest, if using. Make a well in the center of the flour, pour the wet mixture into the center, and mix just until combined. Do not overstir. Fold in the blueberries (draining them a little if the frozen ones start to defrost).

Pour into the prepared pan. Bake for 45 to 50 minutes for a cake, 20 to 25 minutes for muffins. Let cool in the pan for 10 minutes, then invert and cool on a wire rack or plate.

FOOD LORE: *The name "Bundt" comes from the German word bund, which means "a gathering of people." The founder of the Bundt pan, David Dalquist, simply added the letter "t" to the end and trademarked it in 1950. The impetus for creating this style pan was to make kugel, a Jewish side dish or dessert. Dalquist modified some existing pan designs by introducing folds in the outer edge and using aluminum instead of ceramic.*

CINNAMON COFFEE CAKE

YIELD: ONE 9 × 9-INCH (23 × 23-CM) CAKE OR 12 SERVINGS

I grew up eating coffee cake and feel quite nostalgic each time I eat it. The aroma alone will beckon you and your loved ones into the kitchen to enjoy an old-fashioned sit-down breakfast.

INGREDIENTS—CAKE

1 cup (235 ml) nondairy milk

⅓ cup (80 ml) canola oil

1 tablespoon (15 ml) white distilled vinegar

1 cup (125 g) unbleached all-purpose flour or whole wheat pastry flour

½ cup (100 g) granulated sugar

1 teaspoon baking powder

1 teaspoon baking soda

2 teaspoons ground cinnamon

1 teaspoon ground ginger

¼ teaspoon salt

INGREDIENTS—CRUMBLE

¾ cup (94 g) unbleached all-purpose flour or whole wheat pastry flour

¼ cup (50 g) granulated or brown sugar

1 to 2 teaspoons ground cinnamon

½ teaspoon ground ginger

¼ teaspoon salt

¾ cup (115 g) chopped walnuts

⅓ cup (80 ml) canola oil or nondairy butter, melted

Preheat the oven to 350°F (180°C, or gas mark 4). Grease a 9-inch (23-cm) square baking dish/cake pan.

To make the cake, combine the milk, oil, and vinegar in a bowl and set aside. In a large bowl, mix together the flour, sugar, baking powder, baking soda, cinnamon, ginger, and salt. Add the milk mixture and stir until just combined. Pour into the prepared baking dish.

To make the crumble, in a small bowl, combine the flour, sugar, cinnamon, ginger, salt, and walnuts. Add the butter or oil, and use your hands to thoroughly work it into the dry ingredients. Spoon on top of the batter, covering the entire area.

Bake for 35 to 40 minutes, or until a toothpick inserted into the middle comes out clean. Let it cool slightly, and serve warm or at room temperature.

SERVING SUGGESTIONS & VARIATIONS

∗ Add a chopped tart or sweet apple or ½ cup (75 g) blueberries to the cake batter.

∗ Though you'd have to change the name of the recipe, you could replace the cinnamon with cardamom!

VANILLA CUPCAKES

YIELD: 10 TO 12 CUPCAKES

Though you can easily convert this to make one 9-inch (23-cm) cake, I thought this was the perfect recipe for traditional cupcakes—ideal for a birthday celebration.

INGREDIENTS

1 tablespoon (15 g) ground flaxseed (equivalent of 1 egg)

3 tablespoons (45 ml) water

1¾ cups (410 ml) nondairy milk

½ cup (120 ml) water, divided

½ cup (112 g) non-hydrogenated, nondairy butter, melted

1½ cups (300 g) granulated sugar

1½ teaspoons vanilla extract

2½ cups (315 g) unbleached all-purpose flour

2½ teaspoons baking powder

½ teaspoon salt

1 recipe Chocolate Frosting or Chocolate Peanut Butter Frosting (page 242–243)

Preheat the oven to 375° F (190°C, or gas mark 5). Lightly grease standard muffin tins or fill the muffin cups with cupcake liners.

In a food processor or by hand, whip the ground flaxseed and water until it's thick and creamy, about 1 minute. Add the nondairy milk and ¼ cup (60 ml) of the water.

In a large bowl, cream the butter and sugar until light and fluffy. Add the vanilla extract and the remaining ¼ cup (60 ml) water, and beat well to thoroughly combine.

In a separate bowl, stir together the flour, baking powder, and salt. Add this, along with the flax egg/milk mixture, to the butter/sugar combination. Beat until combined.

Fill the muffin cups with the batter and bake for 20 to 30 minutes, or until a toothpick inserted into the center of a cupcake comes out clean. Remove from the oven and place on a wire rack to cool. Make sure the cupcakes have cooled completely before frosting.

FOOD LORE: *In England, birthday cakes are often baked with symbolic objects inside. In medieval times, objects such as coins and thimbles were mixed into the batter, and people believed whoever got the coin would be wealthy and whoever got the thimble would never marry. Today, small figures, fake coins, and small candies are more common.*

COLLEEN'S TIP: *If you've ever frosted a chocolate cake with white icing and ended up with tons of chocolate cake crumbs in it, here's a trick: First frost your cake with a very thin layer of icing. Don't worry if the cake crumbs get mixed in. Then let the cake set for about 15 minutes in the refrigerator. The icing will harden a little and enable you to finish frosting the cake without crumbs getting mixed in.*

CHOCOLATE CREAM CHEESE CUPCAKES

YIELD: 12 CUPCAKES

A decadently delicious combination of flavors, these cupcakes are moist and rich and fun to serve at parties.

INGREDIENTS—CUPCAKES

1 tablespoon ½ ground flaxseed (equivalent of 1 egg)

3 tablespoons (45 ml) water

½ cup (60 g) unsweetened cocoa powder

1 cup (235 ml) boiling water

1 cup plus 6 tablespoons (170 g) unbleached all-purpose flour

1 teaspoon baking soda

¼ teaspoon baking powder

¼ teaspoon salt

½ cup (112 g) non-hydrogenated, nondairy butter, softened

1¼ cups (250 g) granulated sugar

1 teaspoon vanilla extract

INGREDIENTS—CREAM CHEESE FILLING

½ cup (112 g) non-hydrogenated, nondairy butter

8 ounces (225 g) nondairy cream cheese

1½ teaspoons vanilla extract

½ cup (50 g) confectioners' sugar, sifted

Extra confectioners' sugar for sprinkling

Preheat the oven to 350°F (180°C, or gas mark 4). Lightly grease a muffin/cupcake tin or fill with paper liners.

In the small bowl of your food processor or by hand, whip together the flaxseed and water until thoroughly combined and thick.

In a small bowl, combine the cocoa and boiling water. Stir well, and set aside to cool. In a separate bowl, stir together the flour, baking soda, baking powder, and salt. In another bowl, use an electric mixer to beat together the butter and granulated sugar until light and fluffy. Add the "flax eggs" and vanilla and beat for 2 minutes. With the mixer set on low, add the flour mixture alternately with the cocoa/water mixture, beginning and ending with flour. After the last of the flour is mixed in, beat for 1 minute, until smooth. Divide the batter among the 12 liners.

Bake for 20 to 25 minutes, or until a toothpick inserted into the center comes out clean. Cool the cupcakes in the pan for 5 minutes, then carefully loosen the cupcakes from the pan and cool completely on a wire rack.

To make the filling, add the butter and cream cheese to a food processor and blend until creamy, scraping down the sides if necessary. Add the vanilla and confectioners' sugar, and mix until smooth and thick.

When the cupcakes are cool, use a sharp knife to cut out the tops about ½ inch (1.3 cm) from the edge, setting each top beside its cupcake. Use a pastry bag, plastic bag (with a hole snipped out of one corner), or a spoon to fill each cavity with the cream cheese mixture. Replace each lid and sprinkle with confectioners' sugar, if desired.

STRAWBERRY CUPCAKES

YIELD: 12 TO 16 CUPCAKES OR 1 STANDARD-SIZE LOAF CAKE

Enjoy this simple recipe loved by kids and adults alike. After frosting, place a fresh strawberry on top for a pretty presentation, or leave whole and place alongside (as pictured on following page).

INGREDIENTS

1¾ cups (220 g) unbleached all-purpose flour

1 teaspoon baking soda

1 cup (200 g) granulated sugar

½ cup (120 ml) canola oil

1 tablespoon (15 ml) white distilled vinegar

1 teaspoon vanilla extract

8 ounces (225 g) frozen or fresh strawberries, crushed or pureed

1 recipe Buttercream Frosting (page 247)

12 to 16 whole strawberries, stemmed

Preheat the oven to 350°F (180°C, or gas mark 4). Lightly grease standard muffin tins or fill the muffin cups with cupcake liners, or grease a 9-inch (23-cm) loaf pan.

Mix together the flour, baking soda, and sugar in a bowl. In a separate bowl, combine the oil, vinegar, and vanilla. Add the strawberries and stir to combine. Create a well in the center of the dry ingredients, and add the wet ingredients. Stir to combine, but do not overstir. Pour the batter into the prepared muffin tins, filling them halfway.

Bake for 30 minutes for cupcakes or 1 hour for a cake, or until a toothpick inserted into the center comes out clean. Remove from the oven and place on a wire rack to cool. When cool, frost the cupcakes and top each with a whole strawberry.

WHAT'S THE DIFFERENCE?

There seems to be a fine line between a cupcake and a muffin.

* **Cupcake**—*Originally called "cup-cakes," they refer to any small cake. Essentially, cupcakes are miniature cakes and are generally frosted and sweet.*
* **Muffin**—*Derived from yeast-based breads, our modern muffin (except English muffins) relies on baking soda/powder for leavening, tends to be sweet rather than savory, and often has some kind of fruit or nut baked in the batter. These days, commercially prepared muffins are so large and so sweet that the only difference between them and cupcakes is their absence of frosting.*

CHOCOLATE PEANUT BUTTER CUPCAKES

YIELD: 20 TO 24 CUPCAKES

In my opinion, chocolate and peanut butter go together like tea and crumpets, as evidenced by the many recipes in which I feature this combination. Though it may seem like overkill to top these with Chocolate Peanut Butter Frosting, it's not. Trust me.

INGREDIENTS
½ cup (130 g) creamy or crunchy natural peanut butter
1¼ cups (295 ml) nondairy milk
1 ripe banana, mashed
1 teaspoon vanilla extract
2¼ cups (280 g) unbleached all-purpose flour
1½ cups (300 g) granulated sugar
3½ teaspoons (5.4 g) baking powder
1 teaspoon salt
3 tablespoons (25 g) unsweetened cocoa powder
1 recipe Chocolate Peanut Butter Frosting (page 243)

Preheat the oven to 350°F (180°C, or gas mark 4). Line 2 cupcake tins with paper liners. You may also lightly oil your muffins tins.

Using an electric hand mixer, mix together the peanut butter, milk, banana, and vanilla. In a separate bowl, stir together the flour, sugar, baking powder, salt, and cocoa. Add the dry mixture to the wet and stir (by hand) until all the ingredients are combined.

Spoon the cupcake batter into the liners until they are half to two-thirds full. I find that one full tablespoon is enough for each cupcake liner.

Bake for 20 to 25 minutes, or until a toothpick inserted into the center comes out clean.

Cool for 10 minutes in the pans, then remove to a wire rack to cool completely. Once cool, frost the cupcakes.

SERVING SUGGESTIONS & VARIATIONS
✳ Instead of mashing the banana completely, leave a few chunks remaining.
✳ Instead of using Chocolate Peanut Butter Frosting, frost with Chocolate Frosting (page 242) or any other frosting you like. You can even just cream some peanut butter and spread that on top.

CHOCOLATE CHEESECAKE

YIELD: 10 TO 12 SERVINGS

Decadent. Rich. Delicious. This cake is all of these things and more. Many people who have tried this cake declare that they "don't believe it's vegan." Though it's unfortunate that people assume because it's vegan it can't be good, this is definitely the dessert to win them over.

INGREDIENTS

6 teaspoons Ener-G Egg Replacer (equivalent of 4 eggs)
½ cup (120 ml) water
1 cup (175 g) nondairy semisweet chocolate chips
24 ounces (690 g) nondairy cream cheese, at room temperature
¾ cup (150 g) granulated sugar
½ teaspoon vanilla extract
1 Cookie Crust (page 222)

Preheat the oven to 350°F (180°C, or gas mark 4). Lightly oil a 9-inch (23-cm) springform pan.

In the small bowl of your food processor, whip the egg replacer and water together, until it's thick and creamy. (You may also use an electric hand mixer.) Set aside.

Melt the chocolate chips in the microwave or a double boiler. To make your own double boiler, place the chips in a small saucepan. Set this saucepan in a larger pot that is filled with ¼ to ½ cup (60 to 120 ml) water. Heat over a medium flame on the stove and stir the chips in the small pot until they are melted.

In a large bowl with your electric hand mixer or in the large bowl of your food processor, beat together the cream cheese, sugar, and egg replacer mixture at medium speed until smooth and fluffy. You may need to scrape down the sides of the bowl with a rubber spatula. Add the melted chocolate and vanilla and blend thoroughly. Pour into the prepared crust. Then, lick the bowl!

Bake the cheesecake for 50 minutes until the center barely jiggles when the pan is tapped. Remove from the oven and cool completely (about one hour). Transfer to a serving plate, cover with plastic wrap, and chill in the refrigerator for at least 2 hours. It's even better if you can chill it overnight.

COLLEEN'S TIP:
* *See "Cheesecake Secrets" on page 98.*
* *Check out "Resources and Recommendations" on page 270 for information on where to find nondairy cream cheese.*

LEMON CHEESECAKE

YIELD: 10 TO 12 SERVINGS

Cheesecakes are dessert classics that date back to ancient Greece. They are incredibly versatile and handle any flavor you throw at them. In this case, lemons add light freshness, making them perfect for summer or spring, particularly if you choose to add ripe strawberries.

INGREDIENTS

4½ teaspoons (20 g) Ener-G Egg Replacer
   (equivalent of 3 eggs)
6 tablespoons (90 ml) water
24 ounces (690 g) nondairy cream cheese, at
   room temperature
1 cup (200 g) granulated sugar

½ teaspoon vanilla
2 tablespoons (30 ml) lemon juice
1 tablespoon (5 g) lemon zest
1 pie crust (store-bought or the Graham Cracker
   Crust on page 223)
Fresh strawberries for serving, optional

Preheat the oven to 350°F (180°C, or gas mark 4). Lightly oil a 9-inch (23-cm) springform pan.

In a food processor or using an electric hand mixer and a large bowl, whip the egg replacer and water together, until it's thick and creamy. Beat in the cream cheese until creamy, about 30 seconds. Beat in the sugar, vanilla, lemon juice, and lemon zest.

Scrape the batter into the prepared crust, and smooth the top. Bake until the center barely jiggles when the pan is tapped, 50 to 55 minutes. It's okay if it puffs up a bit and turns a golden brown on top. Let cool in the pan on a rack for at least 1 hour, making sure it's cooled completely before unmolding. Cover and refrigerate for at least 2 hours (preferably 24 hours) before serving. Serve with fresh strawberries, if desired.

CHEESECAKE SECRETS:

* *A springform pan (with removable side and bottom) is the most commonly used pan for making cheesecakes.*
* *I tend to use commercial egg replacer powder for my cheesecakes rather than "flax eggs," because I don't want little flecks of flax in the finished cheesecake.*
* *Don't overbeat the batter. Overbeating incorporates additional air and tends to cause cracking on the surface of the cheesecake.*
* *Don't overbake. Cheesecake baking times are not always exact, due to variations in ovens. It is done when the sides of the cake pull away from the pan and the middle is still a little wobbly.*
* *Upon removal from the oven, loosen the cake from the edge of the pan by running the tip of a knife or narrow spatula between the top edge of the cake and the side of the pan. This allows the cake to pull away freely from the pan as it cools.*
* *Cool the cheesecake on a wire rack away from drafts.*
* *Baked cheesecake freezes well for up to a month. Cool completely, remove from the baking pan, and wrap securely in heavy-duty foil or plastic wrap. Do not freeze cheesecake with toppings. Thaw overnight in the refrigerator.*

PUMPKIN CHEESECAKE

YIELD: 8 TO 10 SERVINGS

You can make your own pumpkin puree or use canned pumpkin (I recommend organic). Fortunately, there are excellent brands of canned pumpkin on the market, but if you want to make your own puree, simply use a smaller pumpkin variety, such as Sugar Pie or Baby Bear pumpkin.

INGREDIENTS

$^2/_3$ cup (150 g) firmly packed light brown sugar
½ teaspoon ground cinnamon
½ teaspoon ground ginger
⅛ teaspoon ground cloves
¼ teaspoon ground nutmeg
¼ teaspoon salt
4½ teaspoons Ener-G Egg Replacer (equivalent of 3 eggs)
6 tablespoons (90 ml) water
16 ounces (460 g) nondairy cream cheese, at room temperature
1 teaspoon vanilla extract
1 cup pumpkin puree (canned or homemade)
1 Graham Cracker Crust (page 223) or Pecan Crust (page 223)

Preheat the oven to 350°F (180°C, or gas mark 4).

In a bowl, stir together the brown sugar, cinnamon, ginger, cloves, nutmeg, and salt. In the small bowl of your food processor, whip the egg replacer powder and water for 1 minute. Set aside.

In the large bowl of your food processor, beat the cream cheese until smooth, about 2 minutes. (You can do this with a hand-held electric mixer as well.) Gradually add the sugar mixture and beat until creamy and smooth, 1 to 2 minutes. Add the egg replacer mixture, beating for another minute. Scrape down the sides of the bowl, as needed, and add the vanilla and pumpkin puree.

Pour the filling into the prepared crust. Bake the cheesecake for 30 minutes, then reduce the oven temperature to 325°F (170°C, or gas mark 3) and bake the cheesecake for another 10 to 20 minutes, or until the edges of the cheesecake are puffed but the center is still wet and jiggles when you gently shake the pan.

COLLEEN'S TIP: *See "Cheesecake Secrets" on page 98.*

CHAPTER FIVE

TIMELESS TEMPTATIONS: PIES AND TARTS

A pie refers to a baked food with a baked shell, usually made of pastry that covers or completely contains a filling. A tart, on the other hand, is similar to a pie in that it can be sweet or savory, but it tends to have an open top and is not covered with pastry. A tart is often baked in a tart pan, which is scalloped all the way around, making for a pretty final presentation.

THE RECIPES

No Bake Strawberry Pie with Chocolate Chunks ... 103
No-Bake Chocolate Peanut Butter Pie ... 106
Blueberry Pie ... 107
Apple Pie ... 108
Peach Pie ... 110
Cherry Pie ... 111
Pumpkin Pie ... 113
No-Bake Chocolate Pudding Tart ... 114
Pear Tart ... 115
Fruit Tart ... 116

TIPS FOR MAKING PIES

These classic desserts are perfect for any time of the year and can be made as light or as decadent as you like. Some require no baking at all, which makes them ideal for lazy, hot summer days.

PREBAKING

Sometimes called "prebaking," blind baking refers to the process of baking a pie crust or other pastry without the filling. It's necessary if the pie filling would make the crust too soggy if added immediately. In general, the unfilled pie crust is lined with foil or parchment paper, then filled with dried peas, lentils, or beans, so that the crust will keep its shape while baking. Metal or ceramic pie weights can also be used. After the pie crust is baked for 10 to 12 minutes, the beans are replaced with the proper filling. Frankly, I think it's just as easy to simply poke the unfilled pie crust all over with a fork before baking (also for 10 to 12 minutes) to prevent air bubbles from forming. See page 221 for more tips on preparing the perfect pie crust.

FLOUR VS. CORNSTARCH

Fruit pies are thickened with either cornstarch or flour. Cornstarch slurries tend to be made on the stovetop, while flour slurries are usually created by tossing the fruit with flour. Each has its advantages, the most obvious of which is how quick and easy the flour option is. In terms of aesthetics, cornstarch makes a clearer slurry that results in an attractive shine, whereas flour makes a more milky slurry.

FRESH FRUIT VS. FROZEN OR CANNED

Fresh is always best, but I do use frozen pretty regularly when I'm in a hurry or when I'm making a pie out of season. I tend not to use canned fruit very often, but it's a fine substitute when you're in a pinch.

SHORTENING VS. (NONDAIRY) BUTTER CRUST

Shortening, which makes a more tender crust, creates easy-to-form doughs. Crust made with butter is much more flavorful but can be a little harder to work with. I prefer a combination to get the best of both worlds.

NO-BAKE STRAWBERRY PIE
WITH CHOCOLATE CHUNKS

YIELD: 8 TO 12 SERVINGS

This delicious, easy-to-prepare seasonal pie requires no baking (especially if you pair it with the No-Bake Pecan Crust on page 226) and calls for the ripest, sweetest strawberries, which you can find at your local farmers' market. Feature this special dessert at a summertime soirée.

INGREDIENTS

4 cups (680 g) ripe strawberries, sliced
1 No-Bake Pecan Crust (page 226)
1 cup (110 g) ripe strawberries, whole
5 pitted dates, soaked 10 minutes in warm water and drained
2 teaspoons fresh lemon juice
Nondairy dark chocolate chunks, preferably from a good, organic, fair-trade bar

Arrange the sliced strawberries on top of the prepared crust and set aside. In a food processor or blender, combine the whole strawberries with the 5 soaked dates and lemon juice. Puree until smooth. Pour this mixture over the sliced strawberries. Arrange the chocolate chunks, if using, on top of the sauce and refrigerate for 1 hour before serving. (You will need to refrigerate even if you don't add the chocolate!) This will help the pie set and make it perfect for slicing.

COLLEEN'S TIP: *Because of the freshness of the ingredients, this pie is best when served within an hour or two of preparing it.*

DID YOU KNOW? *Strawberries top the list when it comes to pesticide contamination. Knowing which fruits and vegetables are considered the "dirty dozen" is helpful when deciding between organic and conventionally grown. Other highly contaminated produce includes apples, bell peppers, celery, cherries, imported grapes, nectarines, peaches, pears, potatoes, red raspberries, and spinach.*

Cow's Milk: A Substitute for Human Milk

Not only are we the only animal that drinks another animal's milk, but we are also the only animal that drinks it into adulthood. All female mammals produce milk for the same reason: to feed and nourish their offspring. At a certain age, depending on the mammal, the infant is able to move onto solid food and is weaned off of the mother's milk—every mammal, that is, except humans. Despite the fact that humans don't even continue drinking human milk after being weaned, we're told we have to drink cow's milk. And despite the fact that calves naturally stop drinking cow's milk after they're weaned, humans have been duped into believing that they must drink it as adults. It makes absolutely no sense, but it makes good business and good money.

THE POWER OF THE HERD

Thanks to the dairy industry, whose government-sponsored advertisements pose as public service announcements, humans are taught that we need cow's milk (and goat's and sheep's milk). This stuff is sold as if it contains some magical formula designed just for human bodies, and the truth is it is a perfect formula, designed just for growing babies—bovine babies, that is.

Cattle are herd animals, which means they are easy to control because they move together and stay together. In other words, "cattle" meet certain requirements that make it easy for humans to contain them. Let's not kid ourselves into believing that humans struck nutritional gold when they started drinking cow's milk.

Cow's milk is a commercial product in that it is marketed and sold as if it's natural for humans. It has billions of dollars behind it in advertising and is totally unnecessary for human survival and health. Cow's milk protein is considered a carcinogen (a cancer-causing substance); has been strongly linked to childhood-onset, or type 1, diabetes; and leeches calcium from our bones, according to *The China Study*, by T. Colin Campbell, PhD.

THE CALCIUM CONUNDRUM

The main selling point for cow's milk is its calcium content, and indeed calcium is an important nutrient. But where does it come from? It's a mineral, and minerals are found in the ground. Cows have a lot of calcium in their milk because they eat plants. They eat grass, which, like all green leafy vegetables, contains high amounts of calcium. These days, though, because three out of four cows are not eating grass and are not let out to graze but are confined on dry lots, they aren't getting calcium. So, to ensure that cow's milk has calcium, producers supplement their feed with calcium, and they add vitamin D during processing, according to The Welfare of Cattle in Dairy Production, a summary of scientific evidence that exposes and evaluates common practices in the dairy industry. You can read it online by searching for the title of the report.

If we examined this strictly from a resource perspective, we would recognize how wasteful it is, but it's also incredibly unethical. Just like humans, cows have nine-month-long pregnancies, and like any female, all she wants is to take care of her baby when he or she is born.

To the dairy industry, this newborn is just a by-product of the need to keep her lactating. Male babies are taken away when they're born and either killed immediately or sold to the veal industry. If the cow gives birth to a female, she is taken away to become part of the dairy herd, and the process begins all over again. All so humans can have calcium? Though we have certainly been made to believe this is the reason, the truth is there's money to be made in the reproductive cycles of female animals.

If we really want to get our essential minerals, we can do what the cows do: eat our leafy greens.

Calcium is abundant in kale, broccoli, collard greens, chard, beet greens, and Brussels sprouts, as well as oatmeal, beans, fortified juice, and nondairy milks. All of the nondairy milks I recommend for baking (see "Better Than Cow's Milk" on page 27) are delicious for drinking, cookie-dunking, or pouring on cereal. We can make a huge difference in our own health and in the lives of animals if we leave the cow's milk to the cows.

NO-BAKE CHOCOLATE PEANUT BUTTER PIE

YIELD: 8 TO 10 SERVINGS

This is a rich and delicious no-bake pie that will have your guests clamoring for more!

INGREDIENTS

2 cups (350 g) nondairy semisweet chocolate chips

12 ounces (340 g) silken tofu (firm)

1½ cups (390 g) natural peanut butter, crunchy or smooth

½ cup (120 ml) nondairy milk

1 Graham Cracker Crust (page 223), Brownie Crust (page 227), or Cookie Crust (page 222)

Melt the 2 cups of chocolate chips in the microwave or in a double boiler. In a food processor or high-powered blender, combine the tofu, peanut butter, milk, and melted chocolate chips. Blend until very smooth, adding more milk, if desired. Pour the filling into the crust and refrigerate for 2 hours. Top with chocolate chips and chopped nuts, if desired.

SERVING SUGGESTIONS & VARIATIONS

✳ Spread ½ to 1 cup (130 to 260 g) peanut butter onto the crust.

✳ For a Chocolate Peanut Butter Pie with a hard chocolate topping, after the pie has been chilled for 2 hours, melt 1 cup (175 g) nondairy chocolate chips. Pour the melted chocolate over the top of the pie. If desired, sprinkle on 1 cup (150 g) chopped nuts. Refrigerate for 2 additional hours.

✳ You may substitute 1 (14-ounce or 425-ml) can of coconut milk for the tofu and soymilk. Add a thickener, such as arrowroot or kudzu root dissolved in water, if you go this route. The ratio is usually 1 tablespoon (6 g) of thickener to 2 tablespoons (30 ml) of water.

BLUEBERRY PIE

Though this is a quintessentially summer pie, you can make it throughout the year using blueberries you bought in season and froze yourself.

INGREDIENTS

1 or 2 Flaky Pie Crusts (page 224) or store-bought pie shells

½ to ¾ cup (100 to 150 g) granulated sugar

3 tablespoons (24 g) cornstarch

2 tablespoons (30 ml) fresh lemon juice

1 tablespoon (5 g) lemon zest

5 cups (725 g) fresh or frozen blueberries, picked over

Pinch of salt

1 recipe Tofu Whipped Topping (page 254) or nondairy vanilla ice cream (for serving)

Preheat the oven to 450°F (230°C, or gas mark 8). Prebake your homemade or store-bought crust for 10 to 12 minutes (see page 101 for more on prebaking). Set aside to cool.

Roll out your bottom dough into a 13-inch (33-cm) round and fit it into a 9-inch (23-cm) pie pan. Trim the overhanging dough to ¾ inch (2 cm) all around. Place in the refrigerator while you prepare the filling. Roll out the dough for the top crust, if using, fold it in half, cover, and place in the refrigerator as well.

In a large bowl, mix together the sugar, cornstarch, lemon juice, and zest. Add the blueberries and gently toss to combine. If using frozen blueberries instead of fresh, let stand for 15 minutes until partially thawed. Strain the juice before mixing with the other ingredients. Pour the mixture into the prepared pie shell.

You may bake this as is, or make a covered pie (be sure to cut steam vents in the top), or make a lattice-covered pie. You can also take any excess dough scraps from making your single crust and use a cookie cutter to create pastry shapes, such as stars, that you place directly on top of the berries.

Turn down the heat to 425°F (220°C, or gas mark 7). Bake the pie for 30 minutes, slip a baking sheet underneath it (to catch the juices), reduce the oven temperature to 350°F (180°C, or gas mark 4), and bake for another 25 to 35 minutes, at which point the juices will begin bubbling. If the edges of the pie are browning too much during baking, cover with aluminum foil.

Place the baked pie on a wire rack to cool completely, for at least an hour, preferably 3 to 4. Serve at room temperature with tofu whipped topping or nondairy vanilla ice cream. Store any leftovers for 2 to 3 days at room temperature.

DID YOU KNOW? *The blueberry is the second most popular berry in the United States. (The strawberry is number one.) More than 200 million pounds of blueberries are grown commercially each year.*

APPLE PIE

YIELD: 8 TO 10 SERVINGS

The first time I made my very own homemade apple pie, I was ecstatic. There is nothing as satisfying as making your own pie crust and filling it with crisp apples.

INGREDIENTS

2 Flaky Pie Crusts (page 224) or store-bought pie shells

5 to 6 medium-large apples, peeled, cored, and sliced ¼-inch thick (6 cups [90 g])

½ cup (100 g) granulated sugar (or ¼ cup [50 g] white and ¼ cup [55 g] extra brown)

2 to 3 tablespoons (16 to 24 g) unbleached all-purpose flour

1 tablespoon (15 ml) fresh lemon juice

¾ teaspoon ground cinnamon

¼ teaspoon ground nutmeg

Pinch of salt

2 tablespoons (28 g) non-hydrogenated, nondairy butter, cut into small pieces

2 teaspoons granulated sugar

⅛ teaspoon ground cinnamon

Roll out your bottom dough into a 13-inch (33-cm) round and fit it into a 9-inch (23-cm) pie pan. Trim the overhanging dough to ¾ inch (2 cm) all around. Place in the refrigerator. Roll out the dough for the top crust, fold it in half, cover, and place in the refrigerator as well.

Preheat the oven to 425°F (220°C, or gas mark 7).

Combine your sliced apples with the sugar, flour, lemon juice, cinnamon, nutmeg, and salt. Let it stand for 10 to 15 minutes while the apples soften slightly. Pour the mixture into the bottom crust and gently level it with the back of a spoon. Dot the top with the pieces of nondairy butter.

Brush the overhanging crust with cold water. Cover with the top crust, and tuck any excess pastry under the bottom crust. Crimp the edges using your fingers or a fork. Using a sharp knife or skewer, make 5 slits from the center of the pie out toward the edge of the pie to allow the steam to escape. Sprinkle with sugar and cinnamon and bake for 30 minutes. Slip a baking sheet underneath (to catch the juices), reduce the temperature to 350°F (180°C, or gas mark 4), and bake until the fruit feels just tender when a knife is poked through a steam vent, or 30 to 45 minutes.

Remove the pie from the oven and place on a wire rack to cool for 3 to 4 hours before cutting. This allows the filling to thicken properly, but I always have a hard time waiting that long! If you'd like to serve it warm, place it in the oven at 350°F (180°C, or gas mark 4) for about 15 minutes. Though it will keep for a few days (on the counter—not in the fridge), I think it's best served the day it's baked.

SERVING SUGGESTIONS & VARIATIONS

You may bake this as a single-crust pie with no top crust, or make it a lattice-covered pie. You can also take excess dough scraps you had from making your single crust and use a cookie cutter to create pastry shapes, such as stars, that you place directly on top of the apples before baking.

PEACH PIE

YIELD: 8 TO 10 SERVINGS

What better way to honor summertime than to bake up a luscious peach pie? Best eaten on the day it's baked, pop this pie in the oven before dinner and enjoy it as an evening dessert.

INGREDIENTS

1 or 2 Flaky Pie Crusts (page 224) or store-bought
   pie shells

⅓ cup (40 g) unbleached all-purpose flour

½ cup (100 g) granulated sugar

½ cup (115 g) brown sugar

¼ cup (55 g) non-hydrogenated, nondairy butter

1 tablespoon (8 g) cornstarch

1 teaspoon cinnamon

¼ teaspoon nutmeg

4 to 5 cups (800 to 1000 g) pitted and sliced
   peaches, fresh, frozen, or canned

Preheat the oven to 450°F (230°C, or gas mark 8). Prebake your homemade or store-bought crust for 10 to 12 minutes (see page 101 for more on prebaking). Set aside to cool.

In a bowl, combine the flour, sugars, and nondairy butter until the mixture resembles large crumbs. Mix in the cornstarch, cinnamon, and nutmeg.

If you're using canned peaches, rinse and drain any syrup they may be sitting in. Cut them into slices if they're not already, and pat them dry with a paper towel.

Line the shell with some sliced peaches. Sprinkle some of the butter mixture on top of the peaches, then put more peaches on top of the crumb mixture. Continue layering until both the peaches and the crumbs are gone.

Top with lattice strips of pie crust, with a top crust (create slits for the steam), or leave uncovered.

Bake at 450°F (230°C, or gas mark 8) for 15 minutes, place a cookie sheet under the pie to catch excess juices, lower the temperature to 350°F (180°C, or gas mark 4), and bake for another 30 to 35 minutes. The crust will be golden brown. (If the edges of the pie are browning too much during baking, cover with aluminum foil.) Turn off the oven, and leave the pie in the oven for about 20 minutes (or longer). This helps everything set up properly.

Take the pie out of the oven, and allow it to cool on the counter for an hour before slicing.

FOOD LORE: *The peach tree, a symbol of hope and longevity, is considered the most sacred plant of the Chinese Taoist religion.*

COLLEEN'S TIP: *To peel peaches easily, drop them into boiling water for about 2 minutes, then add them to a bowl of ice water. The skins should slide off easily.*

CHERRY PIE

Enjoy this American tradition with fresh, canned, or frozen cherries and adjust the amount of sugar to your preference. A perfect summer treat.

INGREDIENTS

1 or 2 Flaky Pie Crusts (page 224) or store-bought pie shells
5 cups (775 g) pitted cherries, fresh, canned, or frozen
½ to ¾ cup (100 to 150 g) granulated sugar
4 tablespoons (36 g) cornstarch
1 tablespoon (15 ml) fresh lemon juice
¼ teaspoon vanilla extract

Roll out your bottom dough into a 13-inch (33-cm) round and fit it into a 9-inch (23-cm) pie pan. Trim the overhanging dough to ¾ inch (2 cm) all around. Place in the refrigerator while you prepare the filling. Roll out the dough for the top crust, fold it in half, cover, and place in the refrigerator as well.

Preheat the oven to 425°F (220°C, or gas mark 7). Prebake your homemade or store-bought crust for 10 to 12 minutes (see below). Remove the crust, and set aside.

Rinse and drain the cherries, particularly if you're using canned. Try to find cherries packed in water, not sugar, but rinse either way. Pat them dry with a towel.

In a small bowl, mix together the cherries with the sugar and cornstarch, stirring gently to combine. Let sit for 10 to 15 minutes, then add the lemon juice and vanilla, stirring to combine.

Pour the filling into your prepared crust. Top with lattice strips of pie crust, with a top crust (create slits for the steam), or leave uncovered. It's important that the pie go into the hot oven immediately or the filling will begin to soften the bottom crust.

Bake at 425°F (220°C, or gas mark 7) for 30 minutes, reduce the temperature to 350°F (180°C, or gas mark 4), slip a baking sheet underneath it (to catch the juices), and bake for another 25 to 35 minutes, at which point the juices will begin bubbling. If the edges of the pie are browning too much during baking, cover with aluminium foil.

Turn off the oven, and leave the pie in the oven for about 20 minutes (or longer). This helps everything set up properly. Take the pie out of the oven, and allow it to cool on the counter for about 10 minutes before slicing.

DID YOU KNOW? *Sometimes called prebaking, "blind baking" refers to the process of baking a pie crust or other pastry without the filling. It's necessary if the pie filling would make the crust too soggy if added immediately, as in the case of Cherry Pie, Blueberry Pie (page 107), and Peach Pie (page 110). See "Tips for Making Pies" on page 101 for more on prebaking.*

PUMPKIN PIE

YIELD: 8 SERVINGS

This pie will indeed satisfy, and nobody will miss the eggs. Make the filling and use your own favorite pie crust, for this timeless dessert.

INGREDIENTS

1 Flaky Pie Crust (page 224), Pecan Crust (page 223), or store-bought pie shell

16 pecan halves

12 ounces (340 g) silken tofu (firm)

2 cups (400 g) pumpkin puree

½ cup (170 g) pure maple syrup

½ cup (115 g) firmly packed light brown sugar

¼ cup (32 g) cornstarch or arrowroot powder

1½ teaspoons ground cinnamon

½ teaspoon salt

¼ teaspoon freshly grated nutmeg

¼ teaspoon ground ginger

⅛ teaspoon ground cloves

Preheat the oven to 350°F (180°C, or gas mark 4). Prepare your pie crust or remove a store-bought crust from the freezer/refrigerator. (Thaw the crust if you are using frozen.)

Spread the pecans on a cookie sheet. Toast for 7 to 10 minutes, or until the smell of nuts fills the kitchen. Set aside for garnish.

In a food processor, blend together the tofu, pumpkin puree, maple syrup, brown sugar, cornstarch, cinnamon, salt, nutmeg, ginger, and cloves until the mixture is completely smooth and creamy. You may have to scrape down the sides of the bowl a few times. Pour the filling into the baked crust, and smooth the top with a spatula.

Bake for about 40 to 45 minutes, or until the crust is lightly browned and the outermost inch (2.5 cm) of the filling is set. Don't worry if the center is still soft; it continues to firm up as the pie cools.

Transfer the pie to a wire rack. Gently press the 16 toasted pecan halves into the filling in 2 concentric circles (or any design you like). Cool to room temperature and then chill until set, 1 to 2 hours. Serve chilled or at room temperature.

WHAT'S THE DIFFERENCE?

* Metal, glass, and ceramic pans transfer heat differently and provide varying results.
* Light-colored aluminum pans reflect heat and are not suitable for pies that need a crisp, well-baked crust.
* Heavy, dark steel pans conduct heat evenly and make for a well-baked crust.
* Glass is a good conductor of heat though not as good as dark-colored steel pans.
* Ceramic insulates the crust from the heat and often the crust is not well baked. Ceramic pans are good for prebaked shells and crumb crusts.

NO-BAKE CHOCOLATE PUDDING TART

YIELD: 8 TO 10 SERVINGS

This is a chocolate lover's delight, particularly if you use the Brownie Crust on page 227. The creamy filling satisfies those who love their pudding and want their cake, too. Make this sensuous dessert for your sweetheart on Valentine's Day. It's simply scrumptious.

INGREDIENTS

1 cup (235 ml) water

1 tablespoon (8 g) agar flakes

2 tablespoons (16 g) unsweetened cocoa powder

2 cups (350 g) nondairy semisweet chocolate chips, plus ¼ cup (45 g), chopped into small pieces for garnish

12 ounces (340 g) silken tofu (firm)

¾ cup (150 g) granulated sugar

1 teaspoon vanilla extract

⅛ teaspoon sea salt

1 Brownie Crust (page 227)

1 recipe Raspberry Sauce (page 248)

In a small saucepan, combine the water with the agar flakes and cocoa powder. Heat until the liquid reaches a boil, then lower the heat and gently simmer for 10 to 15 minutes, or until the agar is completely dissolved. At this point, turn off the heat and add the whole chocolate chips. Let them sit for a few minutes in the hot liquid, then whisk thoroughly to blend.

Meanwhile, in a food processor, combine the tofu, sugar, vanilla, and salt and process until smooth. Pour the melted chocolate mixture into the food processor and process until everything is thoroughly combined. Pour the mixture into the tart pan to cover the brownie crust. The chocolate mixture should completely fill the pan.

Let the filling set for a few minutes, then sprinkle the remaining chopped chocolate chips around the edges to line the pan. Place in the refrigerator for 45 minutes, or until completely set and cool. Unmold and serve with raspberry sauce.

DID YOU KNOW? *Agar is a vegetable-based gelatin. (Conventional gelatin is the boiled remnants of animals, including bones, tissue, muscle, and body parts not sold for direct human consumption, such as heads, snouts, hooves, etc.) Agar works just as well for making recipes "gelatinous." Agar can be found in the baking section in natural food stores. Asian markets tend to carry it as well.*

PEAR TART

YIELD: 8 SERVINGS

This is an elegant tart with a creamy cheese custard that is best with pears that are ripe but firm. Use a tart pan for the prettiest presentation.

INGREDIENTS

1 tablespoon (14 g) non-hydrogenated, nondairy butter
3 or 4 pears, peeled, cored, cut in half, and sliced into ½–inch-thick (1.3-cm) slices
⅛ cup (75 g) firmly packed light brown sugar
½ teaspoon ground cinnamon
16 ounces (460 g) nondairy cream cheese
1 tablespoon (8 g) cornstarch
¼ cup (50 g) granulated sugar
1 Shortbread Crust (page 222), cooled

Preheat the oven to 400°F (200°C, or gas mark 6). In a skillet over medium heat, melt the butter. Toss the pear slices with the brown sugar and cinnamon and sauté them in the melted butter for 2 to 3 minutes. Drain off and reserve whatever liquid remains.

In a food processor or by hand, combine the cream cheese, cornstarch, and granulated sugar until smooth and creamy, 1 to 2 minutes. Scrape down the sides, and blend again. It will be thick. Pour the cream cheese custard over the cooled crust, spreading evenly to cover the crust. Place the pears on top so they cover the cream cheese custard.

Bake for 10 minutes. Drizzle with a couple of spoonfuls of the reserved pear liquid, and continue baking for 20 to 25 minutes. Let cool for 30 minutes before serving.

SERVING SUGGESTIONS & VARIATIONS
Use apples in place of pears.

COLLEEN'S TIP: *Use firm but ripe Bosc, Bartlett, or Anjou pears for this tart.*

FRUIT TART

YIELD: 8 SERVINGS

This dessert is surprisingly fast yet incredibly elegant. It's perfect for an outdoor dinner party, picnic, or afternoon tea.

INGREDIENTS

9 tablespoons (180 g) jelly, jam, or preserves, heated, whisked, and divided
1 Shortbread Crust (page 222), cooled
1 cup (200 g) Pastry Cream (page 256)
2½ cups (365 g) whole berries, sliced strawberries, sliced kiwi, or any thinly sliced seasonal fruit
1 ripe banana, thinly sliced
Confectioners' sugar for dusting

Brush 5 tablespoons of the heated jelly over the cooled crust. Refrigerate for 10 minutes to set.
Spread the Pastry Cream over the crust. Arrange the fruit over the cream in a single layer.
Brush the fruit with the remaining 4 tablespoons heated jelly to create a beautiful shine. Just prior to serving, very lightly dust some sifted confectioners' sugar over the top of the tart.
Do not store in the refrigerator for more than 6 hours.

DID YOU KNOW? *The commercial "egg substitutes" in the refrigerated section of grocery stores are not substitutes at all. They are the whites of eggs. Actual egg replacers used to replace eggs in baking are egg-free and are in powdered form. (See "Better Than Eggs" on page 19 for more information.)*

COLLEEN'S TIP: *The purpose of heating and whisking the jelly, jam, or preserves is to thin it out and make it smooth and creamy. Alternatively, you can press it through a strainer.*

CHAPTER SIX

FAMILIAR FAVORITES: COOKIES, BROWNIES, AND BARS

I've never met a cookie that didn't put a smile on someone's face. These homemade goodies are better than any store-bought mix.

TROUBLESHOOTING COOKIES

The guide below is meant to help you identify problems. Also refer to the tips offered on page 121.

IF YOUR COOKIES ARE TOO TOUGH:

* you may have used too much flour.
* you may have used the wrong flour. Unless you want a chewy cookie, do not use bread flour.
* your proportions may have been off. You may have used too much sugar or not enough fat.

IF YOUR COOKIES ARE TOO CRUMBLY:

* you may have used too much sugar, fat, or leavening.
* your dough was not properly or thoroughly mixed.

IF YOUR COOKIES ARE TOO HARD OR TOO DRY:

* they may have baked too long.
* your oven temperature was too low.
* you used too much flour.
* you didn't use enough fat or liquid.

IF YOUR COOKIES ARE NOT BROWNED ENOUGH:

* your oven temperature was too low.
* the cookies were not baked long enough.
* there was too little sugar in the cookie dough.

IF YOUR COOKIES SPREAD TOO MUCH:

* your oven temperature was too low.
* you may have used too much sugar, fat, or leavening.
* your pans were greased with too much oil or nondairy butter.
* you didn't use enough flour.
* you should try chilling your dough before forming the cookies.

IF YOUR COOKIES DIDN'T SPREAD ENOUGH:

* there may not be enough sugar, fat, or leavening in the dough.

* the oven temperature was too high.

IF YOUR COOKIES STICK TO THE PANS:

* you didn't grease the pans adequately.
* there was too much sugar in the batter.
* you let the cookies sit too long on the cookie pan after removing the pan from the oven.

THE RECIPES

Chocolate Chip Cookies ... 118
Chocolate Chip Mint Cookies ... 120
Mexican Wedding Cookies ... 123
Peanut Butter Cookies ... 124
Pine Nut Anise Cookies ... 126
Sugar Cookies ... 127
Oatmeal Raisin Cookies ... 129
Gingerbread Cookies ... 130
Chocolate Crinkles ... 131
Chocolate Brownies ... 132
Raspberry Oatmeal Bars ... 133
Lemon Bars ... 136
Date Bars ... 138
Peanut Butter Chocolate Bars ... 139
Pineapple Walnut Bars ... 140

CHOCOLATE CHIP COOKIES

YIELD: 1 DOZEN COOKIES

I think it's safe to say that this recipe may very well be the most popular of all of the recipes in this book. Although I hope to change people's perceptions of what "vegan" desserts taste like, I still suppose that "I'd never know this was vegan" is the highest compliment for a vegan recipe. It's the most common exclamation I hear after someone bites into this classic cookie.

INGREDIENTS

4½ teaspoons (45 g) Ener-G Egg Replacer or
  3 tablespoons ground flaxseed (equivalent of
  3 eggs)
6 tablespoons (90 ml) water (½ cup water
  [120 ml] if using ground flaxseed)
1 cup (225 g) non-hydrogenated, nondairy butter,
  softened
¾ cup (150 g) granulated sugar

¾ cup (170 g) firmly packed light or dark
  brown sugar
2 teaspoons vanilla extract
2¼ cups (280 g) unbleached all-purpose flour
1 teaspoon baking soda
1 teaspoon salt
1 to 2 cups (175 to 350 g) nondairy semisweet
  chocolate chips
1 cup (150 g) chopped nuts (optional)

Preheat the oven to 375°F (190°C, or gas mark 5). Line a cookie sheet with parchment paper or use a nonstick cookie/baking sheet.

In a food processor or blender, whip the egg replacer (or ground flaxseed) and water together, until it's thick, creamy, and gooey. Blending it in a food processor or blender results in a better consistency than what you could get if you did it by hand.

In a large bowl, cream the butter, granulated sugar, brown sugar, and vanilla. Add the egg replacer mixture to this wet mixture, and thoroughly combine. In a separate bowl, combine the flour, baking soda, and salt. Gradually beat the flour mixture into the wet mixture until it begins to form a dough. When it is almost thoroughly combined, stir in the chips and nuts, if using.

Bake on the cookie sheet for 8 to 10 minutes, or until golden brown. Let stand for 2 minutes; remove to wire racks to cool completely.

COLLEEN'S TIPS:

* *Some brands of "semisweet chocolate chips" add cow's milk. By definition, that's not semisweet! Look for chips in the bulk section of your natural food store, or choose a higher quality brand of semisweet chips.*
* *To create uniform-size cookies, spoon the dough for each cookie into a small measuring cup, then pop it out onto the cookie sheet.*

CHOCOLATE CHIP MINT COOKIES

YIELD: 1½ DOZEN COOKIES

These cookies are so lovely, and the mint extract makes them extra special and particularly good for the winter holidays.

INGREDIENTS

1 tablespoon (15 g) ground flaxseed (equivalent of 1 egg)
3 tablespoons (45 ml) water
¾ cup (170 g) non-hydrogenated, nondairy butter
½ cup (115 g) firmly packed brown sugar
½ cup (100 g) granulated sugar
1 teaspoon vanilla extract
½ teaspoon peppermint extract
1 ½ cups (190 g) unbleached all-purpose flour
¼ cup (32 g) unsweetened cocoa
1 teaspoon baking soda
¼ teaspoon salt
1 cup (175 g) nondairy chocolate chips (semisweet chips are a good choice)

Preheat the oven to 350°F (180°C, or gas mark 4). Line 2 cookie sheets with parchment paper or use 2 nonstick cookie/baking sheets.

In the small bowl of a food processor or by hand, whip together the ground flaxseed and water, until it's thick and gooey. Set aside.

Cream the butter and sugars together by hand or with an electric hand mixer at high speed. Beat in the "flax egg" and the vanilla and peppermint extracts.

In a separate bowl, combine the flour, cocoa, baking soda, and salt. Add to the butter mixture along with the chocolate chips. Stir well until combined, but do not overstir.

Drop by rounded teaspoons onto the cookie sheet. Bake for 10 to 12 minutes, or until golden brown. Remove the cookies from the sheet immediately after baking and cool on a wire rack.

COLLEEN'S TIP : *If the mint is too strong for you, you can certainly leave it out or just put in a couple drops of the extract.)*

Tips for Successful Cookies

Here are a few especially helpful tips for making cookies. Also refer to "Troubleshooting Cookies" on page 117.

CHILL OUT

Any dough that needs to be rolled out should be refrigerated first—for a couple hours or overnight. When ready to roll, lightly flour the rolling pin and the work surface. Be careful, though; too much flour may make the dough too dry.

SHAPE UP

If you're using cookie cutters, dip them in flour first to prevent sticking. Cut the cookie shapes as close as possible to lessen scraps. Press the leftover scraps together and roll, taking care not to handle the dough too much, lest the cookies become tough.

KEEP IT UNIFORM

For drop cookies, make all your cookies the same size so they bake evenly. I like using a dry measuring cup, ice cream scoop, or measuring spoon for this purpose. Leave enough space between each cookie to allow for spreading while baking.

COOL OFF

Always cool the pan before baking another batch. A warm pan can cause the dough to melt, which leads to overspreading, deformed cookies, or altered baking times.

SIGHT TEST

In general, cookies are done when the edges begin to brown or when the cookies turn golden. Because they're still baking somewhat once you remove them from the oven, I always remove them a little early to keep them tender but crisp.

DRESS REHEARSAL

Sometimes I test-bake a couple of cookies before I send the whole batch into the oven. If the cookies spread too much (and you didn't overgrease the pan), then you may need to add a 1 to 2 tablespoons (8 to 16 g) of flour to the batter.

DRY BOTTOMS

Place cookies on a wire rack to cool evenly, so the bottoms don't get soggy. Once I take cookies out of the oven, I let them sit on the sheet for a couple of minutes before I transfer them to the wire rack. If a cookie bends or breaks when transferring, wait another minute before trying again.

STORE IT

Store baked cookies in airtight containers such as tins, cookie jars with tight-fitting lids, zipper-type bags, or clear plastic containers. For delicate or frosted cookies, place parchment paper between the layers.

FROZEN DOUGH

Most cookie doughs freeze extremely well and can be kept frozen for 4 to 6 weeks. Wrap the dough securely. When you're ready to bake, let the dough thaw for a few hours in the refrigerator. Those that freeze best are shortbreads, chocolate chip, peanut butter, refrigerator, and sugar cookies.

FROZEN TREATS

Freezing baked cookies is a great way to preserve their freshness. Securely wrapped, they will keep in the freezer for 3 to 4 weeks. Let them thaw for a few hours prior to serving or defrost them in the microwave. All baked cookies freeze well.

MEXICAN WEDDING COOKIES

YIELD: 3 DOZEN COOKIES

These melt-in-your mouth cookies are called many names: Russian Tea Cakes, Mexican Wedding Cakes, Pecan Balls, Snowdrops, and Snowballs. They're often baked during the winter holidays, but they're also popular at weddings and other festive occasions. This recipe is from my friend and colleague Colleen Holland of VegNews magazine, who reignited my passion for these little gems.

INGREDIENTS

1 cup (225 g) non-hydrogenated, nondairy butter

¼ cup (50 g) granulated sugar

2 teaspoons vanilla extract

2 cups (250 g) unbleached all-purpose flour, sifted

2 cups (250 g) raw pecans, finely chopped

2 cups (200 g) confectioners' sugar, sifted

Preheat the oven to 300°F (150°C, or gas mark 2). Line 3 cookie sheets with parchment paper or use 3 nonstick cookie/baking sheets.

With an electric hand mixer or by hand, cream the butter, granulated sugar, and vanilla until light and fluffy, 1 to 2 minutes. Add the flour, and mix until thoroughly combined. Add the chopped nuts and mix until well blended, about 30 seconds.

Measure out generously rounded teaspoonfuls of dough and roll them into balls. Place the balls about 1 inch (2.5 cm) apart on the cookie sheet. Bake until they just begin to turn golden, about 30 minutes. To test for doneness, remove one cookie from the sheet and cut it in half. There should be no doughy strip in the center.

Roll the cookies in the confectioners' sugar while they are still warm, then cool on the cookie sheets. Serve when cooled.

SERVING SUGGESTIONS & VARIATIONS

Replace the pecans with hazelnuts, almonds, or walnuts.

COLLEEN'S TIP: *The easiest way to coat the warm cookies in the confectioners' sugar is to add the sugar to a large bowl and gently toss the cookies around in the sugar. You can also place everything in a plastic baggie and give them a shake. Just be careful not to knock them around too much.*

DID YOU KNOW? *Confectioners', powdered, or icing sugar is granulated sugar that has been ground to a powder. Cornstarch is added to prevent lumping. Commercially, it comes in several different grades, but 10X (superfine or ultrafine) is the finest grade and what you find in the grocery store. Professionals may use other grades, such as 6X (very fine) and 4X (fine). If you have no confectioners' sugar, you can put some granulated sugar in a blender with a pinch of cornstarch and process it until powdery.*

PEANUT BUTTER COOKIES

YIELD: 2 DOZEN COOKIES

These cookies take me back to my first baking class when I was seven years old, in which we made Peanut Butter Balls. The classic crisscross pattern in these cookies, which dates back to the 1930s, makes them instantly recognizable, and their fabulous flavor and homey aroma may inspire you to have a cookie party!

INGREDIENTS

1 ¾ cups (220 g) unbleached all-purpose flour, sifted

¾ teaspoon baking soda

¾ teaspoon salt

1 tablespoon (15 g) ground flaxseed (equivalent of 1 egg)

3 tablespoons (45 ml) water

1¼ cups (280 g) firmly packed light brown sugar

¾ cup (195 g) natural peanut butter, smooth or crunchy

½ cup (112 g) non-hydrogenated, nondairy butter

3 tablespoons (45 ml) nondairy milk

1 tablespoon (15 ml) vanilla extract

½ cup (62 g) ground peanuts (optional)

½ cup (90 g) nondairy chocolate chips (optional)

Preheat the oven to 375°F (190°C, or gas mark 5). Line 2 cookie sheets with parchment paper or use 2 nonstick cookie/baking sheets.

In a small bowl, combine the flour, baking soda, and salt. Set aside. Whip the ground flaxseed and water together in a blender or food processor, until thick and creamy.

In a large bowl, combine the brown sugar, peanut butter, butter, milk, and vanilla. Beat at medium speed with an electric hand mixer until well blended. Add the "flax eggs". Beat just until blended. Add the flour mixture, ground peanuts, if using, and chocolate chips, if using, and mix just until blended.

Drop by rounded tablespoonfuls 2 inches (5 cm) apart onto the ungreased cookie sheet. Flatten slightly in a crisscross pattern with the tines of a fork.

Bake for 10 to 12 minutes, or until set and just beginning to brown. Do not overbake. Remove from the oven, and let the cookies cool on the sheet for 3 to 5 minutes before removing to let cool on a wire rack.

SERVING SUGGESTIONS & VARIATIONS

If you don't want to add the ground peanuts and chips to the batter, consider dropping a small square of chocolate, a chocolate chip, or some ground peanuts in the center of each cookie before baking or halfway through the baking time.

FOOD LORE:

* Peanut butter was invented in the early twentieth century by a St. Louis doctor, who mashed peanuts into a paste to give to his patients who were unable to chew.
* George Washington Carver (1864-1943), an African-American educator, botanist, and scientist from Alabama's Tuskegee Institute, promoted the peanut as a replacement for the cotton crop that was destroyed by the boll weevil in the 1890s.

PINE NUT ANISE COOKIES

Based on a recipe from *The Millennium Cookbook*, these elegant cookies beg to be served with tea or coffee. Because they're not overly sweet, they're also ideal accompaniments to sorbet.

INGREDIENTS

3 cups (375 g) unbleached all-purpose flour
¼ teaspoon salt
1½ teaspoons baking powder
1 tablespoon (8 g) anise seeds
1 cup (135 g) pine nuts, toasted
¾ cup plus 2 tablespoons (275 g) pure maple syrup
½ cup (120 ml) canola oil
¼ cup (60 ml) water
2 tablespoons (30 ml) anise extract
1 teaspoon vanilla extract

Preheat the oven to 350°F (180°C, or gas mark 4). Line 2 baking sheets with parchment paper or lightly grease with canola oil.

In a large bowl, combine the flour, salt, baking powder, anise seeds, and pine nuts. In a small bowl, stir together the maple syrup, oil, water, anise extract, and vanilla extract.

Pour the wet mixture into the dry mixture and stir until just combined. Form a ball with 2 tablespoons (35 g) of dough and place on the prepared pan. Press with your hand to a thickness of about ⅓ inch (1 cm). Repeat, and place the cookies 3 inches (7.5 cm) apart on the sheet. Bake for 20 to 30 minutes, or until the cookies are golden brown.

Let cool on a wire rack.

FOOD LORE: *Bearing a strong family resemblance to the members of the carrot family, including dill, fennel, coriander, cumin, and caraway, anise (pronounced ANN-is) has a distinct licorice flavor. Native to the Eastern Mediterranean region and Southwest Asia, anise is one of the oldest-known spice plants used for both culinary and medicinal purposes.*

SUGAR COOKIES

YIELD: 20 COOKIES

Break out your cookie cutters and get ready to make these classic cookies, ideal for forming into various shapes.

 ADVANCE PREPARATION REQUIRED

INGREDIENTS

1¾ cups (220 g) unbleached all-purpose flour
½ teaspoon baking powder
½ cup (112 g) non-hydrogenated, nondairy butter, room temperature
¾ cup (150 g) granulated sugar

1½ teaspoons Ener-G Egg Replacer (equivalent of 1 egg)
2 tablespoons (30 ml) water
1 teaspoon vanilla extract
Sprinkles (optional)
1 recipe Royal Icing (page 250), optional

Line 2 baking sheets with parchment paper.

In a bowl, combine the flour and baking powder. Set aside.

In the bowl of your electric mixer (or with an electric hand mixer), beat the butter and sugar until light and fluffy, 3 to 4 minutes. Add the egg replacer, water, and vanilla extract and beat for at least another minute. Finally, add the flour mixture and beat until you have a smooth dough.

Divide the dough in half and wrap each half in plastic wrap. Refrigerate for about 1 hour, or until firm enough to roll. When ready to bake, preheat the oven to 350°F (180°C, or gas mark 4).

Remove one-half of the chilled dough from the refrigerator and, on a lightly floured surface, roll out the dough to a thickness of ¼ inch (6 mm). Keep flipping the dough over as you roll, making sure the dough doesn't stick to the counter. If the dough gets too warm (from handling), making it hard for the cut-out cookies to keep their shape, simply refrigerate it again for about 10 minutes.

Cut out the cookies using cookie cutters and place on the prepared baking sheets. Place the baking sheets with the unbaked cookies in the refrigerator for 10 to 15 minutes to chill the dough, which prevents the cookies from spreading and losing their shape while baking.

Bake the cookies for 12 to 15 minutes, or until they begin to brown around the edges. Remove from the oven and let cool on the baking sheets for a few minutes before transferring to a wire rack to finish cooling. Decorate with sprinkles or frost with Royal Icing, if desired.

Frosted cookies will keep for several days in an airtight container. Store between layers of parchment paper or waxed paper.

OATMEAL RAISIN COOKIES

YIELD: 3½ DOZEN COOKIES

The addition of the nutmeg makes these classics extra-special. Baked just right, they are moist and crispy at the same time. Rolled oats work best in these cookies, but you can use quick-cooking oats if that's what you have on hand—the cookies will just be a little less chewy.

INGREDIENTS

2 tablespoons (30 g) ground flaxseed (equivalent of 2 eggs)

6 tablespoons (90 ml) water

1 cup (225 g) non-hydrogenated, nondairy butter, softened

1½ cups (340 g) firmly packed brown sugar

¼ cup (50 g) granulated sugar

2 teaspoons vanilla extract

1¾ cups (220 g) unbleached all-purpose flour

½ cup (50 g) oat bran

¾ teaspoon baking soda

¾ teaspoon baking powder

½ teaspoon salt

½ teaspoon ground cinnamon

½ teaspoon ground nutmeg

3 cups (240 g) rolled oats

1 cup (145 g) raisins

Preheat the oven to 350°F (180°C, or gas mark 4). Lightly oil 3 cookie sheets or line with parchment paper.

In a blender or food processor, whip together the flaxseed and water until thick and creamy. The consistency will be somewhat gelatinous. By hand or using an electric hand mixer, cream together the butter, sugars, vanilla, and "flax eggs," until well blended.

In a separate bowl, thoroughly combine the flour, oat bran, baking soda, baking powder, salt, cinnamon, and nutmeg. Add to the butter mixture and mix until well blended and smooth. Stir in the rolled oats and raisins until thoroughly combined.

Use a tablespoon to scoop up some dough and, with lightly greased hands, lightly press the cookies to form ½-inch-thick (1.3-cm) rounds. Bake until the cookies are golden brown, 12 to 15 minutes. Remove from the oven and allow the cookies to firm up for a few minutes while still on the cookie sheet. Transfer the cookies to a wire rack to cool.

WHAT'S THE DIFFERENCE?

* *Steel-cut oats are chopped oat groats (the inner portion of the oat kernel), which only have the outer hull removed, so they are nuttier, chewier, and more nutritious than rolled oats.*
* *Rolled oats have been steamed, rolled, re-steamed, and toasted.*
* *Quick-cooking rolled oats have been cut into pieces before being steamed and rolled.*
* *Instant oats have been precooked and dried before being rolled.*
* *Oatmeal is a meal made from crushed, rolled, or cut oats.*
* *Porridge is a simple dish that can be made by boiling oats in water and nondairy milk. In Ireland and Scotland, it's traditional to use steel-cut oats. In England and the United States, rolled oats are used.*

GINGERBREAD COOKIES

YIELD: 3 DOZEN COOKIES

Most associated with gingerbread men, these delicious cookies cry out to be shaped into handsome little people wearing button-down coats. If that's not your style, simply shape into round circles.

 **ADVANCE PREPARATION REQUIRED**

INGREDIENTS

3 cups (375 g) unbleached all-purpose flour

¼ teaspoon salt

1 teaspoon baking soda

2 teaspoons ground ginger

1 teaspoon ground cinnamon

¼ teaspoon ground nutmeg

¼ teaspoon ground cloves

½ cup (112 g) non-hydrogenated, nondairy butter, at room temperature

¾ cup (150 g) granulated sugar

1 tablespoon (15 g) ground flaxseed (equivalent of 1 egg)

⅔ cup (225 g) unsulphured molasses

1 recipe Royal Icing (page 250), optional

In a bowl, sift or whisk together the flour, salt, baking soda, ginger, cinnamon, nutmeg, and cloves. Set aside.

In the bowl of your electric mixer (or with an electric hand mixer), beat together the butter and sugar until light and fluffy, 3 to 4 minutes. Add the ground flaxseed and molasses and beat for another minute. Finally, add the flour mixture and beat until you have a smooth dough. Add a little more water—1 or 2 tablespoons (15 to 30 ml)—as needed to get the right consistency.

Divide the dough in half and wrap each half in plastic wrap. Refrigerate for at least 1 hour or overnight.

When you're ready to bake the cookies, preheat the oven to 350°F (180°C, or gas mark 4). Line 3 baking sheets with parchment paper.

Remove one-half of the chilled dough from the refrigerator and, on a lightly floured surface, roll out the dough to a thickness of ¼ inch (6 mm). Keep turning the dough as you roll, making sure the dough doesn't stick to the counter. If the dough gets too warm (from handling it), making it hard for the cut-out cookies to keep their shape, simply refrigerate it again for about 10 minutes.

Cut out the cookies using cookie cutters and transfer to the prepared baking sheets. Bake for 10 to 15 minutes (depending on size), or until they begin to brown around the edges. Remove from the oven and let cool on the baking sheets for a few minutes before transferring to a wire rack to finish cooling.

SERVING SUGGESTIONS & VARIATIONS

Frost with Royal Icing (page 250) , if desired. Store frosted cookies between layers of parchment paper or waxed paper.

CHOCOLATE CRINKLES

YIELD: 3 DOZEN COOKIES

Also known as Black and Whites, these are perfect little cookies with a delicious, fudgey flavor and a soft texture that remind me of chocolate glazed donuts.

 ADVANCE PREPARATION REQUIRED

INGREDIENTS

2 tablespoons (30 g) ground flaxseed (equivalent of 2 eggs)

6 tablespoons (90 ml) water

½ cup (100 g) granulated sugar

2 teaspoons vanilla extract

4 tablespoons (60 ml) nondairy milk

¼ cup (55 g) non-hydrogenated, nondairy butter

½ cup (90 g) nondairy semisweet or bittersweet chocolate chips

1½ cups (190 g) unbleached all-purpose flour

¼ teaspoon salt

½ teaspoon baking powder

½ cup (50 g) confectioners' sugar, sifted

In a food processor or in a bowl with an electric hand mixer, combine the ground flaxseed and water, until thick and creamy, about 1 minute. Add the granulated sugar, vanilla, and nondairy milk, and beat for another minute.

Melt the butter and chocolate chips on the stove over low heat until the chips are thoroughly melted. Be sure to stay close to the stove and don't let it boil or burn. Stir the sugar and milk mixture into the melted chips until thoroughly combined.

In a separate bowl, whisk together the flour, salt, and baking powder. Once combined, add the wet ingredients and stir, just until incorporated. Cover with plastic wrap and refrigerate until firm enough to shape into balls, at least 1 hour. You may also store in the refrigerator for several hours or even overnight.

When you're ready to bake the cookies, preheat the oven to 325°F (170°C, or gas mark 3). Line 3 baking sheets with parchment paper or lightly grease with canola oil or nondairy butter, and set aside.

Place the sifted confectioners' sugar in a shallow bowl. With lightly greased hands, roll a small amount of chilled dough to form a 1-inch-diameter (2.5-cm) ball. Place the ball of dough into the powdered sugar and roll the ball in the sugar until it is completely coated. Gently lift the sugar-covered ball, tapping off the excess sugar, and place on the prepared baking sheet. Continue forming cookies, spacing them about 1 inch (2.5 cm) apart on the baking sheets.

Bake the cookies for 10 to 15 minutes, or just until the edges are slightly firm but the centers are still soft. For moist, chewy cookies, do not overbake. Remove from the oven and place on a wire rack to cool.

These cookies are best eaten on the day they are baked.

CHOCOLATE BROWNIES

YIELD: 6 TO 8 BROWNIES

Everyone has a different opinion about brownies: some like them cakey, and some like them moist. These fall into the latter category. You may try baking them a little longer for a cakier result. After testing several variations of brownies, I kept coming back to this one from *Sinfully Vegan* by Lois Dieterly. I've adapted it only slightly.

INGREDIENTS

1½ cups (300 g) granulated sugar

¾ cup (185 g) unsweetened applesauce

2 tablespoons water

2 teaspoons ground flaxseed

½ cup (120 ml) water

2 teaspoons vanilla extract

1⅓ cups (165 g) unbleached all-purpose flour

¾ cup (95 g) unsweetened cocoa powder

¾ teaspoon baking powder

¼ teaspoon salt

1 cup (175 g) nondairy semisweet or dark chocolate chips

1 cup (125 g) coarsely chopped pecans or walnuts (optional)

Preheat oven to 350°F (180°C, or gas mark 4). With canola oil, grease an 8 x 5 x 8-inch (20 x 5 x 20-cm) baking pan.

In a medium-size bowl, stir together the sugar, applesauce, and 2 tablespoons water.

In a small bowl or food processor, combine the ground flaxseed with the ½ cup (120 ml) water. Add this to the applesauce mixture, along with the vanilla, and stir to combine.

In a separate small bowl, combine the flour, cocoa, baking powder, salt, chocolate chips, and nuts, if using. Add to the applesauce mixture, and stir just to combine.

Pour into the prepared pan and bake for 40 minutes. The finished product should be moist. Bake longer if you like a cakier result. Remove from the oven and let cool before cutting. Store leftovers in the refrigerator for up to 5 days or in the freezer for up to 3 months.

SERVING SUGGESTIONS & VARIATIONS

Serve warm with nondairy ice cream for brownies à la mode.

FOOD LORE: *The first known mention of a brownie is believed to be in the 1897 Sears and Roebuck catalog.*

COLLEEN'S TIP: *The best way to freeze brownies is to cut them into squares, wrap each square in plastic wrap, and then wrap each in foil. Finally, place the wrapped squares in an airtight freezer bag.*

RASPBERRY OATMEAL BARS

YIELD: 6 TO 8 BARS, DEPENDING ON SIZE

These could easily be called Apricot Oatmeal Bars, Blackcurrant Oatmeal Bars, or Strawberry Oatmeal Bars. It's all a matter of what type of jam or preserves you choose to use. You really can't go wrong, although I do recommend finding as natural a brand as possible.

INGREDIENTS

½ cup (112 g) firmly packed light brown sugar

1 cup (125 g) unbleached all-purpose flour

¼ teaspoon baking soda

⅛ teaspoon salt

1 cup (80 g) quick-cooking oats

½ cup (112 g) non-hydrogenated, nondairy butter, softened

¾ cup (240 g) raspberry (or other fruit) preserves

Preheat oven to 350°F (180°C, or gas mark 4). Lightly oil one 8- or 9-inch (20- or 23-cm) square pan on all sides.

In a medium-size bowl, combine the brown sugar, flour, baking soda, salt, and rolled oats. Add the butter and, using your hands, create a crumbly mixture. Press two-thirds of the mixture into the bottom of the prepared pan. Spread the jam to within ¼ inch (6 mm) of the edge. An offset spatula works well for this. (See "Essential Kitchen Tools" on page 267.)

Sprinkle the remaining one-third of the crumb mixture over the top, and lightly press it into the jam.

Bake for 35 to 40 minutes, or until lightly browned. Allow to cool before cutting into squares.

WHAT'S THE DIFFERENCE?

* *Jams and preserves are similar. Jams are made with whole fruit that is slightly crushed or ground, and boiled with sugar. Jams often contain fruit chunks and have enough jell to hold their shape.*
* *Preserves are made in much the same way as jam. The main difference is that there are larger pieces of fruit in the mixture.*
* *Jelly is made from fruit juice as opposed to whole fruit. It has a smooth consistency and contains no fruit chunks.*
* *Marmalade tends to be a citrus-based preserve, and it often contains pieces of the rind.*
* *Conserves consist of mixed fruits and citrus, along with raisins and chopped nuts.*
* *Fruit butter is a sweet spread made by stewing fresh fruit with sugar and spices until it becomes thick and smooth.*

LEMON BARS

Think lemon meringue pie without the meringue! Who needs whipped egg whites anyway, when you can experience the sweet/tart lemon filling in a buttery shortbread crust?

INGREDIENTS—CRUST

½ cup (112 g) non-hydrogenated, nondairy butter, at room temperature

¼ cup (25 g) confectioners' sugar

1 cup (125 g) unbleached all-purpose flour

INGREDIENTS—FILLING

½ cup (112 g) silken tofu (soft or firm)

1 cup (200 g) granulated sugar

Zest from 2 lemons

⅓ cup (90 ml) fresh lemon juice (2 to 3 lemons)

2 tablespoons (8 g) unbleached all-purpose flour

1 tablespoon (8 g) cornstarch

Confectioners' sugar, sifted

Preheat the oven to 350°F (180°C, or gas mark 4). Grease an 8 × 8-inch (20 × 20-cm) baking pan with canola oil (or use a cooking spray) and sprinkle with just a light dusting of all-purpose flour.

To make the crust, in the bowl of your electric stand mixer, or with an electric hand mixer, cream the butter and confectioners' sugar until light and fluffy. Add the flour, and beat until the dough just comes together. Press into the bottom of your prepared pan and bake for about 20 minutes, or until lightly browned. Remove from the oven and place on a wire rack to cool while you make the filling.

To make the filling, in a food processor or blender, add the tofu and blend until creamy, about 1 minute. Add the granulated sugar and blend until nice and smooth. Add the lemon zest, lemon juice, flour, and cornstarch. Pour the filling over the baked shortbread crust and bake for about 20 minutes, or until the filling is set. Remove from the oven and place on a wire rack to cool.

To serve, cut into squares or bars and dust with the sifted confectioners' sugar. Wait until you're just about to serve the bars before you sprinkle them with the confectioners' sugar. Otherwise, it will soak into the bars and you'll miss out on that pretty presentation. I think these are best eaten the day they are made, but they can be covered and stored in the refrigerator for up to 2 days.

SERVING SUGGESTIONS & VARIATIONS

* Serve these bars along with Classic Currant Scones (page 54), Mexican Wedding Cookies (page 123), or German Apple Cake (page 80).
* Serve with fresh raspberries and blueberries.

COLLEEN'S TIPS:

* Zest two of your lemons first, and then cut them in half and squeeze out their juice. A microplane works incredibly well for zesting lemons. See "Essential Kitchen Tools" on page 267.
* Bottled lemon juice just doesn't cut it. Use fresh lemons to make lemon bars.

DATE BARS

YIELD: 10 TO 12 BARS, DEPENDING ON THE SIZE

I absolutely love dates, and I relish visiting one particular stand at my local farmers' market, whose delicious dates prove that nature provided everything we need, including our desire for something sweet. Medjool and Barhee are my favorites.

INGREDIENTS—FILLING

1¼ cups (295 ml) water
16 to 18 pitted dates, coarsely chopped
½ teaspoon salt
1 teaspoon vanilla extract

INGREDIENTS—TOPPING

3 cups (240 g) quick-cooking oats
1½ cups (190 g) unbleached all-purpose flour
½ cup (100 g) granulated sugar
½ teaspoon salt
½ teaspoon baking powder
½ teaspoon baking soda
1 teaspoon cinnamon
¾ cup (170 g) non-hydrogenated, nondairy butter, melted
¼ cup (60 ml) canola or coconut oil
¼ cup (60 ml) water (optional)

Preheat the oven to 350°F (180°C, or gas mark 4). Lightly grease a 9-inch (23-cm) square or 9 × 13-inch (23 × 33-cm) pan. (The smaller the pan, the thicker your bars will be.)

To make the filling, in a small saucepan, bring the water to a boil. (Chop the dates while you're waiting for the water to boil.) Add the dates and the salt and simmer until the dates are soft and mix easily with the water. Remove from the heat, stir in the vanilla, and set aside to cool.

To make the topping, in a large bowl, thoroughly combine the oats, flour, sugar, salt, baking powder, baking soda, and cinnamon. Add the butter and oil, and stir together until totally combined with the dry mixture. You want it to be moist but not wet. If you need to add more moisture, add some of the optional water until it's the right consistency.

Press half of the crust mixture into the bottom of the prepared pan. Spread the date mixture over the top, spreading it out so it thoroughly covers the crust. Pour the remaining half of the crust mixture over the top of the dates. Bake for 30 to 40 minutes, until the top is lightly browned. Let cool for 5 minutes, then cut into bars.

PEANUT BUTTER CHOCOLATE BARS

YIELD: 12 TO 18 SQUARES, DEPENDING ON SIZE

Enjoy this no-bake bar that both kids and adults will gobble up with zeal. According to my friend Tami Wall, who graced me with this delicious delight, the baking pan should be very well buttered.

INGREDIENTS

2 cups (100 g) crispy rice cereal, crushed

1 ½ cups (390 g) natural peanut butter

2 cups (200 g) confectioners' sugar

½ cup plus 2 tablespoons (140 g) non-hydrogenated, nondairy butter, melted, divided

1 teaspoon vanilla extract

½ cup (90 g) nondairy semisweet or dark chocolate chips

Generously butter a 9 × 13-inch (23 × 33-cm) baking pan.

In a large bowl, combine the cereal, peanut butter, confectioners' sugar, ½ cup (112 g) of the butter, and vanilla. Press the mixture into the prepared baking pan.

In a small saucepan (or double boiler) melt together the chocolate chips and the remaining 2 tablespoons (28 g) butter, stirring constantly. Remove from the heat.

Spread the chocolate mixture over the top of the peanut butter mixture. Set aside for 1 to 2 hours to set.

COLLEEN'S TIP: *I grew up on the type of peanut butter that too many people rely on: the kind with added oil and sugar. The purpose of the oil is to make it easier to stir, but it compromises the taste and the healthfulness of the product. True peanut butter contains only ground peanuts and maybe a little salt. Sugar-free peanut butter may take getting used to, but it's so worth it. Start off by combining half of the old and half of the new until you're fully converted.*

PINEAPPLE WALNUT BARS

YIELD: 15 BARS

This recipe was given to me several years ago by a former student, but it took my writing a cook-book to finally make the bars. And I love them. The apricot puree is something you can use in other recipes in place of butter or oil.

INGREDIENTS

2 cups (250 g) unbleached all-purpose flour
½ teaspoon salt
1½ teaspoons baking powder
½ cup (90 g) dried apricots
⅓ cup (90 ml) water
¾ cup (150 g) granulated sugar
Zest of 1 lemon
1½ teaspoons vanilla extract
1 (20-ounce or 570-ml) can organic, unsweetened, crushed pineapple
½ cup (120 ml) coconut oil
1 cup (150 g) toasted walnuts, coarsely chopped

Preheat the oven to 350°F (180°C, or gas mark 4). Lightly grease a 9 × 13-inch (23 × 33-cm) pan.

In a medium-size bowl, combine the flour, salt, and baking powder. Set aside.

Make the apricot puree by placing the dried fruit in a food processor. Turn it on and slowly add the water until you have a puree. You may add a little more water, if necessary, and you may need to periodically turn off the food processor to scrape down the sides of the bowl. Add the sugar and lemon zest, process until smooth, and transfer to a large mixing bowl.

Add the vanilla and crushed pineapple, and alternately add the flour mixture and the oil. Stir in the toasted walnuts, and stir to combine. Pour into the prepared pan and distribute the batter evenly, spreading the top with a spatula.

Bake for 40 to 50 minutes, rotating the pan once during this time. The sides will be golden brown when finished. Let it cool for 10 minutes before cutting into squares or 1 × 2-inch (2.5 × 5-cm) rectangles.

SERVING SUGGESTIONS & VARIATIONS

Sift a light dusting of confectioners' sugar over the bars just as you are about to serve them.

CHAPTER SEVEN

BEARING FRUIT: CRUMBLES, COBBLERS, CRISPS, AND WHOLE FRUIT DESSERTS

Fruit desserts may very well be even more tempting for me than chocolate! The combination of naturally sweet fruit with earthy ingredients such as nuts, oats, and homey spices fills the home—and belly—with joy!

WHAT'S THE DIFFERENCE?

CRUMBLES

A crumble is a hearty dish of British origin, containing stewed fruit topped with a crumbly mixture of fat, flour, and sugar. The crumble is baked in an oven until the topping is crisp. Popular fruits used in crumbles include apple, blackberry, peach, rhubarb, gooseberry, and plum. The topping may also include rolled oats, ground almonds, or other nuts.

COBBLERS

A cobbler is a traditional American baked dish, consisting of a filling—usually fruit—that's covered by a layer of pastry as a crust. Apples, peaches, and berries are the most common fillings. The name may refer to a shoemaker, who likewise "patches" things together—as in this casual easy-to-prepare dessert.

CRISPS

Crisps are a relatively new American dessert consisting of baked fruit—apples, pears, peaches, berries, or rhubarb—topped with a crispy crust that's often made with oats, nuts, cinnamon, and sugar.

THE RECIPES

Apple Crumble ... 142
Banana Crumble ... 143
Apple Cobbler ... 144
Blueberry Cobbler ... 147
Baked Apples ... 148
Poached Pears ... 149
Bananas in Sweet Coconut Milk ... 150
Sautéed Bananas ... 150
Bananas Foster ... 151
Fall Fruit Crisp ... 152
Peach Melba ... 154
Fruit Compote ... 155
Applesauce ... 156
Mango with Sticky Rice
  (Kow Neuw Mamuang) ... 158
Stuffed Dates ... 159
Chocolate-Dipped Fruit ... 160

APPLE CRUMBLE

YIELD: 6 SERVINGS

The almond and coconut flavors add a special note to this comforting dessert. See "Apples and Their Uses" (page 157) for choosing the right apple(s) for this fall favorite.

INGREDIENTS

4 to 5 large apples, peeled, cored, and sliced
¼ cup (50 g) granulated sugar
¾ cup (94 g) unbleached all-purpose flour, plus 1 tablespoon (8 g)
1 teaspoon cinnamon, divided
1 cup (125 g) finely ground almonds, walnuts, or pecans
½ cup (112 g) firmly packed brown sugar
¼ teaspoon nutmeg
¼ teaspoon salt
½ cup (112 g) non-hydrogenated, nondairy butter, melted

Preheat the oven to 375°F (190°C, or gas mark 5). Lightly grease an 8-inch (20-cm) square baking dish.

In a medium-size bowl, toss together the apples, granulated sugar, 1 tablespoon (8 g) of the flour, and ½ teaspoon of the cinnamon until the apples are completely coated. Arrange the apple pieces in the prepared baking dish.

In another medium-size bowl, combine the remaining ¾ cup (94 g) flour, almond meal, brown sugar, nutmeg, the remaining ½ teaspoon cinnamon, and the salt. Cut in the butter until the mixture is fine and crumbly. Sprinkle the topping over the apples.

Cover with foil, and bake for 45 minutes, until the apples are soft when pierced with a fork. Uncover, and continue to bake until the crumble is crisp and golden in color, about 10 more minutes.

FOOD LORE: *Crumbles originated in Britain during World War II, due to strict rationing when the ingredients for pies were scarce.*

BANANA CRUMBLE

YIELD: 6 SERVINGS

If you're looking for something to warm yourself from the inside out, choose this crumble, and be sure to serve it warm (though room temperature is acceptable).

INGREDIENTS—FILLING
3 to 4 medium ripe bananas, sliced into round discs
¼ to ½ cup (50 to 100 g) granulated sugar

INGREDIENTS—CRUMBLE
½ cup (40 g) quick-cooking oats
½ cup (65 g) whole wheat pastry or unbleached all-purpose flour
½ cup (112 g) firmly packed brown sugar
½ cup (112 g) non-hydrogenated, nondairy butter, melted
½ cup (35 g) unsweetened shredded coconut, toasted
⅛ to ¼ teaspoon nutmeg

Preheat the oven to 350°F (180°C, or gas mark 4). Lightly oil 12 individual ramekins or a 9-inch (23-cm) square or round pan.

To make the filling, mix together the bananas and granulated sugar. Arrange the bananas in the prepared pan, entirely covering the bottom of the pan.

To make the crumble, mix together the oats, flour, brown sugar, butter, and coconut, and distribute it over the bananas, covering them thoroughly. Sprinkle a little nutmeg on top and bake for 20 minutes, or until bubbly.

Serve warm or at room temperature.

SERVING SUGGESTIONS & VARIATIONS
* Add some seasonal berries to the banana mixture.
* Top with nondairy vanilla ice cream or Tofu Whipped Topping (page 254).

COLLEEN'S TIP: *It's easy to toast the shredded coconut, which you shouldn't have any trouble finding in your natural food store. Simply place it on your toaster oven tray and bake on low heat for 5 minutes, or until it turns a golden brown. Keep a close eye on it to prevent burning.*

APPLE COBBLER

Out of all the recipes I tested (and tasted!) for this cookbook, the cobblers were the hardest to resist second and third helpings of! Many different fruits are options for cobblers, and apples are perfect for fall and winter.

INGREDIENTS

5 cups (750 g) peeled and sliced tart apples

¾ cup (150 g) granulated sugar, plus 1 tablespoon for sprinkling over top

2 tablespoons (16 g) unbleached all-purpose flour

½ teaspoon cinnamon

¼ teaspoon salt

1 teaspoon vanilla extract

¼ cup (60 ml) water

1 recipe Cobbler Biscuit Dough (see Blueberry Cobbler, page 147)

1 to 2 tablespoons (15 to 30 ml) nondairy milk or 1 to 2 tablespoons (14 to 28 g)
   non-hydrogenated, nondairy butter, melted, for brushing top of dough

Preheat the oven to 375°F (190°C, or gas mark 5). Have ready an ungreased 8- or 9-inch (20- or 23-cm) square baking pan at least 2 inches (5 cm) deep.

In a large bowl, combine the apples with the sugar, flour, cinnamon, salt, vanilla, and water. Spread evenly in the prepared baking dish, and set aside.

Using a tablespoon, scoop the dough over the fruit. Either leave the dough in shapeless blobs on the fruit or spread it out. There will be just enough to cover the fruit. Brush the top of the dough with the remaining 1 to 2 tablespoons milk or butter and the 1 tablespoon sugar. Bake until the top is golden brown and the juices have thickened slightly, 35 to 40 minutes. Let cool for 15 minutes before serving.

SERVING SUGGESTIONS & VARIATIONS

If you want a flakier dough, the butter should be cold and cut in until the dough resembles coarse bread crumbs.

Tips for Crumbles, Cobblers, and Crisps

These are easy desserts to make—much easier than pies. If you're reluctant to dive into the pie-making arena, start with these delicious fruit-filled goodies. Though they're virtually fool-proof, here are a few tips and guidelines.

BE DARING

Experiment with different filling combinations. Accent apples with cranberries or raspberries. Mix peaches with blueberries and slivered almonds. Combine strawberries with rhubarb. The options are endless.

SPEED IT UP

Use canned fruit in its own juices for a quick and simple filling. To thicken the juice to a slurry, add a little cornstarch or flour. Add any spices you like.

DRIED UP

Small amounts of dried fruits—cranberries, cherries, currants, or raisins—can be added to the fruit mixture. If they've lost some of their freshness, soak them for about 15 minutes in water, fruit juice, or brandy.

ERR ON THE SIDE OF CAUTION

Because a fruit's sweetness can vary so much, the amount of sugar will vary, too. Begin with three-quarters of the sugar required in the recipe and then add more to taste.

FALL FRUIT CRISP, PAGE 152

GLASS BOTTOM

Because fruit is acidic and these desserts don't have a bottom crust as protection, use oven-proof glass or porcelain dishes instead of metal.

ADVANCE PREP

Fruit fillings can be mixed a few hours in advance of cooking. Spread in the pan, cover tightly with plastic wrap, and refrigerate. Put the topping on just before baking.

SERVE WARM

Cobblers and crisps are at their best when served warm the day they're made. Covered with foil, they can be refrigerated for up to 3 days.

BLUEBERRY COBBLER

YIELD: 6 TO 8 SERVINGS

This could easily be called Fruit Cobbler, as it invites the inclusion of any berry or fruit, such as apples or peaches. Because I love biscuits and berries so much, this is one of my favorite desserts.

INGREDIENTS—COBBLER BISCUIT DOUGH

1⅓ cups (165 g) unbleached all-purpose flour

3 tablespoons (40 g) granulated sugar, divided

1½ teaspoons baking powder

½ teaspoon salt

5 tablespoons (70 g) non-hydrogenated, nondairy butter, melted

½ cup (120 ml) nondairy milk

1 to 2 tablespoons (15 to 30 ml) nondairy milk or 1 to 2 tablespoons (14 to 28 g) non-hydrogenated, nondairy butter, melted, for brushing top of dough

INGREDIENTS—FILLING

4 to 5 cups (580 to 725 g) blueberries

½ cup (100 g) granulated sugar

2 tablespoons (16 g) unbleached all-purpose flour

1 teaspoon grated lemon or lime zest (optional)

Preheat the oven to 375°F (190°C, or gas mark 5). Have ready an ungreased 8- or 9-inch (20- or 23-cm) square baking pan or 8 × 10-inch (20 × 25-cm) rectangular baking pan at least 2 inches (5 cm) deep.

To make the biscuit dough, combine the flour, 2 tablespoons (26 g) of the granulated sugar, the baking powder, and salt. When completely combined, add the nondairy butter and milk. Stir just until it forms a sticky dough. Set aside.

To make the filling, wash and pat dry the blueberries. In a large bowl, combine them with the sugar, flour, and lemon zest, if using. Spread evenly in the baking dish.

Using a tablespoon, scoop the dough over the fruit. There will be just enough to cover the fruit. Either leave the dough in shapeless blobs on the fruit or spread it out. Brush the top of the dough with the remaining 1 to 2 tablespoons milk or butter and the remaining 1 tablespoon sugar. Bake until the top is golden brown and the juices have thickened slightly, 45 to 50 minutes. Let cool for 15 minutes before serving.

SERVING SUGGESTIONS & VARIATIONS

If you want a flakier dough, the butter should be cold and cut in until the dough resembles coarse bread crumbs.

BAKED APPLES

YIELD: 4 SERVINGS

This is a delicious dessert that thrills adults as well as children. There simply isn't a better aroma to fill the kitchen than the sweet smell of apples and cinnamon.

INGREDIENTS

4 tart apples

½ cup (112 g) firmly packed light brown sugar

2 tablespoons (28 g) non-hydrogenated, nondairy butter

2 teaspoons cinnamon

⅓ cup (90 ml) apple juice, cider, or dry white wine

Nutmeg for sprinkling

Preheat the oven to 350°F (180°C, or gas mark 4). Have ready an 8-inch (20-cm) square baking dish.

Using an apple corer or the rounded tip of a vegetable peeler, scoop out the core from the top of each apple, leaving a well. Do not cut all the way through to the bottom end. Enlarge the hole slightly for filling.

Using a vegetable peeler, remove the peel from the top half of each apple. This helps the apple "breathe." Place the apples in the baking dish. Stuff each apple with 2 tablespoons (28 g) brown sugar and ½ tablespoon butter. Sprinkle with cinnamon. Pour the juice into the dish.

Cover with foil and bake for 40 minutes, until the sugar begins to caramelize and the apples are tender when pierced with a fork. Transfer the apples to dessert dishes, spoon the liquid over the apples, and sprinkle with nutmeg. Serve warm with Tofu Whipped Topping (page 254), Cashew Cream (page 255), nondairy yogurt, or nondairy vanilla ice cream.

SERVING SUGGESTIONS & VARIATIONS

* Add raisins, chopped dates, or chopped dried apricots.
* Add chopped toasted pecans, walnuts, or almonds and ground ginger.
* If you prefer a firmer apple, bake for less time.

COLLEEN'S TIP:

Several different kinds of apples will do, but here are some that work particularly well for baking:

* *Fuji—Sweet and juicy, firm, red skin*
* *Granny Smith—Moderately sweet, crisp flesh, green skin*
* *Jonathan—Tart flesh, crisp, juicy, bright red on yellow skin*
* *McIntosh—Juicy, sweet, pinkish-white flesh, red skin*
* *Newton Pippin—Sweet-tart flesh, crisp, greenish-yellow skin*
* *Rome Beauty—Mildly tart, crisp, greenish-white flesh, thick skin*
* *Winesap—Firm, very juicy, sweet-sour flavor, red skin*

POACHED PEARS

Poaching is the process of gently simmering food in some kind of liquid, usually water, stock, or wine. This is a light and refreshing dessert that is best with fresh seasonal pears.

INGREDIENTS

4 to 6 ripe pears with stems

1 cup (235 ml) Champagne, white wine, or sparkling cider

5 cups (1175 ml) water

1 cup (200 g) granulated sugar

¼ teaspoon salt

2-inch (5-cm) piece vanilla bean (split lengthwise) or 1 teaspoon vanilla extract

1 cinnamon stick or 1 teaspoon ground cinnamon

2 whole cloves or 1 teaspoon ground cloves

Peel of 1 orange, cut into 4 to 6 pieces

Mint leaves for garnish

Peel the pears, taking care to leave the stems intact, and cut a thin slice from the bottom of each to enable the pear to stand upright when served.

In a large pot (large enough to hold the pears lying on their sides), add the Champagne, water, and sugar. Bring to a boil. Add the salt, vanilla bean, cinnamon, cloves, and orange peel.

Arrange the pears on their sides in the liquid, and add enough water as necessary to just cover the pears. Cover the pot with a smaller-sized lid, making sure that it rests directly on the pears. (The smaller lid keeps the pears submerged, thus ensuring even cooking.)

Reduce the heat to low and simmer, occasionally turning the pears, and cook for 15 to 20 minutes, or until the pears are tender. A sharp knife inserted into the pears should meet no resistance. Don't poach for too long, as the pears will quickly become too mushy.

With a slotted spoon, carefully transfer the pears to serving plates. Cover with plastic wrap and refrigerate the pears until you're ready to serve them.

To prepare the sauce, strain the cinnamon stick, orange peel, and cloves from the poaching liquid, but don't discard the orange peel. Increase the heat to medium-high and boil the remaining liquid for about 30 minutes, or until the liquid is reduced to ¾ to 1 cup (175 to 235 ml) and is slightly syrupy. Watch it carefully, however, so it doesn't burn. Remove from the heat and refrigerate the sauce until ready to serve.

To serve the pears, place each pear on a serving plate and pour approximately ¾ cup (60 ml) of the syrup over each pear. Garnish with the orange peel and a sprig of mint leaves.

SERVING SUGGESTIONS & VARIATIONS
* Any of the following pears will work well: Bosc, Bartlett, Anjou, or Comice.
* Serve with Raspberry Sauce (page 248).

BANANAS IN SWEET COCONUT MILK

YIELD: 4 SMALL SERVINGS (A LITTLE GOES A LONG WAY!)

This is a very rich but delectable dessert that will knock your socks off. My dear friend, Diane Miller, recommended refrigerating it and enjoying it cold. Either way, you'll be delighted.

INGREDIENTS

2 large ripe bananas

1 (15-ounce [440-ml]) can coconut milk

1 to 2 tablespoons (13 to 26 g) granulated sugar

1 teaspoon cinnamon, plus more for sprinkling (optional)

¼ teaspoon ground cloves

¼ to ½ teaspoon nutmeg

Peel the bananas, and cut into bite-size pieces, preferably disk-shaped. In a medium-size saucepan, bring the coconut milk to a boil. Add the sugar, 1 teaspoon cinnamon, cloves, and nutmeg, stirring to dissolve. Add the bananas.

Return to a boil, then turn down the heat and simmer for 3 to 5 minutes, until the bananas are tender but not mushy. The longer you cook the bananas, the thicker it will become.

Serve hot, sprinkling a little cinnamon on top, if desired.

SAUTÉED BANANAS

YIELD: 4 SERVINGS

Anyone who has never cooked fruit is really missing out. The natural fruit sugars caramelize when heated, bringing out the sweetness and depth of the fruit. So yummy! You can use a charcoal, gas, or indoor grill, or simply pan-grill them in a skillet over medium heat.

INGREDIENTS

4 ripe bananas

¼ cup (60 ml) agave nectar or Bee Free Honee

Ground cinnamon for dusting

Peel the bananas and cut them into disk-shaped slices. In a microwave oven or small saucepan, heat the agave nectar until very fluid.

Toss the bananas with the nectar in a shallow bowl until all are coated. This can be done 1 to 2 hours in advance.

Arrange the banana pieces crosswise on the grill, and grill until marked on the bottom. Turn and grill just until the second side is marked. Arrange on a platter and dust lightly with the cinnamon, if using.

BANANAS FOSTER

YIELD: 4 SERVINGS

Bananas are a fruit that I eat every day, and cooking them just adds to their flavor, as they become caramelized and sweeter. This famous dessert is rich and decadent and sure to impress friends and family, particularly if you flambé it.

INGREDIENTS

4 tablespoons (55 g) non-hydrogenated, nondairy butter

½ cup (112 g) firmly packed brown sugar

3 tablespoons (45 ml) dark rum or good-quality brandy

2 tablespoons (30 ml) banana liqueur (optional)

1 ½ teaspoons vanilla extract

1 teaspoon cinnamon

½ teaspoon nutmeg

4 firm, ripe bananas, sliced in half lengthwise

¼ cup (40 g) coarsely chopped walnuts or pecans

Melt the butter in a large, heavy sauté pan. Stir in the brown sugar, rum, banana liqueur (if using), vanilla, cinnamon, and nutmeg and heat until the sugar is completely dissolved and the mixture begins to bubble. Add the bananas and walnuts to the pan and cook until they are well coated with the syrup but not mushy. Serve at once, either on its own or with nondairy ice cream.

SERVING SUGGESTIONS & VARIATIONS

* You can use rum extract instead of rum: 1 tablespoon rum equals 1 teaspoon rum extract plus 2 teaspoons water.
* Serve with nondairy vanilla ice cream.
* This makes a rich topping for French toast or waffles.
* You are essentially cooking off the alcohol by following the instructions above, but if you'd like to have the full "flambé" experience, right after you add the bananas and walnuts, light a long match to ignite the alcohol. Cook until the flame dies out and the alcohol is cooked off.

FOOD LORE: *The dish was created in the 1950s by Paul Blangé, head chef at Brennan's Restaurant in New Orleans, who was challenged by the restaurant's owner (Owen Brennan) to come up with an innovative dish using bananas. It was named for Richard Foster, a friend of Brennan and frequent restaurant patron.*

FALL FRUIT CRISP

YIELD: 6 TO 8 SERVINGS

Any autumn fruit can be used for this delightful dessert that fills the home with an inviting fragrance. I find many crisps to be too sweet. In this version, the flavor and sweetness of the fruit come through, while still satisfying the sweet tooth.

INGREDIENTS—FILLING

6 to 8 cups (900 to 1200 g) cored and sliced or
   chopped pears and/or apples

1 cup (145 g) blueberries, fresh or frozen (optional)

1 cup (145 g) raisins (optional)

Juice from 1 lemon

¼ cup (85 g) pure maple syrup

1 teaspoon cinnamon

½ teaspoon allspice

INGREDIENTS—TOPPING

1 cup (80 g) rolled oats (not quick-cooking)

1 cup (150 g) chopped walnuts or pecans, toasted
   for 10 minutes

½ cup (62 g) whole wheat flour

½ cup (112 g) non-hydrogenated, nondairy butter

¼ cup (55 g) firmly packed light or dark
   brown sugar

1 teaspoon cinnamon

¼ teaspoon allspice

¼ teaspoon nutmeg

¼ teaspoon salt

½ teaspoon anise seeds (optional)

Preheat the oven to 350°F (180°C, or gas mark 4). Have ready an ungreased 8- or 9-inch (20- or 23-cm) square baking pan at least 2 inches (5 cm) deep.

To make the filling, in a medium-size bowl, combine the pears, blueberries (if using), raisins (if using), lemon juice, maple syrup, cinnamon, and allspice and pour into the baking pan.

To make the topping, in a separate bowl (or simply rinse out the one you just used), combine the oats, walnuts, flour, butter, brown sugar, cinnamon, allspice, nutmeg, salt, and anise seeds (if using). The topping should be crumbly (and chunky from the walnuts) and have the texture of wet sand. If it's too dry, add a little more butter or a couple teaspoons of water.

Sprinkle the topping over the fruit mixture, making sure it's evenly distributed. Bake for 35 to 45 minutes, or until the pears and apples are soft when pierced with a toothpick or fork. Remove from the oven and serve hot, warm, or at room temperature; you can also serve it à la mode.

SERVING SUGGESTIONS & VARIATIONS
* Use oat or barley flour for a wheat-free version.
* Use other autumn or winter fruit, such as rhubarb and cranberries.
* You may use canola oil instead of nondairy butter.

COLLEEN'S TIP: *For individual servings, bake the crisp in ramekins or small baking cups. Place on a cookie sheet in case the juices overflow, and cut the baking time in half.*

PEACH MELBA

A classic French dessert, this dish was invented in London to honor an Australian. Combining three summer favorites—peaches, raspberries, and ice cream—this is definitely a seasonal dessert.

INGREDIENTS

1 (16-ounce or 455-g) can peaches halves or 4 fresh pitted peaches, cut in half
2 pints (910 g) nondairy vanilla ice cream
1 recipe Raspberry Sauce (page 248)

In a single-serving dish, place a peach half, cut side up. Top the peach with a scoop of nondairy vanilla ice cream and pour some of the raspberry sauce on top. Serve immediately.

FOOD LORE: *There are many variations of this legend, but it goes something like this: The Peach Melba was created around 1892 by Auguste Escoffier at the Savoy Hotel in London. He had heard Nellie Melba, a renowned Australian opera singer, was performing at Covent Garden and wanted to create a dessert just for her. He heard that she loved ice cream but didn't eat it often, lest it affect her vocal cords. (Dairy-based ice cream creates a lot of phlegm.) Escoffier figured that if the ice cream were only one element of the entire dessert, the diva would eat it. She did. The rest is history.*

FRUIT COMPOTE

Dried fruits, especially apricots, are great for satisfying your sweet tooth (while also providing numerous nutritional benefits). This easy compote is quick, naturally sweet, and very versatile. It can be served alone, topped with vanilla nondairy yogurt, or as a topping over fresh fruit such as pears or apples.

INGREDIENTS

1½ cups fresh (355 ml) orange juice
2 tablespoons (30 ml) agave nectar or Bee Free Honee
2 ½ cups (375 g) dried fruit (a combination of dried dates, raisins, cherries, apricots, and blueberries, for instance)
1 teaspoon cinnamon

Bring the orange juice and nectar to a boil in a small saucepan. Add the dried fruit and cinnamon, reduce the heat to low, and simmer just until the fruit becomes tender and a little syrupy, about 10 minutes. Do not overcook or they will dissolve, and you want to have definition in your fruit.

Remove from the heat, and serve warm or chilled.

SERVING SUGGESTIONS & VARIATIONS

∗ Other sweeteners, liquid or granulated, will work well.
∗ This makes a delicious topping for oatmeal or quinoa.

DID YOU KNOW? *The word "compote" comes from the Latin word meaning "a mixture."*

APPLESAUCE

This can be served either chunky or smooth, as a side dish, a dessert, or a sweet snack. Blending two or three different types of apples makes the best-testing sauce. See "Apples and Their Uses" on the right for help in choosing a combination of tart and sweet apples.

INGREDIENTS

3 pounds (1365 g) apples, peeled if desired, cored, and cut into ½-inch-thick (1.3-cm) slices
½ to ¾ cup (120 to 180 ml) apple cider or apple juice
1 teaspoon cinnamon
¼ to ½ cup (50 to 100 g) granulated sugar
½ teaspoon ground ginger (optional)
½ teaspoon nutmeg (optional)

In a large saucepan, combine the apples, apple cider, and cinnamon. Cover and simmer, stirring often, over low heat until tender but not mushy. After 20 minutes, add the sugar, and ginger and nutmeg, if using, stirring until the sugar is dissolved and blended, about 1 minute. Remove from the heat. For chunky applesauce, break up the apples with a wooden spoon. For medium texture, mash with a potato masher or use an immersion blender. For a totally smooth sauce, puree in a blender or food processor. Serve warm or chilled.

SERVING SUGGESTIONS & VARIATIONS

Top with toasted fennel seeds or pistachio nuts.

COLLEEN'S TIP: *Three pounds of apples equals 8 or 9 apples. See "Common Ingredients: Yields and Equivalents" on page 280.*

Apples and Their Uses

There's nothing sweeter than tasting a fresh apple on a crisp fall day. If your idea of a fresh apple is a Red Delicious from the grocery store, please use this list to expand your apple horizons! Apples are often classified according to how good they are for eating (or dessert or salad), pies, sauces, ciders, and baking whole.

VARIETY	FLAVOR, TEXTURE	EATING	PIE	SAUCE/CIDER	BAKING (WHOLE)
Braeburn	Sweet-Tart, Crisp	Very Good	Good	Good	Good
Cortland	Slightly Tart, Slightly Crisp	Excellent	Very Good	Very Good	Very Good
Crispin/Mutsu	Sweet, Crisp	Excellent	Very Good	Good	Very Good
Criterion	Sweet/Complex, Crisp	Very Good	Very Good	Very Good	Very Good
Empire	Sweet-Tart, Crisp	Excellent	Excellent	Good	Good
Fuji	Sweet, Crisp	Excellent	Good	Good	Good
Gala	Sweet, Crisp	Excellent	Good	Very Good	Good
Golden Delicious	Sweet, Tender	Very Good	Excellent	Very Good	Very Good
Granny Smith	Tart, Crisp	Very Good	Very Good	Very Good	Fair
Gravenstein	Sweet-Tart, Crisp	Very Good	Excellent	Excellent	Good
Jonagold	Sweet-Tart, Crisp	Very Good	Very Good	Good	Very Good
Jonathan	Moderately Tart, Tender	Very Good	Very Good	Very Good	Good
McIntosh	Tart, Tender	Good	Good	Very Good	Poor
Newtown Pippin	Slightly Tart, Firm	Very Good	Excellent	Excellent	Good
Pink Lady	Tart, Firm	Very Good	Poor	Excellent	Poor
Red Delicious	Sweet, Crisp	Excellent	Fair	Fair	Poor
Rome Beauty	Slightly Tart, Firm	Good	Very Good	Very Good	Excellent
Winesap	Slightly Tart/Spicy, Firm	Very Good	Excellent	Excellent	Good

STORING APPLES

Apples store very well and, if properly stored, they can keep for months and months. They can be stored in the vegetable bin of your refrigerator or, if you buy a large quantity, such as a bushel, store them in the coolest area of your house: in a cool or cold garage or basement. The cooler the temperature, the better. The first sign of aging is when the apple peel begins to soften and shrivel. At that time they are no longer appealing for eating fresh, but they may still be good for applesauce and cooking.

MANGO WITH STICKY RICE
(KOW NEUW MAMUANG)

YIELD: 2 SERVINGS

This popular Thai dessert is traditionally served in late spring and early summer when mangoes are in season and ripe for picking.

 **ADVANCE PREPARATION REQUIRED**

INGREDIENTS

1 cup (195 g) sticky rice
1 (15-ounce [440-ml]) can coconut milk
2 tablespoons (25 g) granulated sugar
Pinch of salt
1 ripe mango, peeled and sliced

Put the rice in a bowl, and add enough water to cover the rice. Soak for at least 1 hour or even overnight.

Add a steamer basket to a 3-quart (3.4-L) pot and add just enough water to reach the basket's bottom. If the holes in your steamer basket are large enough that the rice will fall through, simply place a sheet of cheesecloth in the basket. Pour the sticky rice into the basket, cover, and place on the stove. Turn the heat to medium-high. The rice should take about 20 minutes of steaming to cook and will become translucent when done. You may also steam the rice in a bamboo rice steamer or in a rice cooker.

In the meantime, heat the coconut milk in a pot over medium heat. Stir constantly and let the coconut milk simmer. (Don't let it boil too hard, or the coconut milk will curdle.) Add the sugar and salt. Remove from the heat. Pour three-quarters of the hot coconut milk over the hot sticky rice. Let it sit for 5 minutes. The sticky rice will absorb all the coconut milk. The rice should be a little mushy. Spoon the rest of the coconut milk on top of the rice at serving time. Top with the mango, and serve.

COLLEEN'S TIP: *You can find sticky rice in the Asian section of your grocery store, or better yet, in your local Asian grocery. You may find it as "sticky rice," "glutinous rice," or "sweet rice."*

STUFFED DATES

Stuffing fruits and veggies is common in Middle Eastern cuisine. Think stuffed grape leaves (dolmas), stuffed green peppers, and stuffed dates. Medjool dates are the largest and easiest to stuff.

INGREDIENTS

15 dates, pitted
15 whole almonds or halved pecans, toasted
¼ cup (25 g) confectioners' sugar, sifted

Line a baking or cookie sheet with parchment paper.
  Stuff the dates with 1 nut per date. Roll in the confectioners' sugar.
  Place on the lined cookie sheet, and place in the refrigerator until ready to serve.

FOOD LORE: *Dates have been a staple food of the Middle East for thousands of years. Arabs are responsible for bringing dates to northern Africa and Spain, and it was the Spaniards who introduced dates to California in 1765. Truly nature's candy, dates come in 30 to 40 varieties. Next time you visit California (or the Middle East), check out the local farmers' market and choose from a number of delicious varieties.*

CHOCOLATE-DIPPED FRUIT

YIELD: 4 SERVINGS

This is an elegant but easy dessert that's perfect any time of the year.

INGREDIENTS

A variety of fruit for dipping: strawberries, bananas, mangoes, raspberries, oranges, cherries, pears, apples, pineapples, dried fruit, etc.
2 cups (350 g) nondairy semisweet or dark chocolate chips

Rinse the fruit and pat dry.

Melt the chocolate chips in a microwave or double boiler. Dip the fruit into the chocolate mixture and allow the excess chocolate to drip into the bowl. Set on a plate lined with waxed paper. Transfer to the refrigerator to allow the chocolate to harden, 10 to 15 minutes.

Remove from the refrigerator about 20 minutes before serving so the fruit isn't terribly cold. Unless it's an exceptionally hot day, the chocolate shouldn't melt too much, but do provide napkins!

SERVING SUGGESTIONS & VARIATIONS

A fun way to serve chocolate-dipped fruit, which works well for relatively small crowds, is to transfer the melted chocolate to a fondue-type bowl that has a candle underneath it. Arrange a variety of fruit on a plate so people can choose what they want and dip their own fruit into the chocolate.

COLLEEN'S TIP: *Add chopped nuts to the melted chocolate.*

CHAPTER EIGHT

DECADENT DELICACIES AND ELEGANT EATS: STRUDEL, CRÊPES, BLINTZES, AND PASTRIES

People tend to be intimidated by the delicate phyllo dough used to make strudel and by the fancy-sounding crêpes, which are really just thin pancakes. Hopefully, these tips will give you the confidence you need to make these delicious desserts.

THE RECIPES

Apple Strudel (Apfelstrudel) ... 163

Chocolate Cherry Strudel
(Black Forest Strudel) ... 164

Dessert Crêpes ... 166

Crêpes Suzette ... 168

Blueberry Cream Cheese Blintzes ... 169

Rugelach ... 170

Baklava ... 172

TIPS FOR WORKING WITH PHYLLO DOUGH

Phyllo dough, found in the frozen section of your grocery store, is very forgiving and easy to work with as long as it doesn't get soggy or dried out. Here are some tips for preventing these two occurrences.

* Thaw frozen phyllo in the refrigerator for at least 8 hours or overnight; this will prevent the damp spots that cause the sheets of dough to stick together.

* Remove the phyllo from the refrigerator, and leave unopened at room temperature for 1 to 2 hours.

* Clear a large work surface before removing the phyllo from the box. You want to have a lot of elbow room and not have bowls and utensils crowding your space.

* Carefully unroll the sheets onto a dry work surface. Make sure there is no water on the counter.

* Keep phyllo that you're not working with covered with waxed paper and a damp towel. If the dough is left uncovered for even a short period of time, it will dry out.

* Work quickly but with a gentle hand.

* Don't worry if a sheet tears while stacking the layers. No one will notice after the sheets are baked together.

* Cut phyllo sheets with scissors—it's easier than using a knife.

* Lightly brush or spray each sheet with melted nondairy butter or olive oil. Don't drench the sheets.

* Tightly wrap the remaining rolled-up sheets in plastic, and refrigerate for up to 1 month.

APPLE STRUDEL (APFELSTRUDEL)

YIELD: 8 SERVINGS

Working with phyllo dough is not as hard as some might think. The trick is to have all of your ingredients prepared in advance and to work quickly so the pastry sheets don't dry out. I have it on the utmost authority that Germans would never eat the strudel cold but rather enjoy it lukewarm with vanilla sauce, which you can make by combining nondairy milk, cornstarch, and vanilla extract and warming it up.

INGREDIENTS—FILLING AND PASTRY

5 apples, peeled and sliced
½ cup (100 g) granulated sugar
2 teaspoons ground cinnamon
¼ cup (35 g) golden raisins
¼ cup (27 g) slivered almonds, toasted (optional)

1 tablespoon (8 g) all-purpose flour
Juice from 1 small lemon
6 to 8 sheets phyllo pastry
¼ cup (55 g) non-hydrogenated, nondairy butter, melted

INGREDIENTS—TOPPING

2 tablespoons (25 g) granulated sugar
1 tablespoon (8 g) cinnamon

½ cup (65 g) ground almonds, toasted (optional)

Preheat the oven to 400°F (200°C, or gas mark 6). Line a baking sheet with parchment paper.

To make the filling, in a bowl, mix together the apples, sugar, cinnamon, raisins, almonds (if using), flour, and lemon juice, stirring thoroughly to combine.

Place 1 sheet of phyllo on a clean work surface. (It should be placed so you are looking at it vertically.) Keep the remaining phyllo sheets covered with a damp cloth. Brush the entire phyllo sheet with some melted butter. Lay down another phyllo sheet directly on top of the buttered sheet and brush again with some melted butter. Repeat until you use all 6 or 8 sheets.

Spoon the apple filling across the lower third of the phyllo stack, leaving a 2-inch (5-cm) border along the bottom and sides. Roll the phyllo over once to begin creating a log, then fold in the sides. Continue to roll gently until you have a compact log, ending seam side down. Place the strudel seam side down on the prepared baking sheet, and brush the top with butter.

To make the topping, combine the sugar, cinnamon, and almonds, if using, and sprinkle on the top of the strudel.

Bake for 20 minutes, or until golden brown. Allow to cool before slicing with a serrated knife.

FOOD LORE: *Though there are many types of strudel, depending on the filling, apple strudel (apfelstrudel) is the most widely known and is a traditional pastry of southern Germany and the many countries that once belonged to the Austro-Hungarian empire (Austria, Croatia, Hungary, Czech Republic, etc.).*

CHOCOLATE CHERRY STRUDEL (BLACK FOREST STRUDEL)

YIELD: 6 SERVINGS

Cherries and chocolate have always been a favorite combo of mine, and so I give you this decadent treat!

INGREDIENTS
⅓ cup (35 g) crushed graham crackers
1 cup cherries (110 g), rinsed and pitted
⅓ cup (35 g) slivered or ground almonds
⅓ cup (60 g) nondairy semisweet chocolate chips
¼ cup (50 g) granulated sugar
6 to 8 sheets phyllo dough
¼ cup (55 g) non-hydrogenated, nondairy butter, melted
Sugar, nutmeg, and cinnamon for sprinkling on top

Preheat the oven to 400°F (200°C, or gas mark 6). Line a baking sheet with parchment paper.

In a bowl, mix together the graham crackers, cherries, almonds, chocolate chips, and sugar.

Place 1 sheet of phyllo on a clean work surface. (It should be placed so you're looking at it vertically.) Keep the remaining phyllo sheets covered with a damp cloth. Brush the entire phyllo sheet with some melted butter. Lay down another phyllo sheet directly on top of the buttered sheet and brush again with some melted butter. Repeat until you use all 6 or 8 sheets.

Spread the cherry/chocolate filling in a 3-inch-wide (7.5-cm) band along the bottom long edge of the dough, 2 inches (5 cm) in from the bottom and sides. Roll the phyllo over once to begin creating a log, then fold in the sides. Continue to roll gently until you have a compact log, ending seam side down. Place the strudel seam side down on the prepared baking sheet, and brush with butter. Sprinkle the sugar, nutmeg, and cinnamon on top.

Bake for 20 minutes, or until golden brown. Allow to cool before slicing with a serrated knife.

SERVING SUGGESTIONS & VARIATIONS
* You may use fresh, frozen, or canned pitted cherries.
* Instead of graham crackers, use vegan vanilla cookies.
* Add ⅓ cup (40 g) dried sweet cherries.

Suggestions for Making Healthful Transitions

COLLEEN'S TIP #1—BE CONSISTENT

The good news is that our eating habits are just that—habits—and habits are meant to be broken. It takes a little time, but with consistency and commitment, it really doesn't take more than thirty days. (They say it takes three weeks to change a habit, but I like to give people an extra week, hence my 30-Day Vegan Challenge program you can find at my website colleenpatrickgoudreau.com.)

COLLEEN'S TIP #2—TAPER DOWN

When you switch from something like cow's milk to nondairy milk, it may be helpful to taper off the former. If you eat it with cereal, slowly cut back on the cow's milk and make up for the difference with a nondairy milk of choice. Continue to do this until you're at zero percent cow's milk and 100 percent nondairy milk.

COLLEEN'S TIP #3—CHANGE YOUR PALATE

Our palates have been shaped by what we've eaten for so many years. We've grown so accustomed to fat, sugar, and salt that we have forgotten what real food tastes like. When we begin to rely on the flavor of plant foods and naturally reduce the amount of rich foods in our diet, our palates will begin to crave these more wholesome flavors and textures. But we need to give our palates time to adjust.

COLLEEN'S TIP #4—STOCK YOUR PANTRY

Fill your cupboards with healthful, plant-based ingredients. If you have them on hand, you're more likely to make healthier choices. Stocking your cupboards with basic foods that will make it easy and convenient for you to cook and bake healthfully anytime may seem expensive at first, but a lot of the foods you buy will last a long time.

COLLEEN'S TIP #5—MEET THE FARMERS

Whether you're buying ingredients for baking or cooking, find out where your farmers' markets are—and frequent them. I'm lucky enough to live in the San Francisco Bay Area, where there are farmers' markets almost every day of the week—year round. Try new foods, bring home new produce, and ask questions. The more familiar you are with your ingredients, the more apt you are to eat them.

COLLEEN'S TIP #6—PREP IN ADVANCE

Take 10–15 minutes to chop your fruit and veggies when you bring them home. You're more likely to snack on them or use them in cooking when they've already been prepped for use.

DESSERT CRÊPES

YIELD: 6 TO 8 CRÊPES

When my husband and I moved to California several years ago, my sister-in-law graced us with a notebook full of our favorite recipes. This crêpe recipe was one of them. "Veganizing" it was incredibly easy, and the results are the same. Though crêpes are really only thin pancakes, there is something inherently elegant about them.

INGREDIENTS

3 teaspoons Ener-G Egg Replacer (equivalent of 2 eggs)
4 tablespoons (60 ml) water
1 cup (235 ml) nondairy milk
2 teaspoons canola oil or non-hydrogenated, nondairy butter
1 tablespoon (30 ml) vanilla extract
¾ cup plus 1 tablespoon (100 g) unbleached all-purpose flour
1 teaspoon granulated sugar
¼ teaspoon ground nutmeg
Pinch of salt
Nondairy butter for the pan

In a food processor, whip the egg replacer and water together until creamy, at least 2 minutes. (It's important to give this mixture time to get nice and thick.) Add the milk, butter, and vanilla, and blend until thoroughly combined. Add the flour, sugar, nutmeg, and salt. Mix until the batter is the consistency of heavy cream, about 1 minute. Pour the batter into a medium-size bowl.

At this point, the batter can be covered and refrigerated for up to 2 days. Bring it to room temperature before continuing with the recipe.

Melt a small amount of nondairy butter in a nonstick 8- or 9-inch (20- or 23-cm) crêpe or sauté pan over medium heat. You'll find a traditional crêpe pan in any kitchen supply store, but you can also make larger crêpes. You want enough butter to coat the pan but not so much that there is a little puddle of it in the pan.

Using a large serving spoon, pour a small amount of batter into the pan (¼ cup [60 ml] tends to work well for an 8-inch [20-cm] pan). As you pour the batter, lift the pan from the heat and twirl it around. As you twirl the pan, the batter will coat the entire bottom of the pan. If you put in too little batter to begin with, pour in some extra batter to fill in the gaps. If you put in too much batter, just pour any excess back into the bowl.

Return to the heat. As the crêpe cooks, it changes in appearance, and you'll start to notice the edges will begin to look crispy. Loosen the edges with a spatula. You can use a spatula to turn the crêpe, but I usually turn it with my fingers. Using both hands, pick up the loosened edges and quickly flip it over.

Cook on the other side until golden (usually less than 1 minute) and slide it out onto a plate. Fold in half, and cover with waxed paper. Repeat with the remaining batter. (You won't need to add butter before each crêpe; I find it works if it's added between every two crêpes, but you need only a small amount.)

The crêpes may be kept tightly wrapped for up to 3 days in the refrigerator. They may also be frozen. Before freezing, let them cool first, then stack them with waxed paper between each crêpe. Wrap securely in foil and freeze for up to 2 months. Thaw and bring to room temperature before using.

VARIATION

I've used Follow Your Heart's Vegan Egg for this recipe with great success. Just follow the package instructions for making the equivalent of two eggs.

TIPS FOR MAKING CRÊPES

* *You don't need a special crêpe pan. If you have a small nonstick skillet, you will get perfectly sized crêpes, and you'll have one less pan crowding up your kitchen.*
* *Expect to mess up a couple of the crêpes when you make your first batch. Sprinkle some sugar on it and enjoy it as a snack. Don't stress about it.*
* *Purists will say that you absolutely have to let the batter rest for at least 30 minutes at room temperature, and up to 2 hours. I often make crêpes without letting the batter rest at all, and I have success every time.*
* *Finished crêpes can easily be refrigerated for up to 3 days and frozen for up to 2 months. Crêpe batter can be covered and refrigerated for up to 2 days. Bring it to room temperature before continuing.*
* *When making crêpes for sweet applications, sprinkle a little granulated sugar on each crêpe before stacking another fresh one on top.*

COLLEEN'S TIP: *Sometimes the first crêpe is a flop, because it soaks up so much of the butter. You can prevent this by not adding too much butter or by just resigning yourself to this being part of the process. Sprinkle on some confectioners' sugar, and enjoy!*

CRÊPES SUZETTE

YIELD: 6 TO 8 SERVINGS

A traditional French and Belgian dessert, Crêpes Suzette is essentially crêpes with a hot sauce of caramelized sugar, orange juice, and liqueur poured on top and subsequently lit on fire.

INGREDIENTS

¼ cup (55 g) non-hydrogenated, nondairy butter

3 tablespoons (38 g) granulated sugar

Juice and rind from 1 orange

1 recipe Dessert Crêpes (page 166)

Confectioners' sugar for dusting

Orange slices for garnish

⅓ cup (78 ml) liqueur, such as Grand Marnier or Cointreau (optional)

Melt the butter in a large sauté pan. When it starts to foam, add the sugar and stir until it's dissolved. Add the orange juice and rind, and bring to a simmer. Turn the heat to low.

Add 1 crêpe to the pan, making sure to coat it completely with the syrupy sauce. Carefully fold it in half, then in half again. Repeat with the remaining crêpes, arranging them around the pan, working quickly enough so that the first crêpe doesn't absorb all the sauce. At this point, you may serve the crêpes with a dusting of confectioners' sugar and orange slices, if desired. Continue below if you would like to add the alcohol and "flambé" the crêpes.

Pour the liqueur over the crêpes. Using a long match, ignite the sauce. Remove the pan from the heat. When the flames subside, place the crêpes on dessert plates. Dust with confectioners' sugar, and garnish with orange slices. Serve immediately.

FOOD LORE: *The legend—somewhat disputed—behind this dish is that it was created out of a mistake made by a 14-year-old assistant waiter in 1895 at the Maître at Monte Carlo's Café de Paris. Ostensibly, he was preparing a dessert for the Prince of Wales, the future King Edward VII of England, and his companion, whose first name was Suzette.*

BLUEBERRY CREAM CHEESE BLINTZES

YIELD: 6 TO 8 SERVINGS

Blintzes, originating from Russia, differ from crêpes in that they are cooked twice. First, you prepare Dessert Crêpes (page 166), then add ingredients to the middle, then fold the crêpe into a rectangular shape, and finally fry it in hot oil or nondairy butter.

INGREDIENTS

2 cups (290 g) fresh or frozen blueberries, divided
Juice and zest of ½ lemon
3 tablespoons (38 g) granulated sugar, divided
½ teaspoon ground ginger
¼ teaspoon cinnamon
2 ounces (60 g) nondairy cream cheese
1 recipe Dessert Crêpes (page 166)
2 tablespoons (28 g) non-hydrogenated, nondairy butter

Combine 1 cup (145 g) of the blueberries, the lemon juice and zest, 2 tablespoons (25 g) of the sugar, ginger, and cinnamon in a saucepan and bring to a boil over medium heat, stirring constantly. Continue to boil until most of the berries have popped and the mixture is the consistency of jam. Add the remaining 1 cup (145 g) blueberries, and cook, stirring, for 1 minute. Transfer to a bowl and let cool to room temperature.

Meanwhile, in a small bowl, combine the cream cheese and remaining 1 tablespoon (13 g) sugar, until it's nice and creamy. If you choose not to use the sugar, cream the cheese anyway. Spread some cream cheese on one side of each crêpe, and when the blueberry mixture has cooled, spoon it into the center of each crêpe atop the cream cheese.

Fold the sides of each blintz around the filling to form a rectangular package. (At this point, you may wrap and freeze the blintzes for up to 1 month.) In a large nonstick sauté pan, heat the butter. When the butter is melted, add the blintzes and cook for 1 to 2 minutes, until golden brown on both sides. Transfer to paper towels to drain for a moment and serve immediately.

SERVING SUGGESTIONS & VARIATIONS
Top with Sautéed Bananas (page 150), Raspberry Sauce (page 248), Brown Sugar Syrup (page 257), pure maple syrup, chopped toasted nuts, or confectioners' sugar.

FOOD LORE: *The word blin comes from the Old Slavic word mlin, which means "to mill." The word became blintse in Yiddish and finally came into English in the form of blintz. Blintzes are often prepared during Hanukkah.*

RUGELACH

These rich, sweet little pastries, a favorite in Jewish cuisine, have as many spellings (Rugulach, Rugalach, Rogelach, Rugalah) as they do filling options.

✳ **ADVANCE PREPARATION REQUIRED**

INGREDIENTS

1 cup (225 g) non-hydrogenated, nondairy butter, cold

1 (8-ounce or 225-g) package nondairy cream cheese

2 cups (250 g) unbleached all-purpose flour

¼ teaspoon salt

⅓ cup (77 g) nondairy sour cream

½ cup (100 g) granulated sugar

1 tablespoon (8 g) ground cinnamon

1 cup (150 g) finely chopped walnuts

½ cup (75 g) finely chopped raisins

1 cup (320 g) fruit jam or preserves (apricot, strawberry, raspberry)

Cut the butter and cream cheese into small pieces. In the food processor, pulse together the flour, salt, butter, cream cheese, and sour cream until crumbly.

Shape the mixture into 4 equal disks. Wrap each disk and chill for at least 2 hours or up to 2 days.

When you're ready to prepare the pastry, preheat the oven to 350°F (180°C, or gas mark 4). Line 2 cookie sheets with parchment paper. (You may use ungreased cookie sheets, but the jam mixture tends to ooze onto the sheet, making it difficult to clean.) In a bowl, combine the sugar, cinnamon, walnuts, and raisins. Set aside.

Lightly flour a work surface area, and roll each disk into a 9-inch (23-cm) round, keeping the other disks chilled until you're ready to roll them. Spread each circle of dough with a light layer of the jam. Divide the sugar/nut filling among the disks, and press lightly into the jam. With a sharp knife or pizza cutter, cut each round into 12 wedges or triangles. Roll the wedges from the wide end to the narrow end, so you end up with a point on the outside of the cookie. Place on the prepared baking sheets with the point side down.

Bake in the center rack of the oven for 22 minutes, or until lightly golden. Cool on wire racks. Store in airtight containers. They also freeze very well for up to 2 months.

SERVING SUGGESTIONS & VARIATIONS

✳ Roll the rugelach in a mixture of cinnamon and sugar just prior to putting them on the cookie sheets.

✳ Use ground pecans instead of walnuts.

✳ These are often served during the winter holidays.

✳ See "Resources and Recommendations" on page 270 for where to find nondairy cream cheese.

FOOD LORE: *The word "rugelach" is derived from the Slavic word rog, which means "horn"; thus, rugelach are "little horns."*

BAKLAVA

YIELD: 3 DOZEN PASTRIES

Don't be intimidated by the idea of making your own baklava, a rich, sweet pastry found in many cuisines of the Middle East.

INGREDIENTS

1 cup (235 ml) water

1 cup (200 g) granulated sugar

1 teaspoon vanilla extract

½ cup (120 ml) agave nectar or Bee Free Honee

3 cups (450 g) nuts (walnuts, pistachios, almonds, or pecans), toasting optional

1 teaspoon cinnamon

1 tablespoon (13 g) granulated sugar (optional)

1 (16-ounce [455-g]) package phyllo dough (you may use only half this package)

¾ cup (170 g) non-hydrogenated, nondairy butter, melted

Preheat the oven to 350°F (180°C, or gas mark 4). Butter the bottom and sides of a 9 × 13-inch (23 × 33-cm) baking dish. In a small saucepan, heat the water and 1 cup sugar until the sugar is completely dissolved. Add the vanilla and agave nectar. Simmer for 15 minutes. Remove from the heat, and set aside to cool. You want this to be completely cooled before pouring onto the baked baklava.

Pulse the nuts in a food processor until they're a coarse meal. You don't want fine crumbs, so use the pulse button to have better control. Add the cinnamon and 1 tablespoon sugar, if using, and mix to combine. Set aside.

Unroll the phyllo dough from the package. Trim the stack of phyllo into 9 × 13-inch (23 × 33-cm) sheets, so that they will fit comfortably in your prepared pan. Keep the sheets that you're not working with covered with some waxed paper and a damp cloth. Place 2 sheets of dough in the pan, and using a pastry brush, coat the top sheet completely with some of the nondairy butter. Spread a thin layer of the cinnamon/nut mixture, and add 2 more sheets of phyllo. Repeat with the butter, nut mixture, and 2 phyllo sheets, until you have a total of 8 layered sheets. For the top layer, place 2 to 4 phyllo sheets, but this time brush butter between each individual sheet.

Using a very sharp serrated knife, carefully cut the baklava into diamond or square shapes all the way to the bottom of the pan. This is important to do now, because you won't be able to cut the baklava once it's baked without crushing the pastry.

Bake for 45 to 50 minutes, until the baklava is golden. Remove from the oven and immediately pour or spoon the (completely cooled) sauce over it. Cool uncovered for at least 3 hours or over-night before serving.

SERVING SUGGESTIONS & VARIATIONS

* Transfer individual pieces to cupcake papers.
* Add ¼ teaspoon of either cloves, allspice, ground ginger, or nutmeg to the nut mixture.
* Baklava can be stored in the freezer for up to 3 months.

A Word about Sweeteners

Because everyone's sweet tooth is different, the most difficult aspect of creating these recipes was deciding how sweet to make them. A dessert that may be just right for me may be too sweet for someone else and not sweet enough for another. The good news about that is it's easy to adjust. So, please feel free to customize the recipes to your own preference.

My intention in writing this cookbook was to debunk the notion that "vegan" desserts are somehow inferior to those made with cows' milk, chicken's eggs, and dairy-based butter. Though I don't consider desserts "health food," vegan desserts certainly have the benefit of containing no dietary cholesterol and virtually no saturated fat (coconut milk is one of the few plant foods that is high in saturated fat). But a dessert is a dessert is a dessert, and I did not set out to create broccoli. For that reason, I generally recommend plain old granulated sugar for those recipes that require a dry (versus a liquid) sweetener. So, which sugars meet that requirement?

✳ **White Sugar:** Half of the white sugar manufactured in the United States is cane sugar and the other half is beet sugar. There is little perceptible difference between sugar produced from beet and that from cane, except how it is produced.

Though there are no animal products in the sugar, cane sugar (not beet) undergoes a filtration process that may or may not involve the use of animal bones. It is for this reason that some vegans avoid white sugar. Bones are even sometimes used to filter water in treatment plants, so it's very difficult to know when we are using practices that support animal exploitation industries. We each have to decide where to draw this line.

✳ **Turbinado:** This is a type of sugar cane extract. Made by steaming or rinsing (in turbines, hence the name) unrefined raw sugar, it's often called "raw sugar," though it's technically not raw. It's similar in appearance to brown sugar, though it's not as fine and is paler in color. Although turbinado may be used when "granulated sugar" is called for and can replace "white/refined sugar" measure for measure, I recommend looking for a fine variety.

✳ **Sucanat:** Its name is a concatenation of SUgar CAne NATural and refers to the fact that it is a non-refined cane sugar that has not had the molasses removed from it. It is essentially pure dried sugar cane juice. Sucanat is better as a substitute for brown sugar (though you will want to grind it much finer using a high-speed blender) than it is for white sugar. The beautiful brown color and the strong molasses flavor may affect the final outcome of your dessert—sometimes welcome, sometimes not.

✳ **Brown Sugar:** Brown sugar is white sugar (cane sugar or beet) with molasses added back in. It can be used in place of white sugar, but it will impart the flavor of molasses.

✳ **Confectioners' Sugar** (also known as "powdered," "baker's," or "icing" sugar): This is finely ground white sugar that is mixed with cornstarch to improve its flowing ability. Its primary use is for making frosting or icing.

✳ **Granulated or Evaporated Cane Juice and Unbleached Cane Sugar:** Vegans concerned with the bone filters in the processing of some cane sugars sometimes turn to these dry sweeteners as an alternative. Both can generally replace white sugar measure for measure but may darken your finished product or impart a slight molasses flavor.

* **Date Sugar:** Not really a sugar at all, date sugar is made from ground, dehydrated dates and contains all the vitamins, minerals, and fiber found in the fruit. It can be used in equal parts for sugar in most baking recipes but because the tiny pieces don't dissolve. If you find it too sweet using it measure for measure, try substituting 2/3 cup (130 g) date sugar for each cup (200 g) granulated or brown sugar.

* **Alternative Dry Sweeteners:** This is a general term referring to anything that's not cane or beet sugar as well as artificial concoctions that were, for the most part, produced in a laboratory. Just as I don't advocate "Fat-Free Ding Dongs" and "Sugar-Free Twinkies," I am also not a proponent of artificial sweeteners, particularly aspartame, Splenda, cyclamate, and saccharin, either for weight loss or simply as an alternative to sugar. Most of these are chemically or lab produced, which isn't where I want my food to come from.

* **Liquid Sweeteners:** Other sweeteners, such as maple syrup, brown rice syrup, molasses, agave nectar, malt syrup, fruit juice concentrates, and a wonderful liquid sweetener called Bee Free Honee (made from apples and with the same viscosity and flavor of bee honey) are fantastic in their own ways, and each has its place; I do use some of these for certain recipes. It really comes down to a taste preference, but in terms of calories, except for the fruit concentrates, it's really all the same. I don't think making desserts every day with maple syrup is healthier than eating a dessert made with white sugar once a week. From a logistical standpoint, however, never substitute a dry sweetener for a liquid and vice versa.

* **A Word about Honey:** By virtue of it being a secretion from an animal, it is not a "vegan" food. Bees produce and store honey as their sole source of nutrition in cold weather and other times when alternative food sources are not available. Agave nectar and Bee Free Honee (see below left) are wonderful liquid sweeteners that taste and look like bee honey and are used throughout this book. When we can replace animal products with plant-based ones, why wouldn't we?

* **Choosing Organic and Fair Trade:** There are many other factors to consider when purchasing sugar and the products that contain it. The history of sugar cane is built on slavery and, according to a number of recent reports examining the lives of sugar cane workers, the contemporary sugar industry is still rife with inequality. The impact on the Earth is also of great cause for concern, as unsound environmental practices on plantations include heavy pesticide use and crop burning, which are detrimental to the soil, air, and water—not to mention the workers.

CHAPTER NINE

ANCIENT WONDERS: YEAST BREADS AND ROLLS

It is an absolute myth that baking your own bread is time-intensive. Most of the work (the rising!) is done without you. Trust me: you'll spend a lot more time eating these beauties than you will preparing them.

THE RECIPES

Naan (Leavened North Indian Bread) ... 178
Whole Wheat Bread ... 179
Focaccia ... 182
Soft Pretzels ... 184
Cinnamon Rolls ... 185
Chocolate Babka (Polish Bread) ... 188
Melonpan (Japanese Cookie Bread) ... 190

PERFECTING HOMEMADE YEAST BREADS

Making bread from scratch may seem intimidating or time-consuming, but it's really a simple and satisfying process. Most of the time involved stems from waiting for the dough to rise, so you can just go about your business while this takes place. Here are some helpful hints that will make the process go as smoothly as possible—all without the use of a machine.

LEAVE YOUR MARK

Each loaf of bread you bake will be unique—and completely your own. You infuse your very essence into each creation you make. Though your first loaf may not be aesthetically beautiful, it is special because you made it. Besides, if it tastes and smells great, who cares about how it looks?

PROOF YOUR YEAST

It's always a good idea to "proof" your yeast before using it to make sure it's still alive. First dissolve 1 tablespoon (8 g) of sugar in very warm (not hot) water (somewhere between 95° and 115°F [35°C to 46°C]) and then add the yeast. Wait several minutes for it to dissolve and begin to "work," i.e., develop tiny bubbles. If it doesn't show signs of life, discard it and try another packet.

AMOUNT PER PACKET

One envelope or packet of Active Dry Yeast, Instant Yeast, Rapid Rise Yeast, Fast Rising Yeast, or Bread Machine Yeast weighs ¼ ounce or 7 grams and equals 2¼ teaspoons.

STORING FLOUR

If you use your flour fairly quickly, store it in a cool, dry cupboard. If you won't be using your flour right away, particularly whole wheat flour, put it in a secure plastic bag and store it in your freezer.

TYPE OF FLOUR

Breads made with all-purpose flour are fine, but you can also use bread flour—and, of course, whole wheat, which is my favorite. Most bread recipes call for shaping bread into a loaf and baking in a loaf pan, but bread can be made into any shape and baked in almost any pan; you just may need to adjust the baking time.

SWEETEN IT UP

Even though you don't necessarily need it when making bread, a little sugar can bring out flavor, just as salt does. For added moisture and flavor, try agave nectar, pure maple syrup, or unsulphured molasses.

RISE AND SHINE

Bread rises best in a moist, warm environment. An ideal place to raise bread is in an oven next to a pan of steaming water. Don't turn the oven on, but keep the door closed.

SALT IN DOUGH

Follow the directions when it comes to salt. Salt helps strengthen gluten, which gives bread texture, but too much salt can affect how well the yeast works.

INTUITIVE BAKING

There are really only three key ingredients you need to worry about when baking yeast bread: the flour, the liquid, and the yeast. The two other ingredients are sugar and salt, and they just bring out the bread's flavor.

MEASURING YOUR FLOUR

Give your flour a little fluff in the bag or canister with a spoon. Then sprinkle it lightly into a dry cup measure. Scrape any excess off with the back of a knife, but do not pack it down.

HAND KNEADING

If you're not using an electric stand mixer, turn your dough out onto a lightly floured counter. I also flour my hands and my rolling pin. Turn on some music and rock the dough as you would a baby. Give the dough a quarter turn after each push, and add flour as needed.

GIVE IT A REST

When you're kneading dough, whether by hand or in your mixer, after 3 or 4 minutes, just let it rest for a few minutes. This relaxes the dough and makes the remaining kneading easier.

FIRST RISING

After the dough has been kneaded, form it into a nice, round ball and place it in a greased bowl, turning it over so the top has a thin film of grease on it as well. This helps keep it soft so that, as the yeast begins to grow and produce carbon dioxide bubbles, it can expand.

GO PUNCHY

After a couple of hours, give the dough a good punch to knock the gas out. Turn the dough out onto your lightly floured kneading surface and knead for a few minutes to remove any stray bubbles.

REVIVING STALE BREAD

Revive stale bread by placing it inside a brown paper bag, sealing the bag, and moistening a portion of the outside of the bag with water. Place it in a preheated 350°F (180°C, or gas mark 4) oven for about 5 minutes, and the bread will emerge warm and soft.

SLASH THE TOP

Just before you put your loaf in the oven, slash the top diagonally three or four times about ¼ inch (6 mm) deep with a serrated knife. By making these cuts, you enable the bread to expand.

"WASH" YOUR BREAD

If you don't have Follow Your Heart's Vegan Eggs to make an "egg wash," add a nondairy milk wash to the top of your dough and sprinkle on any of the following: sea salt, chopped herbs, sesame seeds, poppy seeds, sunflower seeds, minced garlic or onion, chopped nuts, or anything that will complement the meal your bread will be served with.

Add a brush of melted nondairy butter either before or after baking for a softer, richer flavored crust.

FREEZING DOUGH

Bread dough can be frozen prior to baking, either before or after it has been shaped. Freezing won't kill the yeast, but it does subdue it somewhat, so double the amount called for in the recipe.

STORING BREAD

Bread kept in the fridge goes stale about four times as fast as it does at room temperature. It's best to keep it in a bread box or paper bag. This will hold some of the moisture in, while keeping the crust firm. If you store it in a plastic bag, it will keep the bread softer longer but encourage spoilage by holding moisture in.

WHOLE WHEAT BREAD, PAGE 179

FREEZING BREAD

Finished breads can be frozen successfully in heavy, airtight plastic bags. If you get them into the freezer as soon as they are completely cool, they will taste just as if they had come right out of the oven when they're thawed.

NAAN (LEAVENED NORTH INDIAN BREAD)

YIELD: 4 TO 6 SERVINGS

If you've ever eaten in a traditional North Indian restaurant, no doubt one of your favorites is the bread, especially naan. It is traditionally baked in a tandoor (clay oven), but I found that a very hot oven with a pizza stone works well.

 ADVANCE PREPARATION REQUIRED

INGREDIENTS

1 packet active dry yeast

¼ cup (60 ml) warm water

1 teaspoon granulated sugar (optional)

1 tablespoon (15 g) ground flaxseed (equivalent of 1 egg)

3 tablespoons (45 ml) water

4 cups (500 g) unbleached all-purpose flour

1 teaspoon baking powder

½ teaspoon baking soda

½ teaspoon salt

6 tablespoons (90 g) plain nondairy yogurt

3 to 4 tablespoons (42 to 56 g) non-hydrogenated, nondairy butter, melted, divided

1 cup (235 ml) nondairy milk

Dissolve the yeast in ¼ cup warm water. You may add 1 teaspoon of sugar to help activate the yeast. Let it sit for 5 to 10 minutes. (If the mixture does not start to bubble after 5 minutes or so, it may be inactive.)

In a food processor or by hand, whip the ground flaxseed and 3 tablespoons water together, until creamy and thick, about 1 minute.

Sift together the flour, baking powder, baking soda, and salt in a bowl. Stir in the yeast/water mixture, "flax egg", yogurt, and 2 tablespoons (28 g) of the butter. Gradually stir in enough milk to make a soft dough. You may not need all the milk. Coat the bowl with oil, cover with a damp cloth, and let sit in a warm place for 2 hours.

Preheat the oven to 450°F (230°C, or gas mark 8). If you're using a pizza stone, put it in the oven as you preheat it. You may also use a cookie or baking sheet if you don't have a stone.

Once the dough has risen, knead it on a floured surface for 3 minutes until smooth. You may do this by hand or use your electric stand mixer.

Divide the dough into 8 pieces, and roll each piece into a ball and then into ovals (or circles), about 6 inches (15 cm) long (or round).

If you use a baking sheet, grease it first and brush the underside of the dough with water. Brush the top with the remaining 1 to 2 tablespoons (14 to 28 g) nondairy butter. If you're using a stone, just brush the top with the butter. Bake for 6 to 10 minutes, until puffy and golden brown.

WHOLE WHEAT BREAD

This bread is hearty and wholesome, perfect as sliced sandwich bread or as an accompaniment to a hot bowl of soup.

 ADVANCE PREPARATION REQUIRED

INGREDIENTS

1 envelope active dry yeast
2 ¼ cups (530 ml) warm water
6 cups (750 g) whole wheat flour
1 teaspoon salt
2 tablespoons (30 ml) agave nectar or other liquid sweetener
2 to 3 tablespoons (30 to 45 ml) olive oil (optional)

Add the yeast to the warm water and allow it to dissolve. (You can give it a little stir.) Let it sit for 10 minutes. After this time, the yeast should begin to form a creamy foam on the surface of the water. If there is no foam, the yeast is dead and you should start over with a new packet. This process is called "proofing" to make sure the yeast is alive.

In a large mixing bowl (I use an electric stand mixer, but you can do it by hand), mix together the flour and salt, and make a well in the center. Pour the yeast and water mixture, agave nectar, and oil, if using, into the well. Stir from the center outward, incorporating the liquid ingredients into the flour. Fold in the remaining flour from the sides of the bowl and stir until the mixture forms a soft dough. Add a small amount of water if the dough is too dry or a bit of flour if the dough is too sticky.

Turn out the dough onto a breadboard (or continue using the stand mixer). For best results, knead the dough for about 10 minutes, without adding any more flour. If you're using a stand mixer, you won't need to do this for more than 5 minutes. The dough should be elastic and smooth. Place the dough in a lightly oiled bowl, cover with a damp cloth, and let sit in a warm, draft-free spot so the dough can rise. The dough should double in size. At 70°F (21°C), this should take about 2½ hours.

(continued on next page)

WHOLE WHEAT BREAD (continued)

After the allotted time, test the dough by poking a wet finger ½ inch (1.3 cm) into the dough. The dough is ready if the hole doesn't fill in. Gently press out the air, making the dough into a smooth ball. Return it to the bowl for a second rise, which will take about half as long as the first. Test with your finger again after an hour or so.

After the second rising, turn the dough onto a lightly floured countertop or breadboard. Deflate the dough by pressing it gently from one side to the other. Cut it in half and form each part into a round ball. Let the rounded balls rest, covered, for about 10 minutes.

Shape each ball into a loaf, and place the loaves in one 9-inch (23-cm) or two 8-inch (20-cm) greased loaf pans. Let rise for about 30 minutes. Preheat the oven to 425°F (220°C, or gas mark 7). Bake for 10 minutes, then lower the temperature to 325°F (170°C, or gas mark 3). Bake until done, 45 to 60 minutes, until the loaves turn a golden brown color. The loaves should slip easily out of the pans. When you tap their bottoms, they should sound hollow. Cool slightly before slicing.

SERVING SUGGESTIONS & VARIATIONS

✳ Other liquid sweeteners that can be added include brown rice syrup, pure maple syrup, molasses, and Bee Free Honee.

✳ Make homemade croutons by cubing your bread and tossing it with a light sprinkling of olive oil, fresh herbs, and salt. Bake for 25 to 30 minutes at 350°F (180°C, or gas mark 4).

DID YOU KNOW? *The word crouton comes from the French word croûton, meaning "crust."*

FOCACCIA

Related to pizza, focaccia is a yeast-based flat bread popular in Mediterranean cuisines.

✳ **ADVANCE PREPARATION REQUIRED**

INGREDIENTS

1 packet active dry yeast

½ cup (120 ml) warm water

1 teaspoon granulated sugar (optional)

3½ cups (440 g) unbleached all-purpose flour

2 teaspoons sea salt

2½ tablespoons (5 g) fresh rosemary leaves

5 tablespoons (75 ml) olive oil, divided

2 teaspoons coarse salt

Dissolve the yeast in the water. You may need to add 1 teaspoon of sugar to help activate the yeast. Let it sit for 5 to 10 minutes. (If the mixture does not start to bubble after 5 minutes or so, it may be inactive.)

In the bowl of your electric stand mixer (or by hand), add the flour, the sea salt (not the coarse salt), rosemary, and 2 tablespoons (30 ml) of the oil. Using the dough blade, begin to mix. Add the yeast and continue to mix. Add water as needed to create a smooth ball of dough.

Knead the dough for about 10 minutes (5 minutes in the electric stand mixer), until it's smooth and elastic. Coat the sides of the bowl with some olive oil, turning the dough over once to moisten all sides. Cover the bowl with a damp cloth, and let sit in a warm, draft-free spot so the dough can rise. The dough should double in size in 2 to 2½ hours.

Once the dough has risen, punch it down and knead again for a few minutes. Press into an oiled 9- or 10-inch (23- or 25-cm) round cake pan or a 12 × 16-inch (30 × 41-cm) baking sheet. Create small depressions in the surface of the dough by poking it all over with your fingertips.

Cover the pan with plastic wrap, and leave it in a warm place to rise for 1 hour more. Preheat the oven to 400°F (200°C, or gas mark 6). Remove the plastic wrap and brush the remaining 3 tablespoons (45 ml) oil over the dough. Sprinkle with the coarse salt. Sprinkle on some remaining fresh rosemary, if you like.

Bake for 20 to 25 minutes, until the bread is a golden color. Carefully remove from the pan to cool on a rack. Though it's best the day it is baked, focaccia freezes well.

SERVING SUGGESTIONS & VARIATIONS

* Serve with a hearty green salad and soup.
* Dip pieces of the bread in some quality olive oil and balsamic vinegar.
* Add any of the following to the dough: finely chopped sundried tomatoes, black olives, or dried Italian herbs.
* Top with caramelized onions or roasted garlic.

Troubleshooting Yeast Breads

The guide below is meant to help you identify problems, which is the first step in solving them. Please also refer to "Perfecting Homemade Yeast Breads" on page 175.

IF YOUR DOUGH DID NOT RISE:

* the yeast you used was old.
* the water you used to "proof" your yeast was too cold to activate it or too hot and killed it.

IF YOUR DOUGH IS TOO STIFF:

* the rising location was too cool.

IF YOUR BREAD FALLS WHILE BAKING:

* the dough rose too much. Yes, dough can "over rise."

IF YOUR BREAD DOES NOT BROWN ON THE SIDES:

* your baking pans are too bright and reflect heat away from the sides. Try baking in darker pans.
* your bread was not placed properly in the oven. Try baking it in the center of the oven.

IF YOUR BREAD HAS A SPLIT OR BREAK ON ONE SIDE:

* the oven was too hot.
* the rising time for the dough was not sufficient.

IF YOUR BREAD CRUMBLES EASILY:

* the dough was not thoroughly mixed.
* you may have added too much flour.
* the rising location was too warm.
* the rising time was too long.
* your oven temperature was too low.

IF YOUR BREAD IS TOO DOUGHY OR MOIST ON THE BOTTOM:

* you did not remove your loaf from the pan to cool on a rack after taking it out of the oven.

IF THE CRUST ON YOUR BREAD IS TOO THICK OR HARD:

* there was too much flour in the dough.
* the rising time was insufficient.
* the oven temperature was too low.

IF YOUR BREAD IS HEAVY AND DENSE:

* there was too much flour in the dough.
* the oven temperature was too low.

IF YOUR BREAD IS WET INSIDE AND HAS A COARSE GRAIN:

* the rising time was insufficient.

IF YOUR BREAD IS DRY AND HAS A COARSE GRAIN:

* there was too much flour in the dough.
* the dough was not kneaded long enough.
* the dough rose too much.
* your oven temperature was too low.

IF YOUR BREAD HAS HOLES IN IT:

* the air was not completely pressed out of the dough when the loaves were kneaded.
* the dough rose too long.

IF YOUR BREAD SMELLS AND TASTES OF YEAST:

* your dough rose too much.
* the rising location was too warm.

IF YOUR BREAD HAS A SOUR TASTE:

* the rising location was too warm.
* the dough rose too long.

SOFT PRETZELS

These come out just the way pretzels are meant to be eaten: crispy on the outside and fluffy on the inside.

✳ **ADVANCE PREPARATION REQUIRED**

INGREDIENTS

1 tablespoon (12 g) granulated sugar

3 cups (705 ml) warm water, divided

1 packet active dry yeast

3 cups (375 g) unbleached all-purpose flour

1 teaspoon salt

2 tablespoons (30 ml) canola oil

2 tablespoons (16 g) baking soda

2 tablespoons (36 g) coarse salt

Lightly grease a large cookie or baking sheet or line with parchment paper to prevent sticking.

Stir the sugar into 1 cup (235 ml) of the warm water. Once it has been evenly distributed, add the yeast and allow it to dissolve, then whisk it and let it sit for 10 minutes. After this time, the yeast should begin to form a creamy foam on the surface of the water. If there is no foam, the yeast is dead and you should start over with a new packet.

Combine the flour, salt, and oil in a large mixing bowl. Add the yeast mixture and stir until well combined. Knead the dough for about 3 minutes, then form into a ball. The dough should easily come together in a ball. If it's too wet, add a little more flour. Place the dough in a lightly oiled bowl, cover with plastic wrap and a damp cloth, and let sit for about 2 hours in a warm, draft-free spot so the dough can rise. The dough should double in size.

Divide the dough into 12 pieces and roll each piece into a ball (dust your hands with flour to prevent sticking). Place the balls on a cookie sheet or lightly floured surface. Let rest for 10 minutes or so.

When you're ready to bake, preheat the oven to 400°F (200°C, or gas mark 6).

Roll each ball into a 16-inch (41-cm) length and form into a pretzel or other fun shapes. In a large bowl, dissolve the baking soda in the remaining 2 cups (470 ml) water.

Carefully dip the pretzels (already formed into shapes) into the water. Shake off the excess water, and place each pretzel on the cookie sheet. Sprinkle with coarse salt.

Bake for 15 to 20 minutes, or until golden brown. They're best eaten right out of the oven, but you can freeze and reheat them at 375°F (190°C, or gas mark 5) for 5 minutes.

CINNAMON ROLLS

YIELD: 8 OR 9 ROLLS

Prepare these the night before and let them rise overnight while you slumber. The next morning, finish off the recipe, bake them while your loved ones sleep, and rouse them with the scent of these delectable buns. It's a perfect breakfast treat for out-of-town guests. Absolutely delicious.

 ADVANCE PREPARATION REQUIRED

INGREDIENTS—DOUGH

4½ to 5 cups (565 to 625 g) unbleached all-purpose flour, divided

1 packet active dry yeast

1½ cups (235 ml) nondairy milk

⅓ cup (75 g) non-hydrogenated, nondairy butter

⅓ cup (66 g) granulated sugar

½ teaspoon salt

Nondairy milk for brushing

INGREDIENTS—FILLING

¾ cup (150 g) firmly packed light brown sugar

1 tablespoon (8 g) cinnamon

½ cup (112 g) non-hydrogenated, nondairy butter, softened

½ cup (75 g) raisins (optional)

¾ cup (112 g) chopped walnuts or other nuts

INGREDIENTS—ICING

1 cup (100 g) confectioners' sugar

2 tablespoons (28 g) non-hydrogenated, nondairy butter, melted

½ teaspoon vanilla extract

2 tablespoons (30 ml) nondairy milk

To make the dough, using the paddle attachment in the bowl of your electric stand mixer, combine 2¼ cups (280 g) of the flour and the yeast. In a small saucepan, heat the milk, butter, sugar, and salt, stirring constantly, until warm and the butter is almost melted. Pour the milk mixture into the flour mixture, with the mixer on low speed. Scrape down the sides of the bowl.

Turn the speed to high and beat the mixture for 3 minutes. Replace the paddle attachment with the dough hook (or do this all by hand), and knead in as much of the remaining 2¼ to 2¾ cups (280 to 345 g) flour as necessary until you make a moderately soft dough that is smooth and elastic, 3 to 5 minutes. (The dough will no longer be sticky to the touch.)

Shape into a ball, and place in a greased bowl. Cover and let rise in a warm place for 1 to 2 hours. When the dough has doubled in size, punch it down. Place on a lightly floured surface, cover with a clean towel, and let rest for 10 minutes.

(continued on next page)

CINNAMON ROLLS (continued)

Meanwhile, to make the filling, combine the brown sugar, cinnamon, butter, raisins (if using), and nuts. Set aside.

After the dough has rested for about 10 minutes, roll the dough into a 12-inch (30-cm) square. Brush the filling evenly over the rolled-out dough. Carefully roll the dough into a log and pinch the edges to seal. Slice the log into 8 equal-sized pieces. Arrange these pieces on a greased cookie or baking sheet.

Cover the dough loosely with clear plastic wrap, leaving room for the rolls to rise. Let the dough rise in a warm place until the rolls are nearly double in size, 45 minutes to 1 hour.

Preheat the oven to 375°F (190°C, or gas mark 5). Brush the dough with the nondairy milk. Bake for 25 to 30 minutes, or until they turn golden brown. You'll also know they're done if they sound hollow when you lightly tap on the top of the buns.

While the buns are cooking, prepare the icing by combining the confectioners' sugar, butter, vanilla, and milk in a bowl. When the rolls are ready, remove them from the oven, and let them cool for 5 minutes. Drizzle with the icing. Serve warm or at room temperature.

SERVING SUGGESTIONS & VARIATIONS

Once you've added your filling, rolled the dough into a log, and cut it into your pinwheel-shaped rolls, you can refrigerate the rolls for up to 24 hours before baking them. Just place them on a cookie sheet and wrap with plastic wrap. Once you remove them from the refrigerator, just take off the plastic wrap, and let them come to room temperature for about 30 minutes. Make sure they have risen (doubled in size) before baking them.

FOOD LORE: *Also known as sticky buns, cinnamon rolls were first brought to United States in the 18th century by English and German immigrants. There is even some evidence that the rolls may date as far back as the ancient Egyptians, Greeks, and Romans (we know that cinnamon dates back that far).*

CHOCOLATE BABKA (POLISH BREAD)

YIELD: 1 LARGE BUNDT LOAF

Though this bread can be "stuffed" with delicious fruit-based jam, my favorite is chocolate. Having both Christian and Jewish associations, this wonderful bread, baked in a Bundt pan, is often served during the spring holidays. Even if you don't add a filling, this buttery bread will be enjoyed by all.

 **ADVANCE PREPARATION REQUIRED**

INGREDIENTS

1 cup (235 ml) nondairy milk

5 tablespoons (70 g) non-hydrogenated, nondairy butter

6 tablespoons plus ½ teaspoon (77 g) granulated sugar, divided

¼ cup (60 ml) warm water

1 packet active dry yeast

5½ cups (690 g) unbleached all-purpose flour

1 teaspoon salt

1½ cups (265 g) nondairy semisweet chocolate chips

¼ cup (32 g) unsweetened cocoa powder

In a small saucepan, add the milk and heat it to just the point where it is about to boil. Add the butter, remove from the heat, and give it a little stir. Set aside to cool, or put it in the fridge for 10 minutes.

Stir the ½ teaspoon sugar into the warm water. Once it has been evenly distributed, add the yeast and allow it to dissolve, then whisk it and let it sit for 10 minutes. After this time, the yeast should begin to form a creamy foam on the surface of the water. If there is no foam, the yeast is dead and you should start over with a new packet.

If you have an electric stand mixer, it makes this recipe much easier, but you can do it by hand. To your mixing bowl, add the flour, the remaining 6 tablespoons (75 g) sugar, and the salt, and stir to combine. Pour in the yeast mixture and the cooled milk (the milk should not be hot), and stir from the center outward, incorporating the liquid ingredients into the flour. Mix until you form a soft dough. Add a small amount of water if the dough is too dry or a bit of flour if the dough is too sticky.

Turn out the dough onto a floured counter (or continue using the stand mixer). For best results, knead the dough for 5 to 10 minutes. The dough should be elastic and smooth. Place the dough in a lightly oiled bowl, cover with a damp cloth, and let sit in a warm, draft-free spot so the dough can rise, about 2 hours. The dough should double in size.

Generously grease the bottom, middle, and sides of a standard-sized tube or Bundt pan.

THE JOY OF VEGAN BAKING

Add the chocolate chips to your food processor or blender, and chop them until they resemble a coarse meal. Add the cocoa and stir to combine.

After the dough doubles in bulk, punch it down and return it to the floured surface or your stand mixer. Knead for another 5 to 10 minutes.

Use a rolling pin to roll the dough into a large oval, 9 to 10 inches (23 to 25 cm) wide and 16 to 17 inches (41 to 43 cm) long. Sprinkle the chopped chocolate as evenly as possible over the dough, leaving a ½-inch (1.3-cm) rim around the outer edge. Roll it up tightly the long way, and pinch the edges to seal them.

Lift carefully and ease the dough into the pan, making as even a circle as possible. Pat it firmly into place, and then seal the two ends together with a little water. If you want to bake the babka the same day, cover it with a towel, and let it rise for another hour. If you want to bake it in a day or two, wrap it tightly in a plastic bag, and refrigerate until baking time. (It will rise enough in the refrigerator and can go directly from the fridge to a preheated oven.)

Preheat the oven to 375°F (190°C, or gas mark 5). Bake for 45 to 50 minutes, or until it sounds hollow when tapped.

Remove from the oven and unmold your bread by inverting it onto a plate. Let it cool for 20 minutes.

Because you want the chocolate to be melted when serving it, simply heat up individual pieces in the microwave for 10 to 20 seconds.

SERVING SUGGESTIONS & VARIATIONS

* Add ½ to 1 cup (75 to 150 g) chopped nuts of your choosing.
* Add 1 teaspoon cinnamon.
* Add 1 cup (320 g) fruit preserves or jam instead of chocolate.

FOOD LORE: *Babka, also known as baba, is a sweet "cake" that originated in Eastern Europe. Introduced to North America by early immigrants, traditional babka has some type of fruit filling, often includes raisins, and is glazed with a fruit-flavored icing. Modern babka, as in this one here, may feature a chocolate filling.*

MELONPAN (JAPANESE COOKIE BREAD)

YIELD: 8 TO 12 BUNS

This special sweet bread from Japan contains no melons whatsoever but resembles a melon in appearance.

✳ **ADVANCE PREPARATION REQUIRED**

INGREDIENTS—BREAD

½ teaspoon granulated sugar

¼ cup (60 ml) warm water

1 packet active dry yeast

1¾ cups (220 g) unbleached all-purpose flour

½ teaspoon salt

3 tablespoons (42 g) non-hydrogenated, nondairy butter, melted

INGREDIENTS—TOPPING

1½ teaspoons Ener-G Egg Replacer (equivalent of 1 egg)

2 tablespoons (30 ml) water

1¼ cups (155 g) unbleached all-purpose flour

½ teaspoon baking powder

⅔ cup (150 g) non-hydrogenated, nondairy butter, melted

¾ cup (150 g) granulated sugar

In a bowl, stir the sugar into the warm water. Add the yeast and allow it to dissolve, then whisk it and let it sit for 10 minutes. The yeast should begin to form a creamy foam on the surface of the water (if it doesn't, start over with a new packet).

In your electric stand mixer or by hand, combine the flour, salt, and melted butter. Add the yeast mixture to the flour mixture, and mix until you have a nice, smooth ball. Add a small amount of water if the dough is too dry or a bit of flour if it is too sticky. Knead for 10 minutes.

Lightly grease the bowl and place the dough back in it, turning it over once to moisten all sides. Cover with a damp cloth, and let sit in a warm, draft-free spot so the dough can rise. The dough should double in size. At 70°F (21°C), this should take about 2 hours.

Preheat the oven to 350°F (180°C, or gas mark 4).

When the dough has doubled in size, punch it down and knead lightly for 5 to 10 minutes. Pinch off walnut-sized pieces, and shape them into balls. Place the balls on a lightly greased cookie sheet and let rise in a warm place for 15 minutes.

To make the topping, in a food processor or blender, whip the egg replacer and water together, until creamy, about 2 minutes. In a separate bowl, stir together the flour, baking powder, butter, and sugar until combined. Stir in the egg mixture. Coat the dough balls (which should be puffy now) with the topping. The easiest way to do this is to just grab some topping and add it to the dough ball, just as you would add clay to a sculpture. Don't worry about reducing the size of the balls that have just risen. Each dough ball should have cookie topping added all around.

Bake for 12 to 15 minutes, or until the edges are slightly brown.

CHAPTER TEN

CREAMY CONCOCTIONS: MOUSSES AND PUDDINGS

Some people are incredulous about making mousses and puddings without eggs, but as you'll see—and taste—it's not difficult at all, and the taste is definitely not compromised.

THE RECIPES

Chocolate Mousse ... 193
Chocolate Pudding ... 194
Butterscotch Pudding ... 195
Coconut Pudding ... 196
Rice Pudding (Risgrynsgröt) ... 198
Bread Pudding ... 200
Chocolate Bread Pudding ... 201
Baked Pumpkin Pudding ... 202

TIPS AND TECHNIQUES

It's pretty hard to mess up these simple treats, but here are guidelines to help you out.

TAKE A BATH
Called a bain marie in French, this cooking technique is designed to cook delicate dishes such as custards, sauces, and mousses without burning or curdling them. Not unlike the double boiler technique we employ when melting chocolate chips on the stove, it consists of placing a container (pan, bowl, baking dish, etc.) of food in a large, shallow pan of water, which surrounds the food with gentle heat. The food may be cooked in this manner in an oven or on the stove top. This is a particularly useful way of baking bread pudding.

CHECKING FOR DONENESS
The best way to check for doneness in a baked pudding is to use your fingertips. The center should feel just firm when pressed gently with the fingertips.

MAKING CORNSTARCH/KUDZU PUDDINGS
To avoid lumping and scorching, cook the pudding in a heavy-bottomed saucepan, ensuring gentle, even heat. Stir with a large, flexible, heatproof rubber spatula. A wooden spoon is the next best choice.

DISSOLVE FIRST
Always dissolve your cornstarch or kudzu root powder (or any thickener) in water first before adding it to the main recipe.

DON'T GO STIR CRAZY
Once you remove your pudding from the heat, do not continue to beat, blend, or mix the pudding or it may become very thin.

WITH OR WITHOUT SKIN
When you pour the pudding into cups to cool and thicken, press plastic wrap onto the surface of the warm puddings to prevent a skin from forming. If you like skin on your pudding (as I do!), simply leave the pudding uncovered until cooled and then cover with plastic wrap.

CHOCOLATE MOUSSE

YIELD: 6 SERVINGS

This is a quick and delicious dessert. You won't miss the dairy in this rich and creamy mousse that's also perfect as a pie filling.

INGREDIENTS

1 cup (175 g) nondairy semisweet or dark chocolate chips
12 ounces (340 g) silken tofu (soft or firm)
½ cup (120 ml) nondairy milk
½ teaspoon vanilla extract
Fresh berries for serving (optional)

Melt the chocolate chips by creating your own double boiler. Place the chips in a small saucepan. Set this pan in a larger pot that is filled with ¼ to ½ cup (60 to 120 ml) water. Heat over a medium heat on the stove and stir the chips in the small pot until they are melted. You can also place the chocolate chips in a microwave-safe bowl, and heat it in the microwave for 1 minute. Give the chips a stir, and heat for another minute. They should be melted at this point; just give it another quick stir.

Place the tofu in a blender or food processor. Add the melted chocolate, nondairy milk, and vanilla. Process until completely smooth, pausing the blender or food processor to scrape down the sides and under the blade, if necessary.

Chill the mixture in serving bowls—or in a low-fat graham cracker or cookie crust—for at least 1 hour before serving. Add fresh berries just before serving, if desired.

SERVING SUGGESTIONS & VARIATIONS

* Add Raspberry Sauce (page 248) to the bottom or top of each serving glass before chilling.
* Add a chopped banana to the food processor when you process the tofu and chocolate together.
* Nondairy milks abound, including almond, rice, oat, hazelnut, peanut, and soy. Any will do!
* Use almond extract in place of vanilla. (Or use half of each.)
* Add ½ cup (120 ml) of your favorite brewed coffee. (Cut down on the nondairy milk by one-quarter.)
* Add a few teaspoons of your favorite liqueur or Irish whisky.
* If you like it sweeter, add ⅓ cup (65 g) dry sweetener of your choice.

CHOCOLATE PUDDING

YIELD: 6 TO 8 SERVINGS

The more I cook and bake, the less I prefer store-bought baked goods. It's just so much more satisfying to create my own. This is definitely the case with pudding. However fond my childhood memories are of opening flip-top cans of pudding, I enjoy my own version much more.

INGREDIENTS

3 tablespoons (24 g) ground kudzu root

6 tablespoons (90 ml) water

¾ cup (150 g) granulated sugar

⅓ cup (50 g) unsweetened cocoa powder

2¾ cups (645 ml) nondairy milk, divided

½ cup (88 g) nondairy semisweet or chocolate chips or 4 ounces (88 g) nondairy
    semisweet or dark chocolate, chopped

1½ teaspoons vanilla extract

1 tablespoon (14 g) non-hydrogenated, nondairy butter

Dissolve the kudzu in the water. Stir to combine thoroughly.

In a medium-size bowl, stir together the sugar and cocoa powder. Whisk in ½ cup (120 ml) of the milk until thoroughly combined. Set aside.

In a medium-size saucepan over medium heat, bring the dissolved kudzu and the remaining 2¼ cups (525 ml) milk just to a boil, then begin whisking in the sugar combination until the mixture is smooth. Turn the heat to low, and cook, stirring constantly, until the mixture thickens, 5 to 7 minutes. Remove from the heat.

Immediately add the chocolate, vanilla, and butter, stirring gently with a rubber spatula, until the mixture is smooth. Pour into 6 to 8 small bowls, ramekins, or wine glasses. Serve warm, or if chilling, press plastic wrap onto the surface of the warm puddings to prevent a skin from forming. If you like skin on your pudding (as I do!), simply leave the pudding uncovered until cooled and then cover with plastic wrap. The pudding will store well in the refrigerator for up to 3 days.

SERVING SUGGESTIONS & VARIATIONS

* Add a dollop of Cashew Cream (page 255) or Tofu Whipped Topping (page 254).
* Use coconut milk as your nondairy milk.
* Add 2 dashes of cinnamon and 1 dash of cayenne pepper.
* Substitute mint extract for the vanilla extract.

BUTTERSCOTCH PUDDING

YIELD: 4 SERVINGS

I have fond memories of eating butterscotch pudding, albeit not from scratch, when I was a young-ster. I love the color as well as that slightly burnt flavor, which comes from the cooked molasses in the brown sugar. It brings me right back to my childhood.

INGREDIENTS

3 tablespoons (42 g) non-hydrogenated, nondairy butter

½ cup (112 g) firmly packed dark brown sugar

2 cups (470 ml) nondairy milk, divided

¼ teaspoon salt

3 tablespoons (24 g) cornstarch

3 tablespoons (45 ml) water

1 teaspoon vanilla extract

Melt the butter over low heat in a small but heavy saucepan. Stir in the brown sugar, and cook, stirring constantly, until it's melted and bubbling. Gradually stir in ½ cup (120 ml) of the non-dairy milk. Continue stirring over low heat until the sugar is dissolved. Add the remaining 1½ cups (355 ml) milk and the salt, and stir until blended.

Remove from the heat and let cool to lukewarm. Meanwhile, in a small bowl, dissolve the cornstarch in the water. Mix until smooth.

Stir the cornstarch mixture into the cooled milk mixture, and return to the stove at medium heat. Cook, stirring constantly, until the mixture begins to thicken. Reduce the heat to low, and stirring briskly, bring to a simmer and cook for 1 minute. Remove from the heat, and stir in the vanilla.

Pour the pudding in to 4 bowls, cups, or ramekins. Press plastic wrap onto the surface of the warm puddings to prevent a skin from forming. If you like skin on your pudding, simply leave the pudding uncovered until cooled and then cover with plastic wrap. Refrigerate for at least 2 hours and up to 3 days.

FOOD LORE: *The word "butterscotch" was first recorded in Doncaster, a town in northern England, where Samuel Parkinson began making butterscotch candy in 1817. The jury is still out concerning the origins of the word. Some believe that "scotch" was derived from the word "scorch." Some believe it may be related to the country of Scotland, "scotch" being a nickname for the country; however, the association with Scotland has not been satisfactorily explained.*

COLLEEN'S TIP: *Use a thick nondairy milk, such as oat, soy, or almond. Rice tends to be much too thin for such a purpose.*

COCONUT PUDDING

By definition, a dessert made with coconut milk is rich. By definition, it's also delicious. Enjoy this creamy concoction, and serve it with some colorful fruits.

✳ **ADVANCE PREPARATION REQUIRED**

INGREDIENTS
¾ cup (150 g) granulated sugar
½ cup (64 g) cornstarch, sifted
¼ teaspoon salt
5 cups (1180 ml) canned unsweetened coconut milk, divided
Tropical fruits (papaya, pineapple, mango), chopped

Lightly oil a 1½-quart (1.7-L) soufflé dish or mold or several custard cups or ramekins. Set aside.

In a heavy saucepan, stir together the sugar, cornstarch, and salt. Gradually stir ½ cup (120 ml) of the coconut milk to make a smooth, runny paste.

Stir in the remaining 4½ cups (1060 ml) coconut milk, and cook over medium heat until the mixture begins to thicken. Turn the heat to low and, stirring briskly, simmer for 1 minute.

Pour the pudding into the prepared dish(es) and press plastic wrap onto the surface to prevent a skin from forming. (If you want a skin, let it cool uncovered before putting it in the refrigerator.) Refrigerate for at least 12 hours. Unmold onto a serving plate and serve with the tropical fruits.

COLLEEN'S TIP: *You'll need 3 (14-ounce [425-ml]) cans of coconut milk to make this recipe.*

What About Free-Range Eggs?

Once people learn about the treatment of conventionally raised egg-laying hens, their next thought is often "I'll just buy free-range eggs since the hens aren't harmed or confined." It's a reasonable leap to make; nobody really wants to contribute to the suffering of another, and I think our intentions are good when we seek out foods labeled "free-range," "cruelty-free," or "cage-free."

The problem is that, though these phrases evoke images of happy animals that actually have control over their own lives and their own bodies, they don't necessarily reflect reality. If we truly want to be informed consumers, we owe it to the animals to learn the truth, and we owe it to ourselves so we can make sure that our own values aren't being compromised when we make our purchasing decisions.

Contrary to what most people believe, the term "free-range," especially in the case of birds, doesn't provide you with any information about the animal's quality of life, nor does it ensure that the animal actually lives outdoors.

Free-range chicken eggs have no legal definition in the United States. Likewise, free-range egg producers have no common standard on what the term means. There is no regulation regarding how the word is interpreted or used. Many egg farmers sell their eggs as free-range merely because their cages are 2 or 3 inches (5 or 7.5 cm) above average size, or there is a window in the shed. "Free-range" is not a legal industry term—it is essentially meaningless.

Egg producers know that the public has a desire for guilt-free eating, so they use this term to appease the customer's conscience. They know that if they use this term, it implies that they practice a more humane standard of production. In fact, common cruel industry practices, such as confinement and debeaking used in animal factories, also take place in these "free-range" operations.

"Free-range" producers also tend to buy their chicks from the conventional hatcheries that kill male chicks at birth. All the birds are slaughtered in the end, and the slaughtering process is anything but "humane." Poultry (which covers all birds, including egg-laying hens, chickens raised for meat, turkeys, geese, ducks, and even rabbits) are not covered under the Humane Slaughter Act.

Unless you visit the farm yourself, it's impossible to know for certain how the hens are treated when they're alive, but remember: no matter where she comes from or how she was "raised," every hen is killed for her meat when her egg production wanes, usually after one or two years. In a natural environment, a hen could live up to fifteen years.

RICE PUDDING (RISGRYNSGRÖT)

YIELD: 2 TO 3 SERVINGS

This is simplicity at its best and can be made with any nondairy milk you prefer. If you'd like to be like the medieval Europeans, however, you can use almond milk, which was their top choice.

INGREDIENTS

2½ cups (590 ml) nondairy milk

⅓ cup (65 g) long- or short-grain white or
   brown rice

⅛ teaspoon salt

¼ cup (50 g) granulated sugar

1 teaspoon vanilla extract

1 teaspoon cinnamon, plus more for sprinkling

¼ cup (35 g) raisins (optional)

In a 3-quart (3.4-L) saucepan, combine the milk, rice, and salt. Place the saucepan over high heat and bring to a boil. Stay pretty close to the stove; you don't want it boiling all over the place.

Reduce the heat to medium-low and simmer until the rice is tender, about 25 minutes. Stir frequently using a heatproof rubber spatula or wooden spoon to prevent the rice from sticking to the bottom of the pan.

When the rice is tender, remove from the heat and add the sugar, vanilla, and 1 teaspoon cinnamon. Return to the stove, and cook until the rice pudding thickens, 5 to 10 minutes. Remove from the heat and add the raisins, if using. Spoon the pudding into serving bowls, sprinkle with cinnamon, and cover with plastic wrap. If you want a skin to form on the puddings, allow them to cool before covering with plastic wrap. Refrigerate for 1 to 2 hours and serve.

SERVING SUGGESTIONS & VARIATIONS

Found in nearly every area of the world, rice pudding can be varied by choosing from many different options:

* Rice: long- or short-grain, white, brown, black, basmati, or jasmine.
* Milk: coconut, almond, rice, or soy.
* Spices: allspice, cinnamon, ginger, nutmeg, or mace.
* Flavorings: vanilla, orange, lemon, pistachio extract, or rose water.
* Sweetener: granulated sugar, brown sugar, agave nectar, fruit, or syrups.
* Serve it as a dessert or snack.
* Serve it hot, at room temperature, or cold.

FOOD LORE: *In Sweden, rice pudding, risgrynsgröt, is traditionally served at Christmastime. A "lucky almond" is often hidden inside the pudding, and tradition has it that the one who eats it will be married the following year. Rice pudding is also a traditional Christmas dessert in Norway, Denmark, and Finland.*

BREAD PUDDING

YIELD: 8 TO 10 SERVINGS

Nothing says "comfort" more than bread pudding. You can prepare this in no time with the help of little ones, and it's the perfect excuse to let your bread sit on the counter too long.

INGREDIENTS

6 slices day-old bread (fresh is fine, too), cut into
   ½-inch (1.3-cm) slices

2 tablespoons (28 g) non-hydrogenated, nondairy
   butter, melted

½ cup (75 g) raisins

1 ripe banana

2 cups (470 ml) nondairy milk

½ cup (100 g) granulated sugar

¼ cup (55 g) firmly packed light brown sugar

1 teaspoon ground cinnamon

½ teaspoon nutmeg

2 teaspoons vanilla extract

Preheat the oven to 350°F (180°C, or gas mark 4).

Break the bread into small pieces, and add to a 9-inch (23-cm) square baking pan. Drizzle the melted butter over the bread. Sprinkle with raisins.

In a medium-size bowl, mash the banana. You may use an electric hand mixture, do it by hand, or blend it in a food processor or blender. Add the milk, sugars, cinnamon, nutmeg, and vanilla. Beat until well mixed. Pour over the bread, and lightly push down with a fork until the bread is covered and soaking up the mixture.

Bake for 45 minutes, at which time the bread will be very tender.

WHAT'S THE DIFFERENCE?

* Raisins are dried grapes that are typically sun-dried, but may also be "water-dipped," or dehydrated. The seedless varieties include Thompsons, Flames, and Sultanas. "Golden raisins" are treated with sulfur dioxide to give them their characteristic color.
* Currants are smaller and harder than an average raisin. They're not as sweet, and in fact, in their fresh form are rather tart, tiny "grapes" that look like berries. Where a raisin can be overly sweet and cloying at times, a currant is more subtle.

FOOD LORE: *Stale bread has been used to make sweet puddings for many centuries, merely by soaking it and adding fat and a sweetener. Nondairy butter plays the role beautifully, demonstrating that suet or animal fat is not necessary for a rich dessert. Bread pudding is popular in British cuisine and in the Southern United States, as well in Belgium and France. The French refer to it simply as "pudding" without the word "bread," and the Belgians combine the two words to come up with "Bodding."*

CHOCOLATE BREAD PUDDING

If you like rich chocolatey goodness, then this is the dessert for you. If you don't, then make this decadent dessert anyway and share it with your chocoholic friends. Though the bread requires some time for the chocolate to soak in, this is one of the easiest and richest desserts you'll ever make.

 **ADVANCE PREPARATION REQUIRED**

INGREDIENTS

1 loaf Italian bread, day-old or fresh

3 cups (705 ml) nondairy milk, divided

¾ cup (150 g) granulated sugar

Pinch of salt

8 to 10 ounces (225 to 280 g) nondairy semisweet or dark chocolate chips

1 small ripe banana

1 tablespoon (15 ml) vanilla extract

Cut the bread into ½-inch-thick (1.3-cm) slices and remove the crusts, taking care to preserve as much of the main part of the bread as possible. Cut the bread into ½-inch (1.3-cm) cubes, which will amount to 6 or 7 cups (300 to 350 g).

In a large saucepan, combine 1 cup (235 ml) of the nondairy milk, the sugar, and the salt. Bring to a boil over medium-high heat, stirring constantly. Remove from the heat and add the chocolate chips. Let the mixture stand for a few minutes, then stir until smooth.

In a large bowl, mash the banana, then combine with the remaining 2 cups (470 ml) milk and the vanilla. (You may use a food processor or an electric hand mixer for the best results.) Add this mixture to the chocolate mixture, then stir in the bread cubes. Let this stand for 1 to 2 hours so that the bread thoroughly absorbs the chocolate sauce. Stir and press down the bread periodically.

Preheat the oven to 325°F (170°C, or gas mark 3).

Generously butter a 9-inch (23-cm) square baking pan. Pour the bread mixture into the dish and smooth the top. Bake in a water bath (see page 191) for 55 to 65 minutes. Let cool for 30 minutes before serving.

COLLEEN'S TIP: *The pudding will keep in the refrigerator for up to 3 days. To reheat, simply plate the individual servings and heat in the microwave for about 20 seconds.*

BAKED PUMPKIN PUDDING

<u>YIELD: 6 SERVINGS</u>

Essentially a pie filling in custard cups, this pudding will fill your home with an autumnal aroma.

INGREDIENTS

1 (15-ounce or 420-g) can pumpkin puree
¾ cup (175 ml) nondairy milk
½ to ¾ cup (100 to 150 g) firmly packed brown sugar
1 tablespoon (8 g) cornstarch
¼ teaspoon salt
½ teaspoon ground ginger
½ teaspoon nutmeg
1 teaspoon cinnamon
½ teaspoon vanilla extract

Preheat the oven to 350°F (180°C, or gas mark 4). Lightly oil four 6-ounce (175-ml) custard cups or ramekins. Set the cups in a baking dish deep enough to hold the ramekins and the water that will surround them. Pour some water around the cups, until it reaches halfway up the sides of the ramekins.

In a medium-size bowl, by hand or using an electric hand mixer, combine the pumpkin, milk, brown sugar, cornstarch, salt, ginger, nutmeg, cinnamon, and vanilla, mixing until smooth. Distribute the pudding among the prepared cups.

Bake for 30 to 35 minutes, or until the top begins to turn golden brown. Allow to cool uncovered and serve warm or chilled.

SERVING SUGGESTIONS & VARIATIONS
Add a dollop of Tofu Whipped Topping (page 254) or Cashew Cream (page 255).

CHAPTER ELEVEN

SWEET SOMETHINGS: CONFECTIONS AND CANDY

You don't have to be Willy Wonka to make candy. These treats are so easy to prepare, and they make lovely gifts. The popcorn, pralines, panforte, and coconut candies travel particularly well, as they don't require refrigeration to keep their form.

THE RECIPES

Caramel Popcorn ... 205
Chocolate Fudge ... 206
Caramelized Pecans (Pralines) ... 207
Chocolate Almond Brittle ... 208
Chocolate Coconut Macaroons ... 209
Panforte ... 210
Dried Fruit and Coconut Candies ... 212

TIPS FOR CONCOCTING CONFECTIONS

Only a few of the recipes in this chapter actually require you to boil the sugar water to candy-making temperature, but it's helpful to know how it's done.

SLOW AND STEADY

Candy mixtures should boil at a moderate, steady rate. Cooking too quickly or slowly makes candy too hard or too soft. When stirring a hot candy mixture, use a wooden spoon or silicone nonstick spatula.

USING A CANDY THERMOMETER

The most accurate way to test the stage of the hot mixture is to use a candy thermometer. Attach the thermometer to the side of the saucepan, and make sure it doesn't touch the bottom of the pan. Read the thermometer at eye level. Be sure to test the accuracy of your thermometer every time you use it. To test it, place the thermometer in a saucepan of boiling water for a few minutes, then read the temperature. If the thermometer reads above or below 212°F (100°C), add or subtract the same number of degrees from the temperature specified in the recipe and cook to that temperature.

COLD WATER TEST

If a thermometer is not available, use the cold-water test. The time to test the candy is shortly before it reaches the minimum cooking time. Spoon a few drops of the hot candy mixture into a cup of very cold (but not icy) water. Using your fingers, remove the cooled candy, and form it into a ball. The firmness will indicate the temperature of the candy mixture. If the mixture has not reached the correct stage, continue cooking and retesting, using fresh water and a clean spoon each time.

Thread stage (230°F–233°F or 110°C–112°C): When a teaspoon is dropped into the hot mixture, then removed, the candy falls off the spoon in a 2-inch-long (5-cm), fine, thin thread.

Soft-ball stage (234°F–240°F or 112°C–116°C): When the ball of candy is removed from the cold water, the candy instantly flattens and runs between your fingers.

Firm-ball stage (244°F–248°F or 118°C–120°C): When the ball of candy is removed from the cold water, it is firm enough to hold its shape, but flattens quickly at room temperature.

Hard-ball stage (250°F–266°F or 121°C–130°C): When the ball of candy is removed from the cold water, it can be deformed by pressure, but it doesn't flatten until pressed.

CARAMEL POPCORN

YIELD: 14 SERVINGS

Package this treat as a winter holiday gift for friends, neighbors, and coworkers. This is a tasty, easy-to-make, and easy-to-double recipe. You'll never resort to store-bought again.

INGREDIENTS

14 cups (1400 g) popped popcorn (air- or oil-popped)
1 cup (145 g) dry roasted peanuts (optional)
1 cup (225 g) firmly packed light brown sugar
¼ cup (75 g) light organic corn syrup
½ cup (112 g) non-hydrogenated, nondairy butter
½ teaspoon salt
¼ teaspoon baking soda
½ teaspoon vanilla extract

Lightly grease a shallow pan, such as a roasting pan, jellyroll pan, or high-sided cookie sheet.

Place the popped popcorn in the pan. Add the peanuts, if using, to the popped corn. Set aside.

Preheat the oven to 250°F (120°C, or gas mark ½). Combine the brown sugar, corn syrup, butter, and salt in a saucepan. Bring to a boil over medium heat, stirring enough to blend. Once the mixture begins to boil, boil for 5 minutes, stirring constantly.

Remove from the heat, and stir in the baking soda and vanilla. The mixture will be light and foamy. Immediately pour over the popcorn in the pan, and stir to coat. Don't worry too much at this point about getting all of the popcorn coated.

Bake for 1 hour, removing the pan every 15 minutes and giving the popcorn and nuts a good stir. Line the countertop with waxed paper. Dump the popcorn out onto the waxed paper and separate the pieces. Allow to cool completely, then store in airtight containers or resealable bags. Package as gifts!

COLLEEN'S TIP: *Give the popcorn an entire hour in the oven (stirring every 15 minutes); otherwise, the caramel will be too sticky and difficult to eat. Follow the instructions exactly, and you'll have a hit every time!*

CHOCOLATE FUDGE

YIELD: 2 TO 3 DOZEN FUDGE SQUARES

This recipe will debunk anyone's notion that eliminating eggs and dairy means sacrificing flavor. This classic fudge is soft, creamy, and rich. Have a nice cold glass of nondairy milk on hand to enjoy it with.

 ADVANCE PREPARATION REQUIRED

INGREDIENTS

12 ounces (340 g) nondairy semisweet chocolate chips or a dark chocolate bar
6 tablespoons (84 g) non-hydrogenated, nondairy butter
3½ cups (350 g) confectioners' sugar
½ cup (64 g) unsweetened cocoa powder, sifted
1 teaspoon vanilla extract
¼ cup (60 ml) nondairy milk or culinary coconut milk (the thick version that comes in a can)
1 cup (150 g) chopped nuts (optional)

Lightly grease an 8-inch (20-cm) square baking pan with nondairy butter.

Place the chocolate chips, butter, confectioners' sugar, cocoa powder, vanilla, and milk in a double boiler. (Create your own double boiler by placing a small saucepan inside a larger pot that's filled with a ¼ to ½ cup [60 to 120 ml] water.) Stir until the chips are melted and the mixture is smooth. Add the nuts, if desired, and quickly pour the mixture into the prepared pan. Chill thoroughly for at least 3 hours, then cut into squares.

SERVING SUGGESTIONS & VARIATIONS

Add 1 to 2 tablespoons (16 to 32 g) natural peanut butter for chocolate peanut butter fudge!

CARAMELIZED PECANS (PRALINES)

YIELD: 2 CUPS

These sweet treats are commonly enjoyed in New Orleans. They make great gifts and dangerous snacks. Be sure to invite friends over when you make these, or you'll eat the whole batch!

INGREDIENTS

2 cups (200 g) pecans, toasted (see below)

1½ cups (300 g) granulated sugar

¾ cup (170 g) firmly packed light or dark brown sugar

½ cup (120 ml) nondairy milk

6 tablespoons (84 g) non-hydrogenated, nondairy butter

½ teaspoon salt

1 teaspoon vanilla extract

Line a baking sheet with waxed paper and add a thin layer of nondairy butter to the paper. Fill a large bowl or casserole dish about halfway with cold water. Set aside.

In a large saucepan over medium heat, combine the toasted pecans, sugars, milk, butter, and salt. Bring to a boil and boil for 5 minutes (between 234°F and 240°F or 112°C and 116°C if you have a candy thermometer). If you don't have a thermometer, you want the mixture to reach the soft-ball stage (see page 203). Stir occasionally, taking care not to burn the mixture.

When the mixture has reached a thick, syrupy consistency, remove it from the heat. Stir in the vanilla, and rest the entire pot in the bowl of water. Continue to stir. You will notice the mixture will get much thicker and begin to become the consistency of caramel. However, you don't want the pecans to just sit in the pot while the mixture thickens. Instead, spoon the pecan mixture onto your greased waxed paper and spread them out a bit.

Let cool and serve, or package up and give as gifts.

SERVING SUGGESTIONS & VARIATIONS

* Spice up the mixture by adding ¼ teaspoon cayenne pepper or sweeten it with ½ teaspoon cinnamon.
* To toast the pecans, simply spread them on a toaster oven tray and bake at 250°F (120°C, or gas mark ½) for 5 minutes. Keep a close watch on them. You want to smell their nutty aroma, but you don't want them to burn!

FOOD LORE: *A praline refers to a family of confections made from nuts and sugar syrup. In Europe, the nuts are usually almonds or hazelnuts. In Louisiana and Texas, the nuts are almost always pecans. While sugar-coated nuts were known in the Middle Ages, food historians generally attribute the "invention" of the praline to a French officer in the seventeenth century. Presumably, these confections were transported by French settlers to Louisiana, where they remain a popular treat.*

CHOCOLATE ALMOND BRITTLE

I thought "brittle" was a good name for this easy-to-make treat, since it resembles peanut brittle in its rough-hewn appearance and buttery flavor. It takes much less time to make, however, and is simply delicious.

✳ **ADVANCE PREPARATION REQUIRED**

INGREDIENTS
½ cup (112 g) non-hydrogenated, nondairy butter, room temperature
½ cup (88 g) nondairy semisweet or dark chocolate chips
4 ounces (115 g) graham crackers (about 6 rectangles)
1¼ cups (180 g) raw almonds, toasted and chopped (see below)

Lightly butter a 9-inch (23-cm) square or round cake pan.

In a medium-size saucepan over low heat, melt the butter and chocolate chips.

Meanwhile, break up the graham crackers into small pieces. They tend to break easily, so you want them to be small pieces but not crumbs.

Once the butter and chocolate are melted, remove from the heat and stir in the graham crackers, along with their crumbs, and the chopped nuts.

Spread this mixture into your prepared baking pan. Cover and refrigerate for at least 2 hours or until set. Store in an airtight container.

SERVING SUGGESTIONS & VARIATIONS
Use chopped hazelnuts in place of the almonds.

COLLEEN'S TIP: *To toast the almonds, preheat the oven to 350°F (180°C, or gas mark 4). Bake the almonds for 8 to 10 minutes, or until lightly brown and fragrant. Let cool, then chop coarsely.*

CHOCOLATE COCONUT MACAROONS

YIELD: 2 DOZEN PIECES

Since coconut macaroons are often dipped in chocolate, this version just gets to that end result a lot faster by including cocoa in the recipe itself. This is an incredibly easy recipe that requires no baking.

INGREDIENTS

¾ cup (170 g) non-hydrogenated, nondairy butter
½ cup (120 ml) nondairy milk
2 cups (400 g) granulated sugar
1 cup (70 g) unsweetened shredded coconut
3 cups (240 g) quick-cooking oats
½ cup (64 g) unsweetened cocoa powder
½ teaspoon vanilla extract (optional)

Line a cookie or baking sheet with waxed paper.

In a large saucepan over medium heat, combine the butter, milk, and sugar. Stirring constantly, bring the mixture to a boil and continue to boil and stir for 2 minutes. Remove from the heat, and add the coconut, oats, cocoa powder, and vanilla, if using. Stir the mixture until thoroughly combined.

Drop teaspoon-sized dollops onto the prepared cookie sheet. Place the cookies in the refrigerator or freezer to set up, which they will do in about 15 minutes. Store in an airtight container. I think they're best kept in a cool location or in the refrigerator.

FOOD LORE: *The coconut macaroon, a cross between a cookie and a confection, is a purely American invention. The cookie version of the macaroon originated in Italy and was made with powdered almonds. The name comes from the Italian word for macaroni (maccherone), which is a kind of pasta that resembles almond macaroon paste in color. Because they are unleavened, macaroons are a common treat during Passover.*

PANFORTE

YIELD: 8 TO 10 SERVINGS

Though this is considered a cake (its name means "strong cake"), its chewy texture aligns it more with candy. Panforte (pronounced pan-FOR-tay), originated in Siena, Italy, and is a favorite winter holiday treat—along with Panettone, Torrone, and Pandoro—throughout the country.

INGREDIENTS

¾ cup (110 g) almonds, toasted and coarsely chopped (see opposite)
½ cup (125 g) hazelnuts, toasted and coarsely chopped (see opposite)
1¼ cups (95 g) chopped candied citrus (citron, lemon, and/or orange peel)
⅓ cup (40 g) unbleached all-purpose flour
1 teaspoon cinnamon
¼ teaspoon ground cloves
½ teaspoon ground coriander
¼ teaspoon ground nutmeg
¼ teaspoon allspice
⅛ teaspoon white pepper
½ cup (120 ml) agave nectar
¼ cup (50 g) granulated sugar
Confectioners' sugar for dusting

Preheat the oven to 325°F (170°C, or gas mark 3). Lightly grease an 8-inch (20-cm) round cake pan or springform pan.

In a bowl, combine the chopped nuts, chopped candied citrus, flour, cinnamon, cloves, coriander, nutmeg, allspice, and white pepper.

In a small saucepan, combine the agave nectar and granulated sugar. Turn the heat to medium, and stir until the sugar melts completely.

Add the agave-sugar mixture to the nuts mixture, and stir well until thoroughly combined. Transfer the mixture to the cake pan, using wet hands to spread the mixture evenly in the pan.

Bake for about 30 minutes, or until golden. Remove from the oven, and place inverted on a rack to let cool. If you're using a springform pan, simply release the hinge, and let it cool on the rack. Dust with confectioners' sugar.

The cake will keep for months in a dry airtight box.

COLLEEN'S TIP: *You may use all almonds or all hazelnuts for this recipe. If you use hazelnuts, be sure to remove the thin skin after they're toasted and cooled. To toast the nuts, preheat the toaster oven to 350°F (180°C, or gas mark 4). Spread the nuts on a baking sheet and bake for 5 to 10 minutes, until lightly brown. Let cool before chopping.*

FOOD LORE: *The origins of this cake are ancient and can be traced back to the honey-fruit cakes prepared during the Middle Ages. Those were made by combining nuts, honey, and a lot of spices. In those times, the nunneries and later the chemists assumed the preparation of panforte, and some of the most famous brands today still have the names of those old pharmacists' families.*

DRIED FRUIT AND COCONUT CANDIES

YIELD: 2 DOZEN PIECES

You have to give this treat a try, particularly if you are looking for a "healthier" dessert. It's hard to eat just one of these sweet, satisfying "candies."

INGREDIENTS

1 cup (175 g) dried apricots

1 cup (175 g) dates, pitted

1 cup (145 g) raisins

1 cup (150 g) walnuts

1½ to 2 cups (105 to 140 g) unsweetened shredded coconut, divided

3 tablespoons (45 ml) lemon or orange juice

In the bowl of a food processor, combine the apricots, dates, raisins, and walnuts, and process for 1 minute to finely chop the ingredients. Add 1 cup (70 g) of the coconut and the lemon juice and process an additional 1 to 2 minutes, or until the mixture comes together to form a ball. Place the remaining ½ to 1 cup (35 to 70 g) shredded coconut on a plate and set aside. Dampen your hands with water, roll the mixture into 1-inch (2.5-cm) balls, and then roll the shaped balls in the shredded coconut. Store the candies in an airtight container.

COLLEEN'S TIP: *These candies can be frozen for up to 3 months.*

DID YOU KNOW?: *Some dried fruit may contain added sulfur dioxide, which can trigger asthma in people who are sensitive to it. Visit your local health food store for sulfur-free dried fruit.*

CHAPTER TWELVE

FROZEN TREATS:
SORBETS, SHAKES, AND SMOOTHIES

I wanted to include creamy frozen desserts without expecting readers to own an ice cream maker. Enjoy!

THE RECIPES

Strawberry Sorbet ... 214
Raspberry Sorbet ... 215
Chocolate Banana Shake ... 216
Vanilla Shake ... 216
Berry Smoothie ... 219
Tropical Smoothie ... 219
Date and Almond Butter Smoothie ... 220

TIPS FOR MAKING AND SERVING FROZEN TREATS

FOR SORBET:

* For the freshest flavor, sorbets should be eaten within 1 to 2 days of being made. If you need to store them longer, press a piece of waxed paper on the surface before sealing in airtight containers. This will help prevent ice crystals from forming and preserve the flavor.

* Serve sorbet in chilled bowls, since it tends to melt rather quickly.

* Garnish with a few slices of the same fruit the sorbet is made with, or combine some fruit chunks with the puree before you freeze it.

* When serving, think of contrasting colors. A scoop of strawberry sorbet on top of a slice of mango or a raspberry sorbet on a bed of kiwis makes for a beautiful presentation.

* Serve sorbet on top of a fruit coulis (sauce), such as lemon sorbet on top of a raspberry coulis.

FOR SMOOTHIES AND SHAKES:

* Freeze ripe bananas to make thick smoothies (and shakes). If you freeze them whole in their peel, you will have to wait for them to "defrost" before being able to break them up. Whole, unpeeled bananas will turn black on the outside when they're frozen, but they're fine. The easiest way to freeze ripe bananas is to just peel them and break them into chunks then store them in the freezer in a freezer bag or container.

* Make smoothies or shakes in advance and take them on the road with you. Give them some time to thaw and a little stir, and you're good to go.

* Invest in a large stainless steel–lined to-go cup. That way, even when you're in a rush or on the go, you can take your smoothie with you.

* Add 2 teaspoons of ground flaxseed to your smoothies and shakes daily. Buy whole flaxseeds and grind them in a coffee grinder. Keep them in the fridge or freezer and aim to consume 2 teaspoons daily (for omega-3 fatty acids).

* Experiment with different natural juices and nectars, and add a variety of nuts and seeds to your smoothie. The options are endless.

STRAWBERRY SORBET

YIELD: ABOUT 3½ CUPS OR 4 TO 6 SERVINGS

A timeless dessert that is naturally "vegan," sorbet, by definition, contains fresh fruit, sugar, water, and lemon or lime juice—never dairy or eggs. Use fresh organic strawberries from the farmers' market in the summer and frozen at other times of the year. In fact, if you buy a large amount at the market, you can freeze them yourself and have a supply on hand all year for smoothies, sorbets, and sauces.

 ADVANCE PREPARATION REQUIRED

INGREDIENTS

⅔ cup (135 g) granulated sugar

⅔ cup (155 ml) water

3 cups (330 g) fresh or frozen and thawed unsweetened strawberries

1 tablespoon (15 ml) lemon juice

1 tablespoon (15 ml) Grand Marnier or other
  liqueur (optional)

Place the sugar and water in a small saucepan over low heat, and stir until the sugar is completely dissolved, 3 to 5 minutes. Boil the mixture for 1 minute, then remove from the heat. You've just made a simple syrup, which you can use for other desserts. (See below.) Pour the sugar syrup into a heatproof container, and place in the refrigerator until completely chilled (about 1 hour).

Meanwhile, place the fresh or thawed strawberries in a food processor or a high-speed blender and process until the strawberries are puréed. Transfer to a large bowl, add the lemon juice and liqueur (if using), and refrigerate until the mixture is thoroughly chilled.

Once the simple syrup and pureed strawberries are completely chilled, combine a portion of the simple syrup with the pureed strawberries. Taste for desired sweetness, and add more syrup depending on your preference. You will most likely have leftover sugar syrup, which you can store in the fridge. Pour the mixture into a stainless steel pan (sorbets freeze faster in stainless steel), cover with plastic wrap, and place in the freezer.

When the sorbet is completely frozen (3 to 4 hours), remove from the freezer and let stand at room temperature until partially thawed. Transfer to a food processor, and process to break up the ice crystals that have formed on the sorbet. This step gives the sorbet its wonderful fluffy texture. Place the sorbet back into the pan and refreeze for at least 3 hours and up to several days.

COLLEEN'S TIP:

* *If you taste the sorbet after freezing and find the amount of sugar is not right, adjust the level of sugar by adding a little more syrup to make it sweeter or a little water to dilute the sweetness, then refreeze the sorbet. The sorbet is not affected by thawing and refreezing.*

* ** Sugar or simple syrups often have a flavoring added, such as extracts, juices, or liqueurs, and are used as a glaze and in confectionery and to soak cakes, poach fruit, and flavor sorbets.*

RASPBERRY SORBET

YIELD: 3 TO 4 CUPS OR 4 TO 6 SERVINGS

No need to purchase expensive pints when you can make your own at home with just a few ingredients.

 ADVANCE PREPARATION REQUIRED

INGREDIENTS

⅔ cup (155 ml) water

⅔ cup (135 g) granulated sugar

1 pound (455 g) frozen and thawed unsweetened raspberries

2 tablespoons (30 ml) lemon juice

Place the water and sugar in a small saucepan over low heat, and stir until the sugar is completely dissolved, 3 to 5 minutes. Boil the mixture for 1 minute, then remove from the heat. You've just made a simple syrup, which you can use for other desserts. Pour the sugar syrup into a heatproof container, and place in the refrigerator until completely chilled (about 1 hour).

Place the raspberries in a saucepan, along with the cooled sugar syrup, bring to a boil, and then simmer for 2 to 3 minutes. Allow the raspberries to cool for a few minutes, then transfer to a blender or food processor and process until puréed. Using a fine mesh strainer, strain the mixture to remove the seeds. Add the lemon juice, stir, cover, and place in the freezer.

When the sorbet is completely frozen (3 to 4 hours), remove from the freezer and let stand at room temperature until partially thawed. Transfer to a food processor, and process to break up the ice crystals that have formed on the sorbet. This step gives the sorbet its wonderful creamy, fluffy texture. At this point, if it's too sweet you can add more water, or if it isn't sweet enough you can add more sugar syrup (if you have some left). Place the sorbet back into the pan and refreeze for at least 3 hours and up to several days.

FOOD LORE: *Sorbets were very popular in the nineteenth and early twentieth centuries, when they were served as a palate cleanser between courses (called "intermezzo," which means "in between the work"). Today they are sometimes served between courses but, more often than not, are served for dessert.*

WHAT'S THE DIFFERENCE?

* *Sorbet: A frozen dessert made from iced fruit puree that may or may not include alcohol in the form of a liqueur.*
* *Agraz: A type of sorbet associated with Spain and North Africa. It is made from almonds, verjuice (a bitter juice), and sugar.*
* *Granita: A semi-frozen Sicilian dessert made of sugar, water, and flavorings from Sicily. Related to sorbet and Italian ice, granita in most of Sicily has a coarser, more crystalline texture.*

CHOCOLATE BANANA SHAKE (PICTURED AT RIGHT)

YIELD: 2 SERVINGS

Enjoy this easy-to-make shake that doesn't require any ice cream. It tastes much richer than you would expect from just a few simple ingredients, and you can reduce some of the cocoa powder if you like. Just make sure to use frozen bananas.

INGREDIENTS

2 cups (470 ml) nondairy milk

2 ripe bananas, cut into chunks and previously frozen

4 tablespoons (32 g) unsweetened cocoa powder

1 to 2 teaspoons granulated sugar (optional)

Banana slices for garnish (optional)

Grated chocolate for garnish (optional)

Combine the milk, banana chunks, and cocoa in a blender, and blend until everything is mixed together and there are no lumps of cocoa.

Taste the shake. If desired, add 1 to 2 teaspoons sugar, blending and tasting again after each addition.

Pour the shake into 2 tall glasses. Garnish with banana slices and a sprinkling of grated chocolate, if desired. Share with a friend and enjoy!

VANILLA SHAKE

YIELD: 2 SERVINGS

Consider the measurements as starting points, and adjust the ice cream, milk, and flavoring to taste. With very high-quality ice cream, less flavoring is required.

INGREDIENTS

4 scoops nondairy vanilla ice cream

1 tablespoon (15 ml) vanilla extract

1½ cups (350 ml) nondairy milk, cold

Freshly grated nutmeg for garnish (optional)

Add the ice cream, vanilla, and milk to a blender. Mix just enough to blend. Do not overmix, or you risk making a very thin shake. (When the ice crystals become pulverized, they break down and thin out the final result.)

Pour into glasses, and grate some nutmeg over the top before serving, if desired.

DID YOU KNOW? *Whether it's the whole pod, the powder, or the extract, vanilla is derived from orchids in the genus Vanilla. The word is Spanish for "little pod."*

BERRY SMOOTHIE (PICTURED AT LEFT)

YIELD: 2 SERVINGS

It's difficult to create a "recipe" for smoothies, because there are so many options and variations depending on your likes and dislikes. Berries are the most healthful option, as they're packed with antioxidants and nutritional goodness; bananas add much-needed potassium as well as thickness, and flaxseed adds the ever-important omega-3 fatty acids.

INGREDIENTS

1 or 2 ripe bananas, frozen or fresh
½ cup (75 g) or more frozen blueberries
¼ cup (75 g) frozen strawberries
2 teaspoons ground flaxseed

¼ cup (60 ml) fresh orange juice
½ cup (120 ml) nondairy milk
1 to 2 tablespoons (16 to 32 g) almond butter
  (optional)

Place all the ingredients in a blender and blend just until combined. You can make it thinner or thicker depending on your preference. Just vary the juice and milk for the consistency you prefer. Yummy!

SERVING SUGGESTIONS & VARIATIONS

Add any of the following: frozen cherries, mixed berries, a dash of chocolate nondairy milk, or 3 or 4 dates (pitted).

TROPICAL SMOOTHIE

YIELD: 2 SERVINGS

If you'd like a smoothie with a tropical flair, try a variation of these fruits. Frozen fruit works best when making a smoothie, as it adds thickness.

INGREDIENTS

1 banana, fresh or frozen
½ cup (75 g) pineapple chunks, frozen
½ cup (90 g) mango chunks, frozen
½ cup (80 g) cantaloupe pieces, frozen
½ cup (70 g) papaya pieces, frozen

½ cup (120 ml) orange juice
¼ cup (60 ml) coconut or pineapple juice
½ to 1 cup (120 to 235 ml) nondairy milk
2 teaspoons ground flaxseed

Blend all (or some) of the ingredients until thoroughly combined. You can make it thinner or thicker by varying the amounts of juice and milk. Also, if you use frozen bananas, your final result will be much thicker.

DATE AND ALMOND BUTTER SMOOTHIE

YIELD: 2 SERVINGS

I just love the depth of flavor that comes from some of my favorite foods on the planet
(i.e., almond butter, bananas, and dates).

INGREDIENTS

2 cups (470 ml) nondairy milk

1 or 2 ripe bananas, cut into chunks and previously frozen

2 to 3 heaping tablespoons (32 to 48 g) almond butter

1 teaspoon cinnamon

3 dates, chopped

1 tablespoon (20 g) pure maple syrup

1 teaspoon vanilla extract

Combine all the ingredients in a high-speed blender and blend until you have a creamy smoothie.

SERVING SUGGESTIONS & VARIATIONS

You may use fresh bananas (as opposed to frozen), but you may want to add 1 or 2 ice cubes so
it's cold.

COLLEEN'S TIP: *If you find the dates remain chunky, then add the dates and bananas to the blender
first and purée those separately. Then add the remaining ingredients and blend until smooth.*

CHAPTER THIRTEEN

FUNDAMENTAL FOUNDATIONS: CRUSTS FOR PIES AND TARTS

PREPARING THE PERFECT PIE CRUST

Making traditional pie crust from scratch is intimidating for many people, but I highly recommend trying it just once. It's a very satisfying experience. Here are some tips that will help make it easier and hopefully demystify what too many people presume is a baking skill reserved for only the bravest and most accomplished pastry chefs.

KEEP IT COLD

Keep ingredients and tools as cold as possible to produce the flakiest crust. I freeze the shortening, flour, and even my rolling pin for 30 minutes before making the crust.

CUT IT IN

Cut in the fat until your mixture resembles small peas or gravel. The more you incorporate the fat past that point, the less flaky your crust will be.

EXTRA PADDING

If you are making a double-crust pie, it helps to have a little extra dough for the bottom crust. Divide the dough in two, making one part slightly larger than the other.

CHILL OUT

The dough will be easier to handle if you refrigerate it for 30 to 45 minutes before rolling it out.

You can keep it in the fridge for up to 3 days if it is wrapped well. Let it sit at room temperature for 5 to 10 minutes before rolling to allow the dough to become more pliable.

EASY PEASY

Roll your pastry on a sheet of lightly floured waxed paper. Invert the pastry right over the pan, or filling, and peel the paper off.

PATCH IT UP

You can easily patch tears in pastry by pinching or pressing it back together. Large gaps can be patched with excess dough you cut from the rim.

NO STRETCHING

Tempting though it is, don't stretch the pastry when you're adding the bottom crust to the pie pan. Instead, just ease the pastry into the pan and gently tuck it into the bottom crease.

SHAPE FIRST, FREEZE SECOND

If you would like to freeze the unbaked pie crust you've already put in the pie pan, that's easy. Put the pie pan in the freezer. When it's solid, pry it out of the pan, wrap in plastic wrap, and freeze for up to 2 months.

STOP, DROP, AND ROLL

The simplest way to roll out your dough is on a lightly floured surface with a floured rolling pin. You can also roll your dough between two sheets of floured waxed paper, which gives you a bit more control and makes it easier to get the crust into a pie plate.

FROM THE INSIDE OUT

Always gently roll—without pushing—the dough from the center to the outside edge in all directions. Use a spatula or dough scraper to loosen it if it begins to stick to the counter, and throw a bit of flour underneath to keep it loose. I also continually add flour to my rolling pin.

THE RECIPES

Cookie Crust ... 222
Shortbread Crust ... 222
Graham Cracker Crust ... 223
Pecan Crust ... 223
Flaky Pie Crust ... 224
No-Bake Pecan Crust ... 226
Fat-Free Crust ... 226
Brownie Crust ... 227

COOKIE CRUST

YIELD: ONE 9-INCH (23-CM) PIE CRUST

A very simple recipe, this crust does not need to be prebaked before using. This crust goes well with No-Bake Chocolate Peanut Butter Pie (page 106), Chocolate Cheesecake (page 97), and No-Bake Chocolate Pudding Tart (page 114).

INGREDIENTS

1 cup (100 g) crumbled or crushed vegan cookies
¼ cup (55 g) non-hydrogenated, nondairy butter, melted

Lightly oil a pie pan or springform pan. In a medium-size bowl, mix together the cookie crumbs and melted butter until well blended. Press into a 9-inch (23-cm) springform pan. Add whatever pie ingredients you're using, and follow the baking directions for that recipe.

SHORTBREAD CRUST

YIELD: ONE 8- OR 9-INCH (20- OR 23-CM) PIE CRUST

If you're intimidated by a traditional pie crust (see page 221), this is the recipe for you. It's a simple, delicious buttery crust that can be used for anything, such as the base of a cheesecake, fruit pie, or tart.

INGREDIENTS

½ cup (112 g) non-hydrogenated, nondairy butter, at room temperature

¼ cup (25 g) confectioners' sugar
1 cup (125 g) unbleached all-purpose flour

Preheat the oven to 350°F (180°C, or gas mark 4). With canola oil or nondairy butter, lightly grease your pie pan. You may use an 8- or 9-inch (20- or 23-cm) square cake pan or an 8- or 9-inch (20- or 23-cm) round pie pan.

In the bowl of your electric stand mixer, or with an electric hand mixer, cream the butter and confectioners' sugar until light and fluffy. Add the flour, and beat until the dough just comes together. Even if it's still a little crumbly, as long as it's moist enough to form a crust when you put it in your pan, it's fine. Press the mixture into the bottom of your prepared pan and bake for about 20 minutes, or until lightly browned. Remove from the oven and place on a wire rack to cool while you make your pie filling.

DID YOU KNOW? *The word "shortbread" is derived from the word "shorten," which means "easily crumbled." The word "shortening" shares the same root.*

GRAHAM CRACKER CRUST

YIELD: ONE 9-INCH (23-CM) PIE CRUST

Whenever I visited my paternal Irish grandparents, one thing I could be sure of was that I would be served a bowl of graham crackers (and a shot of whiskey, but that's another story) every time. Needless to say, I loved visiting Nanny and Poppy, and not just because of the whiskey. This simple crust can be used for a variety of pies, but it cries out for Lemon Cheesecake (page 98).

INGREDIENTS

1½ cups (150 g) fine graham cracker crumbs

5 tablespoons (70 g) non-hydrogenated, nondairy butter, melted, warm or cool

¼ cup (50 g) granulated sugar

¼ teaspoon cinnamon (optional)

Preheat the oven to 350°F (180°C, or gas mark 4). Lightly oil a 9-inch (23-cm) pie pan or spring-form pan.

Mix together the graham cracker crumbs, melted butter, sugar, and cinnamon (if using) with a fork or pulse in a food processor until all the ingredients are moistened. Spread the mixture evenly in the pan. Using your fingertips, firmly press the mixture over the bottom of the pan. Bake until the crust is lightly browned and firm to the touch, 10 to 15 minutes.

PECAN CRUST

YIELD: ONE 9-INCH (23-CM) CRUST

This fabulous crust is perfect for any autumn or winter pie.

INGREDIENTS

¾ cup (75 g) raw pecan halves

¾ cup (60 g) quick-cooking oats

¾ cup (95 g) whole wheat pastry flour

½ teaspoon cinnamon

Pinch of salt

¼ cup (60 ml) canola oil

3 tablespoons (45 ml) pure maple syrup

Preheat the oven to 350°F (180°C, or gas mark 4). Lightly oil a 9-inch (23-cm) pie plate.

Spread the pecans on a cookie sheet. Toast for 7 to 10 minutes, or until the smell of nuts fills the kitchen.

Combine the oats, flour, toasted pecans, cinnamon, and salt in a food processor bowl. Pulse until the mixture becomes a coarse meal. Pour in the oil and maple syrup and pulse until the dry and wet ingredients are just combined. Press this mixture into the prepared pie plate. Bake for 10 minutes, then set aside to cool.

FLAKY PIE CRUST

YIELD: TWO 9-INCH (23-CM) PIE CRUSTS OR ONE 9-INCH
(23-CM) COVERED PIE CRUST.

I recommend first reading the tips for "Preparing the Perfect Pie Crust" on page 221. You can halve this recipe if you need only a single pie crust, but because dough freezes so well, it's almost easier to make this double batch and freeze half for later use.

INGREDIENTS

2½ cups (315 g) unbleached all-purpose flour
1 teaspoon white sugar or 1 tablespoon (80 g) confectioners' sugar
½ teaspoon salt
1 cup (225 g) vegetable shortening or ½ cup (122 g) shortening and
   ½ cup (112 g) nondairy butter
⅓ cup plus 1 tablespoon (105 ml) ice water

NOTE: This can be made by hand or using a food processor, and I recommend the latter. However, make sure you don't overprocess the ingredients, which could make for a tough and inedible crust. Follow the directions as I have written them, and you should have no problems.

MAKING THE DOUGH

Prior to beginning, make sure all the ingredients are cold. I usually stick everything in the freezer for 30 minutes prior to preparing my dough. When I say everything, I mean everything: the flour, the shortening, the butter, and of course the water, measuring out more than ⅓ cup (90 ml) just in case I need a little extra. I also cut the shortening and butter up into ½-inch (1.3-cm) chunks prior to freezing it, so I have to fuss with it as little as possible once it's frozen. You want the fat to stay as cold as possible.

Combine the flour, sugar, and salt in a food processor and process for 10 seconds. Scatter the (already cut up) shortening over the dry ingredients, and pulse in 1- to 2-second bursts until most of the fat is the size of peas. With the machine turned off, slowly drizzle the ice water over the top. Pulse until no dry patches remain and the dough begins to clump into small balls.

Try to press the dough together with your fingers. If it does not hold together, sprinkle on a bit more ice water, and pulse again. Don't allow the dough to gather into a single mass during processing. You want the dough to hold together, but you're not making bread or pizza dough, in which case you want a smooth, high-gluten dough. For flaky pie crust, you want it to hold together, but you don't want a smooth, solid mass of dough. It should look rather rough.

Divide the dough in half, press each half into a round flat disk, and wrap tightly in plastic. Refrigerate for at least 30 minutes and up to several days before rolling. The dough can also be tightly wrapped and frozen for up to 6 months. Thaw completely before rolling.

ROLLING OUT THE DOUGH

The secret to rolling out pastry dough is that you're not rolling it! It's more like you're using the rolling pin to press it out from the middle so it naturally extends outward.

Start by clearing a large work surface, as you will need a lot of room. You can roll dough on a pastry board or directly on a clean countertop. If the dough has been chilled for longer than 30 minutes, let it stand at room temperature until it feels pliable enough to roll.

Flour the work surface. (Excessive flouring may toughen the dough, but you don't want the dough to stick to the work surface, so try to find a happy medium.) Place the dough in the center of the floured surface and flour the dough as well. (I also often sprinkle my rolling pin with some flour.) With uniform pressure on the pin, roll the dough from the center out in all directions, stopping just short of the edge. To keep the dough in a circular shape, each stroke should be made in the opposite direction from the one that preceded it. You can do this by rotating the dough itself rather than by moving the pin. Periodically, make sure the dough isn't sticking to the work surface by sliding your hand (or a pastry scraper) beneath it and sprinkling some flour on the counter, if necessary.

Don't worry if you see cracks and splits; all of these can be easily mended by just pushing the dough together with your fingers. If a split reopens, your dough may be too dry. Dab the edges of the split with cold water to "glue" it together.

Roll the dough 3 to 4 inches (7.5 to 10 cm) wider than your pan so you will have plenty of dough for covering the entire pan and for creating a rim. (Place your pan upside down in the center of the dough to calculate the width.)

TRANSFERRING THE DOUGH TO THE PIE PAN

To transfer the dough, roll it loosely around the pin, center the pin over the pan, and then unroll the dough. You can also just fold the dough in half or in quarters, place it in the pan, and unfold it to cover the pan. Patch any holes or cracks with dough scraps by first lightly moistening the scraps with cold water. When the dough completely covers the pan, trim the edges with scissors, leaving an overhang of ¾ inch (2 cm) all around the sides of the pan.

To relax the dough and avoid shrinkage, chill the crust for 30 minutes before baking. (You can chill it for up to 24 hours. You may also freeze the crust. See "Preparing the Perfect Pie Crust" on page 221.) Follow the instructions for whatever pie you're making.

NO-BAKE PECAN CRUST

YIELD: ONE 8- OR 9-INCH (20- OR 23-CM) PIE CRUST

This is an incredibly simple crust that requires absolutely no baking and pairs well with a fresh fruit pie that would also require no baking.

INGREDIENTS

2 cups (200 g) raw pecans or almonds

¾ to 1 cup (130 to 175 g) pitted dates, preferably Medjool

¼ teaspoon salt

Canola oil for greasing pan

Place the nuts in a food processor, and grind them until they are a coarse meal. Add the dates and salt and process until thoroughly combined. Press the mixture into a nonstick or very lightly oiled 8- or 9-inch (20- or 23-cm) tart pan or springform pan.

DID YOU KNOW? *The word "date" comes from the Greek word dactylus, which means "finger or toe," because of the resemblance between the oblong fruit of the date palm and human digits.*

FAT-FREE CRUST

YIELD: ONE 8-INCH (20-CM) PIE CRUST

For those times when you want a healthier foundation for your pies, this is an easy one to prepare.

INGREDIENTS

2 cups (200 g) Grape Nuts cereal (whole-grain or flakes)

½ cup (142 ml) apple juice concentrate, thawed

Preheat the oven to 350°F (180°C, or gas mark 4).

Add the cereal to the food processor, and process until finely crushed. (If using the regular Grape Nuts cereal, you can just leave it whole. It becomes soft when mixed with the liquid.)

Transfer to a bowl and mix in the apple juice concentrate. Press the mixture into the bottom and onto the sides of an 8-inch (20-cm) nonstick pie pan. Bake for 10 minutes if you plan to use a no-bake filling, or just pour your filling into the pie pan and bake according to the recipe instructions.

BROWNIE CRUST

YIELD: ONE 9-INCH (23-CM) TART OR PIE CRUST

Though you may use any granulated sugar, I like the molasses flavor Sucanat gives off in this very simple crust.

INGREDIENTS

½ cup (65 g) whole wheat pastry flour
¼ teaspoon baking powder
¼ cup Sucanat (see below) or granulated sugar
3 tablespoons (24 g) unsweetened cocoa powder
¼ cup (60 ml) canola or coconut oil
¼ cup (85 g) pure maple syrup
2 tablespoons (30 ml) nondairy milk
1 teaspoon vanilla extract
¼ teaspoon salt

Preheat the oven to 350°F (180°C, or gas mark 4). Oil a 9-inch (23-cm) tart or pie pan.

In a medium-size bowl, combine the flour, baking powder, Sucanat, and cocoa powder.

In a small bowl, thoroughly whisk together the oil, maple syrup, nondairy milk, vanilla, and salt. Pour the wet ingredients into the dry, mixing just until the dry ingredients are thoroughly moistened. Pour the batter into the prepared tart pan and spread evenly with a metal spatula or your fingers to cover the bottom of the pan. It will be a thin layer. Bake for about 10 minutes, or until a toothpick inserted into the crust comes out clean. Let cool before adding any kind of filling.

SERVING SUGGESTIONS & VARIATIONS

You may use another granulated sugar such as white or turbinado in place of the Sucanat. For more on sugars and other sweeteners, see "A Word about Sweeteners" on page 173.

DID YOU KNOW? *Sucanat is a dry sweetener made from evaporated sugar cane juice that retains the natural molasses from the sugar cane. "Sucanat" is derived from the words "SUgar CAne NATural." It can be found in health food stores or in the bulk section of any large natural food supermarket.*

By Any Other Name

The language we use and the words we choose reflect our beliefs and biases, our values and perceptions, and reveal much about who we are and where we come from. In our everyday use of language, we choose words that ease our discomfort and inure us to that which might be ugly, dirty, violent, or just discomforting. We speak of "friendly fire" and refer to victims of war as "collateral damage." Dumps are now "transfer stations" and "used cars" are "previously owned vehicles."

Similarly, we tend to sugarcoat what we eat with language that conceals what we're actually putting in our mouths. The euphemisms we use to refer to meat, dairy, and eggs contribute to our disconnection with the source of these products: the animals themselves. The result is a totally desensitized population, not only unaware of the animals' suffering but also completely ignorant of the biological processes that create such products in the first place.

There are also certain words and phrases that make vegetarian food seem déclassé, that make the consumption of animal products seem normal, and that cause even the most open-minded of citizens to cast derisive looks in the direction of certain "vegetarian" foods.

The culprits are "fake," "faux," "mock," "imitation," and "substitute." Some mildly less offensive albeit not altogether appetizing-sounding variations include "analog," "alternative," and "replacement."

Plant foods are not "fake foods." They're the real thing. You'll notice throughout the book that I use the terms "nondairy," "plant-based," "dairy-free," "egg-free," and "eggless" instead of "egg substitute" or "milk substitute." Nondairy milks aren't substitutes for cow's milk—they're simply beverages made out of plant foods. We have no nutritional need to consume these milks, but they're wonderful, nutritious options and add flavor and richness to baked goods. Many are fortified and add additional nutrients to our diets.

At the same time, I refer to cow's milk as such. As a result of brilliant, pervasive, and expensive ad campaigns, we've all come to associate "milk" with cows. And yet, when I use the phrase "cow's milk," many people are taken back. Some may even be offended, but I'm simply calling it what it is to distinguish it from the lactation fluids of other mammals, such as sheep, goats, hyenas, lions, dogs, and humans. In terms of "substitutes," if you think about it, it's cow's milk that has become the substitute for human milk.

Using euphemisms to refer to the anonymous victims of our appetites desensitizes us to our own truth, our own values, and our own compassion. It also belittles and commodifies animals, minimizes their suffering, and legitimizes and conceals our institutionalized use and abuse of them. That's a pretty high price to pay for a few old habits that can easily be replaced with just a little effort.

RESTORATIVE REFRESHMENTS: HOT AND COLD BEVERAGES

The word "beverage" comes from the Latin word bib-ere, which means "to drink; to imbibe." Sweet beverages are a fantastic way to satisfy your sweet tooth; Ginger Tea (page 239) is good for what ails you, Mulled Cider (page 236) warms chilly bones, and homemade Almond or Cashew Milk (page 234) is an economical alternative to the store-bought versions.

THE RECIPES

Hot Cocoa ... 230
Hot Chocolate ... 231
Mexican Hot Chocolate I ... 231
Mexican Hot Chocolate II ... 232
Mexican Horchata ... 233
Chocolate Milk ... 233
Almond or Cashew Milk ... 234
Holiday Nog ... 235
Mulled Cider ... 236
Wassail ... 237
Chai Tea ... 238
Ginger Tea ... 239
Party Punch ... 240

WHAT'S THE DIFFERENCE?

CHOCOLATEY GOODNESS:

* **Hot cocoa** is made by mixing cocoa powder (chocolate pressed free of the fat of the cocoa butter), sugar, and vanilla and heating them up together.

* **Dutch-processed hot cocoa** simply uses Dutch-processed cocoa, which is a little less acidic than regular cocoa. Having been treated with an alkalizing agent to modify its color and give it a milder flavor, it—as you may have guessed—was first developed in the Netherlands.

* **Hot chocolate** is a rich, dec-adent drink made with dark, semisweet, or bittersweet chocolate that is chopped into small pieces and stirred into hot milk with the addition of sugar.

AUTUMN BREWS:

* **Apple Cider**—Often made from a variety of apples, apple cider is produced in the United States and parts of Canada by a process of pressing. Retaining the tart flavor of the apple pulp, it is slightly cloudier and more sour than conventional apple juice.

* **Apple Juice**—Produced by the crushing of apples, apple juice is then filtered and usu-ally pasteurized.

* **Hard Cider**—This is an alcoholic drink made from fermented cider; it is partic-ularly popular in the United Kingdom.

* **Mulled Cider**—The history of mulling cider dates back to medieval times. The drink is popular in autumn and winter. "Mulled" simply refers to a drink that is sweetened, heated, and spiced.

* **Wassail**—This beverage is a hot, spiced punch often associated with the winter celebrations of northern Eu-rope. Particularly popular in Germanic countries, wassail is a corruption of the Anglo-Sax-on phrase often used for toasting, waes hael, which means "good health."

* **Sparkling Cider**—This is a carbonated nonalcoholic beverage made from filtered apple cider or apple juice.

HOT COCOA

Whatever it is, homemade is always better, including hot cocoa which is just as fast, infinitely less expensive, and definitely more satisfing than store-bought hot cocoa powder.

INGREDIENTS

¼ cup (32 g) unsweetened cocoa powder

½ cup (100 g) granulated sugar

⅓ cup (90 ml) hot water

⅛ teaspoon salt

4 cups (940 ml) nondairy milk

1 teaspoon vanilla extract

Combine the cocoa, sugar, water, and salt in a saucepan. Over medium heat, stir constantly until the mixture boils. Cook, stirring constantly, for 1 minute. Stir in the milk and heat, but do not boil. Remove from the heat and add vanilla; stir well. Serve immediately.

SERVING SUGGESTIONS & VARIATIONS

* Use almond extract instead of vanilla.
* When you stir in the vanilla, add some brewed coffee, amaretto, hazelnut liqueur, brandy, or crème de menthe. The amount is up to you.
* After pouring into individual mugs, sprinkle the top with cinnamon, cayenne pepper, or cocoa powder—and don't forget the vegetarian marshmallows!

DID YOU KNOW? *Marshmallows were originally made without gelatin. The traditional recipe used an extract from the gelatinous root of the marshmallow plant, a shrubby herb whose extract was also used as a cough suppressant.*

HOT CHOCOLATE

YIELD: 4 SERVINGS

There's nothing like homemade hot chocolate, the flavor of which you can vary depending on the type of chocolate you use.

INGREDIENTS

6 ounces (170 g) nondairy dark or semisweet
  chocolate chips or chocolate bar, chopped

2 cups (470 ml) nondairy milk
Granulated sugar, to taste (optional)

Place the chocolate, milk, and sugar to taste, if using, in a saucepan over medium heat and whisk periodically until the mixture comes to a boil and is foamy. Remove from the heat and, if more foam is desired, use a wire whisk or hand-held blender to whip the hot chocolate.

MEXICAN HOT CHOCOLATE I

YIELD: 4 SERVINGS

Chocolate and chile were a favorite combination among the Mesoamericans, who discovered chocolate. The word "chocolate" comes from the Aztec Nahuatl words xocol, meaning "bitter," and atl, meaning "water."

INGREDIENTS

2 cups (470 ml) nondairy milk
6 ounces (170 g) nondairy dark or semisweet
  chocolate chips or chocolate bar, chopped
½ teaspoon cinnamon

Pinch of chile powder
Pinch of cayenne pepper
Granulated sugar, to taste (optional)

Place the milk, chocolate, cinnamon, chile powder, cayenne pepper, and sugar to taste (if using) in a saucepan over medium heat and whisk periodically until the mixture comes to a boil and is foamy. Remove from the heat and, if more foam is desired, use a wire whisk or hand-held blender to whip the hot chocolate.

MEXICAN HOT CHOCOLATE II

YIELD: 4 SERVINGS

Chocolate was so revered it was used by the Aztecs as both a food and a currency. In this version of Mexican Hot Chocolate, the spicy flavor comes from the Mexican chocolate itself, which you can purchase at a variety of stores— online and off.

INGREDIENTS

4 cups (940 ml) nondairy milk

8 ounces (225 g) Mexican chocolate, chopped or broken into pieces

¼ teaspoon cinnamon

¼ teaspoon vanilla extract

In a saucepan, heat the milk and then add the chocolate. After the chocolate is incorporated, add the cinnamon and vanilla. Simmer for 10 minutes and then whisk briskly to a foam right before serving. Divide evenly among 4 cups and serve.

SERVING SUGGESTIONS & VARIATIONS

Alternatively, you can heat the milk in a saucepan and then add it and the other ingredients to a blender. Blend on high until the ingredients are combined and the milk is frothy.

MEXICAN HORCHATA

YIELD: 5 TO 6 SERVINGS

Horchata is a traditional rice drink first developed in Spain and modified in Mexico. This is a delicious, sweet drink that has been around for thousands of years and is best served cold. This recipe enthusiastically passed the authenticity test with my amigo Mark Arellano. I can't ask for more than that.

 ADVANCE PREPARATION REQUIRED

INGREDIENTS

1 cup (185 g) long-grain rice
4 cups (940 ml) nondairy milk
¼ to ½ cup (50 to 100 g) granulated sugar

1 teaspoon vanilla extract
½ teaspoon cinnamon
Ice for serving

Place the rice in a bowl and add enough hot water to cover the rice completely. Let cool, and then place the rice in the refrigerator and let it sit overnight.

The next day, drain the water from the rice. (The rice will still have some crunch/texture; it will not be completely soft, but that's fine.)

Place ½ cup (93 g) of the rice and 2 cups (470 ml) of the non-dairy milk in a blender, and blend until the rice is all ground up. Add the remaining ½ cup (93 g) rice and the remaining 2 cups (470 ml) milk, and blend for another minute. Finally, add the sugar to taste, vanilla, and cinnamon, and blend until the rice is all ground up and the ingredients are completely combined.

Strain through cheesecloth, a fine sieve, or a small strainer, and serve over ice.

CHOCOLATE MILK

YIELD: ONE 8-OUNCE (235-ML) SERVING

A cold version of its sister Hot Chocolate (page 231), chocolate milk is simply a drink made from milk, cocoa, and a sweetener. At home, chocolate milk can easily be prepared by using chocolate syrup.

INGREDIENTS

3 tablespoons Chocolate Sauce (page 252), or more if needed
1 cup (235 ml) nondairy milk, cold

Combine the chocolate sauce and milk, and stir. Add more chocolate sauce, if needed.

ALMOND OR CASHEW MILK

YIELD: 5 TO 6 SERVINGS

My favorite of all nondairy milks, almond milk is easy to make and absolutely delicious. Though there are very good commercial brands out there, making your own is less expensive, and you can purchase organic almonds.

This same recipe can be used to make Cashew Milk with just a few modifications.

✳ **ADVANCE PREPARATION REQUIRED FOR ALMOND (NOT CASHEW) MILK**

INGREDIENTS

1½ cups (220 g) raw almonds, soaked in water overnight, or 1½ cups (220 g) raw cashews (no need to soak)

4 cups (940 ml) water

1 vanilla bean, seeds scooped out, or ½ teaspoon vanilla extract

3 to 5 soft dates, pitted

¼ teaspoon salt (optional)

Liquid sweetener (optional; see below)

Ater soaking the almonds, discard the water. In a high-speed blender, blend the almonds or cashews in the 4 cups water. Add the vanilla, dates, and salt (if using), and blend well. Add liquid sweetener to taste if you want more sweetness than what the dates provide.

If making almond milk, strain the mixture through cheesecloth, a fine sieve, or a strainer over a large bowl. This isn't really necessary with cashews.

Store in the refrigerator for up to 5 days . Give a little shake before serving.

SERVING SUGGESTIONS & VARIATIONS

✳ Add some liquid sweetener, such as pure maple syrup or agave nectar, if desired.

✳ Add a ripe banana and ¼ teaspoon nutmeg to make a winter holiday almond or cashew nog.

✳ Add ¼ cup (32 g) cocoa for Chocolate Almond or Cashew Milk.

COLLEEN'S TIPS:

✳ *If the dates are hard, soak them in a bowl of warm water for 15 minutes. Drain the water.*

✳ *Reserve the almond pulp and use in cookie recipes calling for almonds, or mix with rice or sautéed veggies.*

FOOD LORE: *Botanically speaking, the almond tree is part of the plum family and is native to North Africa, western Asia, and the Mediterranean. Prized for its high protein content and its ability to keep better than milk from animals, which sours if it isn't used right away, almond milk has no choles-terol and no lactose and is high in fiber, protein, vitamin E, and monounsaturated fats.*

HOLIDAY NOG

YIELD: SIX ½-CUP (120-ML) SERVINGS

Though commercial varieties of vegan nog are available, why not make your own? That way, you can adjust the sweetness and spices to your liking or use the type of sweetener that you prefer. This is best if served within a day or two of making it.

INGREDIENTS

12 ounces (340 g) silken tofu (soft or firm)

1 ripe banana

2 cups (470 ml) nondairy milk

½ cup (170 g) pure maple syrup

1 tablespoon (15 ml) vanilla extract

1 teaspoon cinnamon

½ teaspoon cardamom

¼ teaspoon nutmeg, plus more for sprinkling

¼ teaspoon ground cloves

Combine all the ingredients in a blender until smooth. Refrigerate for at least 1 hour, as the nog should be well chilled. Serve with a sprinkling of nutmeg on top.

SERVING SUGGESTIONS & VARIATIONS

* For a thicker, richer drink, use a frozen banana.
* Add ½ to 1 cup (120 to 235 ml) rum, whisky, cognac, or brandy.
* Use granulated sugar instead of maple syrup.

MULLED CIDER

Mulled cider, like mulled wine, has become a cold-weather tradition in many homes. This warm, comforting drink is easy to prepare and is a great finale to a winter meal. This recipe is for 1 quart (1.1 L), which will serve up to three people; the amounts can easily be multiplied.

INGREDIENTS

1 quart (1.1 L) apple cider or apple juice

Peel from 1 lemon

1 cinnamon stick

6 to 8 whole cloves

Pour the cider into a saucepan, and turn the heat to low. Lightly pound the lemon peel to release the aromatic oils, and place it in the cider. Place the cinnamon and cloves in the cider and continue to steep over low heat, stirring occasionally. When the cider is very hot and has begun to steam, it's ready to serve. Shut off the heat and ladle the cider into mugs using a strainer to catch the whole spices.

WASSAIL

YIELD: 12 SERVINGS

Although the contemporary beverage referred to as "wassail" during winter holiday feasts most closely resembles Mulled Cider (left), traditional wassail was more likely mulled beer. Enjoy this variation, and feel free to modify it with your own additions.

INGREDIENTS

1 quart (1.1 L) cranberry juice cocktail

1 quart (1.1 L) apple cider

2 cinnamon sticks, plus 8 for garnish

10 dried whole allspice berries

8 whole cloves

2 tablespoons (25 g) granulated sugar

1 Granny Smith apple, cut into ¼-inch-thick (6-mm) slices

1 cup (235 ml) rum or apple liqueur (optional)

Combine the cranberry juice, apple cider, 2 cinnamon sticks, allspice, and cloves in a large soup pot. Bring to a boil. Reduce the heat, and simmer uncovered for 10 to 15 minutes. Add the sugar, apple slices, and rum (if using) and simmer another few minutes. You want the apple slices to remain crisp. Serve hot and garnish with the remaining 8 cinnamon sticks.

SERVING SUGGESTIONS & VARIATIONS

Wassail recipes vary, but they all usually call for a base of either wine or fruit juices (apple being popular) simmered with mulling spices, and sometimes fortified with spirits such as brandy. Orange slices may also be added to the mixture.

FOOD LORE: *More than just the name of a mulled cider, a wassail is a traditional ceremony carried out to ensure a good crop of cider apples for the coming harvest. It is an old Anglo-Saxon expression, waes hal, that literally means "be in good health." By the twelfth century, it had become the salutation one offered as a toast, to which the standard reply was drinc hail, "drink good health."*

Wassail-themed songs were once sung by winter carolers, who went from house to house, singing to the residents in exchange for small gifts of money, food, and drink, which was often wassail in which toast would be soaked, hence the first stanza of the traditional medieval carol:

Wassail! wassail! all over the town,
Our toast it is white and our ale it is brown;
Our bowl it is made of the white maple tree;
With the wassailing bowl, we'll drink to thee.

CHAI TEA

YIELD: 2 SERVINGS

The word chai, which rhymes with pie, is the word for tea in South Asia, mainly India, Pakistan, Bangladesh, and Nepal. Though it may seem redundant to say "chai tea," which essentially means "tea tea," in English, the term is used to refer to what is more properly known in Hindi as masala chai, or "spiced tea."

INGREDIENTS

2½ (590 ml) cups water

1 teaspoon cardamom

4 whole black peppercorns

¼ teaspoon ground ginger or

2 slices fresh ginger, peeled

¼ teaspoon cinnamon or 1 large cinnamon stick

2 whole cloves

⅔ cup (155 ml) nondairy milk

4 teaspoons granulated sugar

3 teaspoons loose black tea (or 3 tea bags)

¼ teaspoon vanilla extract

Add the water, cardamom, peppercorns, ginger, cinnamon, and cloves to a medium-size saucepan. Bring to a low boil. Turn down the heat and let simmer for 5 to 10 minutes. Add the milk and sugar and bring to a heavy simmer. Add the tea, turn off the heat, and let steep for at least 3 minutes. Add the vanilla, and stir to combine.

Strain using a sieve or fine strainer, and serve hot.

SERVING SUGGESTIONS & VARIATIONS

The recipe calls for "black tea," of which there are many varieties, including Darjeeling, English Breakfast, and Irish Breakfast.

DID YOU KNOW? *"Chai" or "cha" is also the word for tea in Chinese, Russian, Swahili, and Arabic- and Persian-speaking countries, albeit with a slightly different pronunciation.*

FOOD LORE: *Chai from India is a spiced milk tea that has become increasingly popular throughout the world. It is generally made up of:*

* *rich black tea*
* *milk (nondairy, in our case)*
* *a combination of various spices*
* *a sweetener*

The spices used vary from region to region and among households in India. The most common are cardamom, cinnamon, ginger, cloves, and pepper.

GINGER TEA

YIELD: 3 SERVINGS

A healing, refreshing tea, it can be served hot or cold.

INGREDIENTS

3 cups (705 ml) water
½ cup (50 g) peeled and sliced or coarsely
  chopped fresh ginger root

Agave nectar
Lemon juice (optional)

Choose one of these three methods for preparing your tea:

* **Using a kettle and a teapot:** Bring the water to a boil. Place the ginger in a glass or porcelain teapot. Pour the boiled water into the teapot, and secure the lid. Steep for 10 to 15 minutes. Strain as you pour into individual cups. Add agave nectar and lemon juice, if using, to taste.
* **Using a saucepan:** Add the water and ginger to a saucepan. Bring to a boil. Lower the heat, and simmer for 15 minutes. Let it sit for 5 minutes before straining and serving. Add agave nectar and lemon juice, if using, to taste.
* **Using a tea ball:** Use a tea ball to hold the ginger and steep in boiled water for 15 minutes. Make sure you use a saucer to cover the top of the cup (or a lid if you're steeping it directly in a saucepan) to prevent the aromatic elements from escaping. Add agave nectar and lemon juice, if using, to taste.

SERVING SUGGESTIONS & VARIATIONS

* Store leftover tea in the refrigerator. Reheat or drink as iced tea.
* To make only one cup of tea, grate 1 tablespoon (8 g) ginger to 1 cup boiling water.
* If the steeped tea is too strong for you, simply add more water to dilute it.

WHAT'S THE DIFFERENCE?

* *Fresh ginger—Though commonly referred to as a root, it is actually the rhizome of the Zingiber plant. (A rhizome is the underground, horizontal stem of a plant that sends out roots and shoots from its nodes. This is how running bamboo spreads, for instance.)*
* *Ground ginger—Also referred to as "dry ginger," it's typically used to add spiciness to such recipes as gingerbread and pumpkin pie.*
* *Candied ginger—Also called "crystallized ginger," it's used as a flavoring for candy, cookies, and cake and is the main flavor in ginger ale.*
* *Ginger ale—A soft drink flavored with candied ginger, it was invented in Ireland around 1851.*
* *Ginger beer—Though today it is typically a nonalcoholic carbonated soft drink, it was originally a fermented—hence, alcoholic—beverage when it originated in eighteenthth-century England. Similar to ginger ale, ginger beer has a stronger ginger taste and a distinct sour citrus flavor, and it tends to be cloudier in appearance than ginger ale.*

PARTY PUNCH

YIELD: 6 SERVINGS

Though this is a warm drink that might be more appropriate for chillier days, I've included suggestions for modifying it so it's perfect for summer soirées.

INGREDIENTS

1 to 2 apples
1 tablespoon (7 g) whole cloves
4 cups (940 ml) apple juice
1 to 2 cups (235 to 470 ml) pineapple juice
2 tablespoons (30 ml) lemon juice
1 cinnamon stick

Make apple balls using a melon scoop. Spike the apple balls with the whole cloves.

In a medium-size saucepan, combine the apple juice, pineapple juice, lemon juice, apple balls, and cinnamon stick. Stir and gently simmer for 5 to 10 minutes. Turn off the heat and let cool. Serve.

SERVING SUGGESTIONS & VARIATIONS

* Reduce the apple juice to 2 cups (470 ml), eliminate the pineapple juice, and add 4 cups (940 ml) cranberry juice.
* Cut mandarin oranges or clementines into quarters and pierce with cloves instead of or in addition to the apple balls.
* To modify this to make a Spring or Summer Party Punch, simply use pineapple chunks instead of apples, don't heat the punch, add ice, and eliminate the cloves. You can also vary the type of juice you use. Play with different combinations; you can't go wrong.

FOOD LORE: *The word "punch" derives from the Hindi word panch, which means "five," alluding to the fact that the original punch recipe contained five ingredients: spirits, water, lemon juice, sugar, and spice. There are endless variations of this mixed drink, limited only by your imagination and access to different flavored juices!*

CHAPTER FIFTEEN

OVER THE TOP: FROSTINGS, SAUCES, SYRUPS, AND SPREADS

Though it's not difficult to find "vegan" frosting in the grocery store, it is difficult to find one that isn't laden with preservatives, partially hydrogenated oil, or corn syrup. Making your own is so easy to do, and though I would never call frosting "health food," it is a much healthier choice than that which you'll find on a supermarket shelf.

THE RECIPES

Chocolate Frosting ... 242
Chocolate Peanut Butter
    Frosting ... 243
Cream Cheese Frosting ... 246
Buttercream Frosting ... 247
Raspberry Sauce (Coulis) ... 248
Lemon Sauce ... 248
Pomegranate Sauce ... 249
Royal Icing ... 250
Chocolate Fudge Sauce ... 252
Chocolate Sauce ... 252
Tofu Whipped Topping ... 254
Cashew Cream ... 255
Pastry Cream (Custard) ... 256
Brown Sugar Syrup ... 257
Chocolate Almond Spread ... 257

TIPS FOR MAKING FROSTING AND GLAZES

* If you've ever frosted a chocolate cake with white icing and ended up with chocolate cake crumbs inadvertently mixed in, here's a trick: First frost your cake with a very thin layer of icing. Don't worry if the cake crumbs get mixed in. Then let the cake set for about 15 minutes, preferably in the refrigerator. The icing will harden a little and enable you to finish frosting the cake without crumbs getting mixed in.

* Frosting recipes may include a range for the amount of certain ingredients; for example, "2 to 3 tablespoons (30 to 45 ml) of nondairy milk." For better control over the consistency, start with the smallest amount, and then add more if necessary.

* The best tool for frosting cakes is a flexible or offset metal spatula. Try to avoid lifting your spatula so you don't pull the crumbs away from your cake.

* To drizzle a glaze with very little mess, pour it into a plastic food-storage bag. Snip off a tiny corner and squeeze gently, moving the bag back and forth over the top of the cake. Do the same for thicker frostings—just make your hole a little larger.

* Allow your cake to cool completely for at least 2 hours before frosting. After you frost, let your frosted cake stand for at least 1 hour before you slice it.

* If the frosting becomes too thick to spread easily, stir in a few drops of water or nondairy milk.

* For a basic glaze, combine 1 cup (100 g) of confectioners' sugar with 1 to 2 tablespoons (15 to 30 ml) of water, more for a thinner glaze. Stir until smooth.

CHOCOLATE FROSTING

YIELD: ENOUGH FOR ONE 9-INCH (23-CM) CAKE OR 8 CUPCAKES

A chocolate lover's dream! Though many of the commercial brands of frosting are "vegan," they're also made with unsavory ingredients, such as partially hydrogenated oil and high-fructose corn syrup. This recipe is as easy as it is delicious.

INGREDIENTS

½ cup (112 g) non-hydrogenated, nondairy butter, softened

3 cups (300 g) confectioners' sugar, sifted

⅛ cup (42 g) unsweetened cocoa powder, sifted

1 teaspoon vanilla extract or ½ teaspoon peppermint extract

3 to 4 tablespoons (45 to 60 ml) water or nondairy milk, or more as needed

With an electric hand mixer, cream the butter until smooth. With the mixer on low speed, add the confectioners' sugar, and cream for about 2 minutes. Add the cocoa, vanilla, and milk, and turn the mixer to high speed once all the ingredients are relatively well combined. Beat on high speed until the frosting is light and fluffy, about 3 minutes. Add I to 2 tablespoons (15 to 30 ml) more milk if it's too dry. Cover the icing with plastic wrap to prevent drying until ready to use. Store it in a covered container in the refrigerator for up to 2 weeks. Rewhip before using.

CHOCOLATE PEANUT BUTTER FROSTING

YIELD: 1½ TO 2 CUPS (350 TO 470 ML)

Need I say more? Most of us agree there is no better combination on the planet, and you'll taste why when you make this frosting.

INGREDIENTS

½ cup (130 g) natural peanut butter
⅓ cup (40 g) unsweetened cocoa powder
½ cup (120 ml) nondairy milk, or more as needed
2½ cups (250 g) confectioners' sugar, sifted
¼ teaspoon salt
1 teaspoon vanilla extract

Cream together the peanut butter and cocoa. Add the milk, and beat until smooth. Add the sifted confectioners' sugar, salt, and vanilla, then add a little more milk at a time to reach a good spreading consistency.

CREAM CHEESE FROSTING

The foundation of this simple icing is a store-bought nondairy cream cheese, which can be found at large natural food stores. Tofutti brand is the best. Look for the version made without trans fats and partially hydrogenated oil.

INGREDIENTS

8 ounces (225 g) nondairy cream cheese, cold
2 teaspoons vanilla extract

1 cup (100 g) confectioners' sugar, sifted

Combine the cream cheese, vanilla, and confectioners' sugar in a food processor and pulse all the ingredients until smooth and creamy. If you don't have a food processor, you can use a hand-held mixer or just whisk vigorously by hand. If the frosting is too stiff, pulse for a few seconds longer, but do not overprocess.

SERVING SUGGESTIONS & VARIATIONS

If desired, stir in an additional flavoring to taste, such as grated lemon or orange zest, ground cinnamon, or a liqueur of your choice.

BUTTERCREAM FROSTING

YIELD: ENOUGH FOR ONE 8- OR 9-INCH (20- OR 23-CM) CAKE

This is a great frosting to use when filling and frosting cakes and cupcakes. Make sure the baked good has cooled before frosting or the frosting will melt and won't adhere to the baked good properly. Once frosted, cover to prevent the frosting from becoming hard.

INGREDIENTS

½ cup (112 g) non-hydrogenated, nondairy butter, at room temperature

2 cups (200 g) confectioners' sugar, sifted

1½ teaspoons vanilla extract

2 tablespoons (30 ml) nondairy milk, or more as needed

Food coloring (optional)

With an electric hand mixer, cream the butter until smooth. With the mixer on low speed, add the confectioners' sugar, vanilla, milk, and food coloring (if using). Once all the ingredients are relatively well combined, beat on high speed until the frosting is light and fluffy, 3 to 4 minutes. Add I to 2 tablespoons (15 to 30 ml) more milk if it is too dry. Cover with plastic wrap to prevent drying until ready to use. Store in a covered container in the refrigerator for up to 2 weeks. Rewhip before using.

RASPBERRY SAUCE (COULIS)

YIELD: 2¼ CUPS (530 ML)

This is a simple but elegant sauce that perfectly accompanies many desserts, particularly if they contain chocolate. Because of the ease of preparation, it's ideal for sprucing up last-minute desserts.

INGREDIENTS
2 cups (220 g) fresh or 10 ounces (310 g) frozen raspberries, thawed
¼ cup (50 g) dry sweetener (Sucanat is a great option)

In a blender, thoroughly blend the raspberries and sweetener. Store in an airtight container in the refrigerator for up to 1 week.

SERVING SUGGESTIONS & VARIATIONS
Serve this delicious sauce with anything chocolate, such as the No-Bake Chocolate Pudding Tart (page 114) or Chocolate Mousse (page 193). It's also a great accompaniment to Poached Pears (page 149).

LEMON SAUCE

YIELD: 1 CUP (235 ML)

Enjoy this simple sauce on Light Lemon Bundt Cake (page 86) or gingerbread cake or muffins.

INGREDIENTS
½ cup (100 g) granulated sugar
1 tablespoon (8 g) cornstarch
1 cup (235 ml) boiling water
Zest and juice from 2 lemons

In large saucepan, stir together the sugar and cornstarch. Gradually stir in the boiling water, and simmer over low heat until thick, stirring occasionally. Stir in the lemon zest and juice, and remove from the heat. Serve warm or at room temperature over cake.

POMEGRANATE SAUCE

YIELD: 1 CUP (235 ML)

This is a gorgeous complement to many different desserts and flavors, including those made from chocolate, lemons, apples, and other fruit.

INGREDIENTS

3 large pomegranates
1 tablespoon (8 g) cornstarch, mixed with a little water
½ cup (100 g) granulated sugar

Cut the pomegranates in half and then into quarters. Using a spoon or your fingers, scrape the seeds into a large bowl. Discard the white flesh.

Using a high-powered blender or food processor, puree the seeds until smooth. Strain the sauce using a fine strainer, pushing the pureed seeds with a wooden spoon to speed up the process. You should be left with about 1 cup (235 ml) of smooth, seedless pomegranate juice.

In a small saucepan, combine the pomegranate juice, sugar, and cornstarch, and mix well. (You may also use another thickener, such as arrowroot powder or kudzu root.) Cook the sauce over medium-low heat, stirring constantly, until the sauce begins to thicken and darkens to a deep wine color.

Remove from the heat and let cool. The sauce may be made ahead and stored in a jar in the refrigerator. It will thicken somewhat if stored. When ready to use, thin with a little warm water, if necessary.

DID YOU KNOW?

* Grenadine syrup is thickened and sweetened pomegranate juice and is used in cocktail mixes. (Remember "Shirley Temples"?)
* One pomegranate delivers 40 percent of an adult's daily vitamin C requirement, and it's also a rich source of folic acid and antioxidants.

FOOD LORE: The pomegranate has been cultivated around the Mediterranean region for several millennia. It can be very sweet, or it can be very sour or tangy, but most fruits lie somewhere in between. Pomegranate juice is a popular drink in the Middle East and is also used in Iranian and Indian cuisines.

Grenada, an island off the coast of South America, was named after the Spanish and French word for "pomegranate." The pomegranate also gave its name to the hand "grenade" due to its shape and size.

COLLEEN'S TIP: When pomegranates are out of season, you can make this sauce using store-bought pomegranate juice. Just make certain it's pure unsweetened juice.

ROYAL ICING

YIELD: ABOUT 1½ CUPS (350 G)

This is a pure white icing that dries to a smooth, hard, matte finish, perfect for frosting cakes and cookies and for piping such decorations as flowers, borders, and lettering. It is typically made with an egg white, but even that practice is questioned by traditional bakers because of the risk of salmonella. This version sets up perfectly, invites food coloring, and tastes yummy, particularly with the addition of vanilla or almond extract.

INGREDIENTS

1½ teaspoons Ener-G Egg Replacer (equivalent of 1 egg)

2 tablespoons (30 ml) water

1 teaspoon fresh lemon juice

¼ teaspoon almond extract (optional)

1½ cups (150 g) confectioners' sugar, sifted

Food coloring

Even though it's easy to "make an egg" by hand by whisking the egg replacer powder and water in a bowl, because you want the egg to be super frothy for this recipe, I recommend you use an electric hand mixer or the small bowl of your food processor. Beat for about 2 minutes, until it's nice and thick.

In a medium-size bowl, using an electric hand mixer, beat the egg replacer mixture with the lemon juice and almond extract, if using. Add the sifted confectioners' sugar and beat on low speed until combined and smooth. Add food coloring if you're making a batch of just one color. To make multiple colors, separate the icing into separate bowls, add a color to each bowl and combine each thoroughly. Cover with plastic wrap when not using.

The icing can take several hours, or even overnight, to set up completely on the cookies. Store the cookies in containers, stacking them between sheets of parchment paper.

COLLEEN'S TIPS:

* *To prevent the Royal Icing from drying out while you're working with it, keep the icing covered with a damp towel. It the icing is too runny, it will run over the sides of the cookies; if it's too stiff, it won't spread easily. You want just the right consistency for icing the cookies.*
* *Scoop some icing onto a spoon, then lift the spoon, letting the icing drip back into the bowl. The proper consistency is when the ribbon of icing that falls back into the bowl remains on the surface for about 5 seconds before disappearing.*

CHOCOLATE FUDGE SAUCE

YIELD: 1½ CUPS (350 ML)

Similar to the Chocolate Sauce (below), this version is thicker because of the addition of kudzu and is perfect for making hot fudge sundaes!

INGREDIENTS

1 tablespoon (8 g) ground kudzu root
2 tablespoons (30 ml) water
1 cup (200 g) granulated sugar
⅛ teaspoon salt

3 tablespoons (24 g) unsweetened cocoa powder
1 cup (235 ml) nondairy milk
1 teaspoon vanilla extract

In a small bowl, dissolve the kudzu in the water. Stir well to combine, and make sure it's well dissolved.

Add the sugar, salt, and cocoa to a saucepan. Whisk these dry ingredients thoroughly before adding the milk, vanilla, and dissolved kudzu. Stir over medium heat. Boil for 3 minutes, stirring occasionally. Remove from the heat and either serve hot or allow to cool. You can easily heat it up in the microwave anytime you want hot fudge sauce.

SERVING SUGGESTIONS & VARIATIONS

If you cannot find kudzu (see page 265 for more information), you may use cornstarch instead.

CHOCOLATE SAUCE

YIELD: 1½ CUPS (350 ML)

This rich sauce is perfect for pouring over Bundt or tube cakes or any dessert for which frosting would be too thick. It's also ideal for pouring over ice cream or for making chocolate milk!

INGREDIENTS

1 cup (200 g) granulated sugar
1½ tablespoons (12 g) unbleached
all-purpose flour
⅛ teaspoon salt

3 tablespoons (24 g) unsweetened
cocoa powder
1 cup (235 ml) nondairy milk
1 teaspoon vanilla extract

Add the sugar, flour, salt, and cocoa to a saucepan. Whisk these dry ingredients thoroughly before adding the milk and vanilla. Stir over medium heat. Boil for 3 minutes, stirring occasionally. Remove from the heat and cool.

Re-Viewing the Negative

I've often described myself as a joyful vegan because it reflects what I believe and experience day to day. Not long ago, I came across an essay that beautifully and poignantly expresses what this means. It's written by a philosophy professor named Robert Bass, Ph.D., and reprinted with permission.

If you look at a photographic negative, the colors are reversed, nothing seems quite as it should, and the image may be unrecognizable. Once you see the picture developed, you recognize the face of your best friend.

That's a bit like a common impression of vegans. We don't eat dead animals. Or their products. Pork and beef, seafood and fowl are out. So are milk and cheese, eggs, and caviar. And it doesn't stop with what we don't eat. We try to avoid leather, wool, and fur. We don't use them to cover our bodies or our furniture or our floors. It sounds like a long list of negatives, of don'ts: Thou shalt not this; thou shalt not that. Why would anybody want that?

You get a better picture by reversing the colors and developing the negative. The incomprehensible prohibitions turn out to be the boundaries of something positive, visible in its true colors and proper proportions. Instead of a list of don'ts, we see an abundance of healthy, delicious foods, with plenty of options for home and clothes and personal care. We do not grudgingly practice a creed of self-denial. We select from an embarrassment of riches.

But that is still just a flat, two-dimensional picture instead of the solid, three-dimensional reality. At the heart of being vegan is a kind of compassionate awareness. We share this planet not only with billions of human beings, but also with billions of other creatures, many with lives, wants, enjoyment, and suffering as real as our own. Humans have had and used the power to crowd them out, push them aside, sometimes driving them to extinction, and often, making them into tools for our use, servitors of our desires, food for our tables, clothes for our backs. As vegans, we look, we pay attention, we see the unnecessary suffering imposed on our fellow creatures. We respond in compassion, refusing to pretend that might makes right, refusing to turn away and ignore what we know. The vegan message is ultimately very simple:

Look. Pay attention. See the unnecessary death and suffering. We don't have to contribute or help to keep it going. We can stop being a part of this. And so, that's what we try to do.

TOFU WHIPPED TOPPING

YIELD: 1 CUP (235 ML)

Thick and creamy, this is perfect for topping warm fruit, pies, hot chocolate, or ice cream.

INGREDIENTS

12 ounces (340 g) silken tofu (soft or firm)
¼ cup (60 ml) canola oil
⅛ cup (112 g) pure maple syrup
1 tablespoon (15 ml) nondairy milk
1½ teaspoons vanilla extract
1½ teaspoons lemon juice
Pinch of salt

Blend all the ingredients together in a food processor or blender until VERY smooth. Refrigerate for several hours before serving.

SERVING SUGGESTIONS & VARIATIONS
Add 1 to 2 tablespoons (15 to 30 ml) of your favorite liqueur.

A WORD ABOUT TOFU: *There are many different types of tofu available, ranging from silken and soft to firm and extra firm, but there are also differences within those variations depending on the brand you buy or the way it's packaged. The perfect tofu for this recipe is the silken tofu that's packaged in an aseptic, vacuum-packed box. This means that you'll find it on the grocery store shelf as opposed to in the refrigerated section, and it can stay in your own cupboard for up to a year because of the way it is packaged. Don't be confused if the box of "silken" tofu says "firm" or "extra firm." There is a small difference between "silken firm" and "silken extra firm," so either one will do. (See "Resources and Recommendations" on page 270.)*

CASHEW CREAM

YIELD: 1 CUP (235 ML)

Put this delicious cream in the freezer for a short while before serving to increase its thickness. A friend of mine even serves it as ice cream.

INGREDIENTS

1 cup (145 g) raw cashew pieces

½ to ¾ cup (120 to 180 ml) water

¼ to ½ cup (60 to 120 ml) canola or coconut oil

¼ cup (85 g) pure maple syrup

½ teaspoon vanilla extract

Pinch of salt

In a high speed blender, blend the cashews and ¼ cup (60 ml) water until combined. Gradually add the remaining ¼ to ½ cup (60 to 120 ml) water as you begin to form a thick cream. Slowly add the oil in a fine stream until the cream thickens.

Blend in the maple syrup, vanilla, and salt. Chill in the refrigerator for at least 1 hour. The cream will thicken substantially when chilled.

PASTRY CREAM (CUSTARD)

YIELD: 1½ CUPS (350 ML)

Whether you call it pastry cream or custard cream, you will be thrilled with this recipe's texture and flavor.

INGREDIENTS

⅓ cup (65 g) granulated sugar

2 tablespoons (16 g) unbleached all-purpose flour

4 tablespoons (32 g) cornstarch

¼ cup (60 ml) water

1⅓ cups (315 ml) nondairy milk

2 teaspoons vanilla or lemon extract

1 ripe banana, sliced (optional)

In a medium bowl, beat together the sugar, flour, cornstarch, and water on high speed until creamy, about 2 minutes. Set aside.

In a medium-size saucepan, bring the milk to a simmer. Pour about ⅓ cup (80 ml) of the hot milk into the sugar mixture and stir to thoroughly combine. Add the sugar and milk mixture back to the saucepan that contains the remaining milk. Return to the stove, and heat over medium-low heat, whisking constantly. It will begin to thicken immediately.

Scrape the bottom and sides of the pan as you whisk. Cook until it begins to bubble, then whisk (as vigorously as you can) for 30 seconds, and remove from the heat. Stir in the vanilla and the banana, if using.

Transfer to a bowl, cover with a piece of waxed or parchment paper, and let cool to room temperature. Place in the refrigerator to cool completely. (It can remain in the fridge for up to 3 days.)

DID YOU KNOW?: *The average American consumes about 250 eggs a year. Total U.S. production during 2004 was 76.26 billion eggs. As of January 1, 2006, there were 291 million hens being used and abused for their egg production, and that number continues to rise. That's one hen for every man, woman, and child in this country.*

BROWN SUGAR SYRUP

YIELD: ¾ TO 1 CUP (180 TO 235 ML)

Here is a simple little recipe for when you get caught without any syrup for your pancakes. Try it over nondairy ice cream, as well.

INGREDIENTS
½ cup (112 g) firmly packed brown sugar
¼ cup (60 ml) nondairy milk
3 tablespoons (42 g) non-hydrogenated, nondairy butter
¼ cup (40 g) toasted walnuts, chopped (optional)

Combine the brown sugar, milk, and butter in a saucepan. Bring to a full boil and boil for 3 minutes. Reduce the heat and simmer vigorously until thickened to a syrupy consistency, 10 to 15 minutes. Stir in the nuts, if using. Let cool slightly (it will thicken more as it cools) and serve. It will keep in the refrigerator for up to 1 month.

CHOCOLATE ALMOND SPREAD

YIELD: ¾ CUP (180 G)

Inspired by a certain commercial chocolate nut spread sold on crêpes on the streets of Paris, this simple recipe is dedicated to my good friend Stephanie Arthur, with whom I shared these treats during our visit to Europe many moons ago. Spread on warm crêpes, rice cakes, or with fresh fruit!

INGREDIENTS
½ cup (125 g) natural almond butter (or peanut, cashew, or hazelnut butter)
½ cup (90 g) nondairy semisweet chocolate chips, melted
½ teaspoon vanilla extract

Combine the nut butter, melted chips, and vanilla in a food processor and blend until smooth and creamy. If you store it in the refrigerator, it may get hard. Once you return it to room temperature, it will get soft and spreadable again.

SERVING SUGGESTIONS & VARIATIONS
Spread on Dessert Crêpes (page 166) or rice cakes. For an extra-special treat, serve as a dip for dried or fresh fruit.

APPENDIX I: STOCKING YOUR VEGAN PANTRY

Baking Staples: A Guide to Ingredients

AGAR: A vegetable gelatin made from various kinds of algae or seaweed. The algae are collected, bleached, and dried. Then the gelatin substance is extracted with water and made into flakes, granules, powder, or strips that are brittle when dry.

AGAVE NECTAR: Pronounced "uh-GAH-vay," this sweet nectar comes from the agave plant, which resembles an aloe or a cactus plant. Sustainably harvested primarily in southern Mexico, this liquid sweetener is slightly less viscous than honey but used in just the same way. (See note about honey on page 174.) It is available in most grocery stores, large and small.

BAKING POWDER, DOUBLE ACTING: I recommend using double-acting baking powder, instead of single acting. See page 282 for a detailed discussion on each as well as the difference between baking soda and baking powder.

BAKING SODA: This is a leavening agent activated by interacting with an acidic agent. Liquid ingredients, such as nondairy sour milk, sour cream, buttermilk, and yogurt; molasses and lemon juice, help baking soda produce the gases that make a batter rise. The batter must be baked as soon as possible after the liquid has interacted with the baking soda to produce the desired results. See page 282 for a detailed discussion on the difference between baking soda and baking powder.

BUTTER, NONDAIRY: Though different brands of margarine are often vegan, there are two problems: they tend to have trans fat (which contributes to heart disease), and they're often synthetic-tasting. In my opinion, the best nondairy butter on the market is Earth Balance. It is non-hydrogenated (meaning there are no trans fats), no genetically modified ingredients are used to make it, and it's absolutely delicious. Available in organic, whipped, sticks, and shortening, you can use it the same way you use dairy butter. Look for it in large natural food stores, health food stores, or ask your local grocery to carry it.

CHOCOLATE: Derived from the cacao bean, which grows on the tropical cacao tree, chocolate is a plant-based food, and it's rich in cancer-fighting phytochemicals and antioxidants. The botanical name of the tree means "food of the gods." The cacao tree has grown wild in Central America since prehistoric times and also grows in South America, Africa, and parts of Indonesia. Because many people are most familiar with milk chocolate, they mistakenly assume that chocolate is not vegan. Being plant-derived, it is indeed vegan and is only dairy-based once you add cow's milk. Cocoa butter, cocoa powder, and bittersweet, semisweet, and dark chocolate are all—by definition—vegan. That doesn't mean some large chocolate companies don't add cow's milk to their dark and semisweet chocolates. Some do. Look for chocolate chips and bars without cow's milk for the real thing. Here are some more chocolate-related terms:

Cacao: The tropical evergreen tree and its dried and partially fermented beans that are processed to make chocolate, cocoa powder, and cocoa butter.

Cocoa butter: The ivory-colored, naturally occurring fat in cacao beans. Cocoa butter is the basis of white chocolate.

Chocolate: The general term for the products of the seeds of the cacao tree, used for making beverages and confectionery.

Cocoa powder (unsweetened cocoa: Made when chocolate liquor is pressed to remove most of its cocoa butter.

Bittersweet, dark, and semisweet chocolates: All dark chocolates made when the chocolate liquor, pressed from the cacao bean, is combined with cocoa butter, sugar, vanilla, and lecithin. The only difference between them is the amount of sugar.

Baking chocolate: Pure, unsweetened chocolate liquor, pressed from the cacao bean during processing, usually with lecithin and vanilla added. Baking chocolate is also called unsweetened and bitter chocolate.

Dutch-processed cocoa: This cocoa is treated with an alkalizing agent to modify its color and give it a milder flavor. As its name indicates, it was first developed in the Netherlands.

COCONUT: The fruit from the coconut palm tree, coconuts have many uses. The recipes in this book call for coconut flakes, which are just the dried white fleshy part of the coconut, and coconut milk, which is made by processing grated coconut with hot water or hot milk, which extracts the oil from the fiber. This should not be confused with what is called "coconut water" or "coconut juice," which is the juice found naturally in young coconuts. If you've never tasted it, I highly recommend giving it a try. It's scrumptious.

COOKING OILS: Purified fats of plant origin, which are liquid at room temperature. Some of the many different kinds of oils include olive, soybean, canola, corn, sunflower, safflower, peanut, grape seed, cashew, coconut, and sesame. Here is some information on different oils, but for our purposes—baking!—stick with canola.

Canola oil: "Canola" is a combination of two words, "Canadian" and "oil." Canola's history goes back to the rapeseed plant, but canola and rapeseed are not the same. In the 1970s, Canadian plant breeders produced canola through traditional plant breeding techniques. Canola oil is a good, all-purpose oil, especially suitable for baked goods, as it has a mild flavor that lets the taste of other ingredients shine through. It's high in monounsaturated fat and omega-3 fatty acids and low in saturated fats.

Olive oil: Because it's derived from olives, which are high in monounsaturated fats, olive oil is considered a healthful choice. In baking, I find it most suitable for bread.

Extra-virgin olive oil: This comes from the first pressing of the olives and is judged to have a superior taste. There can be no refined oil in extra-virgin olive oil.

Virgin olive oil: It has a good flavor and contains no refined oil.

Fine olive oil: This is a blend of virgin oil and refined virgin oil and commonly lacks a strong flavor.

Vegetable oil: When the generic term "vegetable oil" is on the label of cooking oil, it refers to a blend of a variety of oils often based on corn, soybean, and sunflower oils. Because these are high in polyunsaturated fats, they're not the oils I recommend.

CORNMEAL: Dried corn kernels ground to a fine, medium, or coarse texture. The traditional stone-ground method produces a more nutritious meal than the steel-ground method. When purchasing cornmeal, look for what might be labeled "coarse cornmeal," "polenta," or "polenta cornmeal." Here are some other cornmeal-related foods:

Corn flour: Finely ground cornmeal.

Polenta: A mush made from cornmeal and a staple of northern Italy.

Hominy: Dried white or yellow corn kernels from which the hull and germ have been removed.

Grits: A common dish in the southern United States. Similar to polenta, grits are usually made from coarsely ground hominy as opposed to cornmeal.

DATES: A staple food of the Middle East for thousands of years, dates are the incredibly sweet, edible, oblong or oval fruit of the date palm tree. Dry or soft dates, which contain a narrow, hard seed, can be eaten as a snack or may be de-seeded and stuffed with fillings such as almonds, candied orange and lemon peel, and marzipan. Dates can also be chopped and used in a range of sweet and savory dishes, such as breads and cakes. They're also processed into cubes, paste, spread, date syrup, powder (date sugar), vinegar, and alcohol. Several different dates are available, some of which you may find in your natural food store, but if your local farmers' market has a date vendor, by all means, run as fast as you can and try a variety of dates, such as Medjool, Barhee, and Deglet Noor.

FIGS: The edible fig is one of the first plants cultivated by humans. Native to southwest Asia and the Eastern Mediterranean region, figs can be eaten fresh or dried, and used in jam or breads. Most commercial production results in dried or otherwise processed forms, since the ripe fruit does not transport well, and once picked does not keep. Visit your farmers' market during fig season, usually in September or October, depending on where you live.

FLAXSEEDS: The most concentrated source of essential omega-3 fatty acids, these pretty little brown seeds should be a staple in your diet even if you're not using them for baking! Always buy whole flaxseeds (golden or brown) and grind them yourself, using a coffee grinder for best results. Once you grind them, put them in a glass container and store them in the freezer. Consume 2 teaspoons a day by adding them to a fruit smoothie, oatmeal, cereal, soup, or salad, or eating them just on their own. (See "Better Than Eggs" on page 19 for making "flax eggs.")

HERBS AND SPICES: Little jars of herbs and spices are—right now—collecting dust in people's kitchens all around the world. Afraid to use the wrong combination of spices, people shy away from using them at all and miss out on all the flavor they provide. Allspice: A single spice, rather than a combination of "all spices," its fragrance is reminiscent of nutmeg, cloves, juniper berries, pepper, and cinnamon.

Anise (Aniseed): Pronounced ANNis. One of the oldest cultivated spices and native to the Middle East, these small greenish-gray seeds have a mild licorice taste. Use aniseed to flavor sweets, creams, cakes, and breads.

Arrowroot: An easy-to-digest starch from the rhizomes of a West Indian plant that acts as a thickener in cooking and baking.

Capers: The unopened green flower buds of a Mediterranean (and Californian) bush, capers are sun-dried, then pickled in a vinegar brine. Rinse the salt before using them in a variety of dishes. They're great to use in Caesar salad dressing instead of anchovies.

Caraway: Caraway seeds are the fragrant seeds of an herb in the parsley family. They have a sharp, delicate anise flavor, and just a small amount adds a lot of flavor to bread.

Cardamom: These wonderfully aromatic seeds are a member of the ginger family and can be used in cooking and baking whole or ground. With a piquant but sweet flavor, it's used in desserts and in curry powders; in fact, it's an essential ingredient of garam masala, the Indian spice mix.

Chili powder: A spice mix consisting of various dried ground chile peppers, it also tends to include cumin, garlic, and oregano. Depending on the type of chile peppers used, the mix may be mild or hot.

Cinnamon: One of the most familiar spices in kitchens around the United States, cinnamon was once an exotic and expensive spice. Harvested from the tree of the same name, it is the dried pale brown inner bark of the aromatic tree.

Cloves: Cloves derive their name from their nail shape; clavus is Latin for "nail." These strongly scented, dried, unopened buds of the clove were first used by the Chinese as far back as the third century.

Coriander: Coriander seeds come from the cilantro plant. The plant and seeds have very different flavors, and both are used in a variety of cuisines.

Cream of tartar: An acid salt obtained from sediment produced in the wine-making process, cream of tartar is often the acidic ingredient in baking powder. It's also used to thicken some desserts.

Cumin: Cumin dates back to biblical times and is even mentioned several times in the Bible. Use ground or whole seeds, and if using the latter, lightly roast the seeds in a dry frying pan before using to bring out the flavor and aroma.

Curry powder: This spice mixture, which is more popular in the West than in India, usually consists of coriander, turmeric, fenugreek, cumin, and chile.

Fennel: The fragrant, feathery leaves are used as an aromatic herb, and the seeds, which have a light aniseed flavor, are used as a seasoning.

Ginger: Ground and fresh ginger have quite different tastes, and ground ginger is a poor substitute for fresh ginger. However, fresh ginger can be substituted for ground ginger at the ratio of $1/8$ teaspoon ground ginger to 1 tablespoon fresh grated ginger.

Mint: Used in sweet and savory dishes and for adding a refreshing flavor to tea and other beverages, the most common and popular mints are peppermint and spearmint.

Nutmeg and mace: Nutmeg is the seed of an evergreen tree; mace is the dried "lacy" reddish covering of the seed. Though their flavors are similar, nutmeg is slightly sweeter.

Marjoram: Similar in taste and fragrance to oregano, it is used both dried and fresh.

Oregano: Native to the Mediterranean region, it is used widely in Greek and Italian cuisines. Dried oregano is often more flavorful than the fresh.

Paprika: Though there are many kinds of peppers, only two of them are used to make paprika. The name "paprika" comes from Hungary, where it is popular and essential ingredient.

Parsley: Imparting a much milder flavor than its relative, cilantro, parsley is used in much the same way. It's also used as a breath freshener, particularly to counter the strong smell of garlic.

Rosemary: A woody, perennial herb with fragrant evergreen needle-like leaves, rosemary is native to the Mediterranean region. Both dried and fresh leaves are used, and a little goes a long way.

Saffron: Saffron is derived from the flower of the saffron crocus. Too much saffron in a dish can impart a bitter flavor, and just a small amount is enough to give food a rich golden-yellow hue.

Sesame: These little flavorful seeds pack a lot of punch and come in a variety of colors from creamy white to jet black. Sesame seed paste (tahini) is the basis for hummus, a popular Middle Eastern spread.

Tarragon: An herb that is used dried or fresh, it makes a wonderful accompaniment to potatoes. Its flavor is slightly reminiscent of anise.

Thyme: Thyme is widely cultivated as an herb that retains its flavor after drying better than many other herbs. Often used in French cuisine, it's also used in Caribbean and Middle Eastern cuisines.

Turmeric: One of the great Indian spices, turmeric has been used since antiquity as a spice, perfume, and dye. This bright yellow powder comes from the rhizome (or root) of a ginger-like plant. The rhizome is boiled, dried, and ground to a fine yellow powder before use.

Vanilla: A flavoring derived from orchids in the genus Vanilla, whose name comes from the Spanish word vainilla, which means "little pod." Vanilla flavors many desserts in the form of extract or crushed vanilla beans or pods.

JAM/JELLY/PRESERVES: These sweet fruit-based spreads vary in terms of how they are prepared, but whatever your preference, have a jar around for adding flavor and sweetness to various desserts, muffins, or quick breads.

KUDZU (KUZU): Sometimes referred to as "Japanese arrowroot," kudzu is a high-quality starch made from the root of the kudzu plant that grows wild in the mountains of Japan and in the Southern United States. When added to water and heated, kudzu powder becomes clear and thickens whatever you've added it to. The name comes from the Japanese word meaning "vine."

Kudzu is more expensive than other thickeners, such as arrowroot and cornstarch, but I prefer it for its effectiveness and for its lack of flavor. I find that arrowroot can sometimes have a chalky aftertaste if not mixed properly. All of these thickeners, however, can be used interchangeably for thickening liquids, sauces, and gravies, by first dissolving the powder in a small amount of cool liquid.

To prepare kudzu, follow the instructions on the package. In general, you will dissolve 1 tablespoon in 2 tablespoons of cool liquid, mix well, then stir slowly into whatever sauce you are cooking. Once it begins to heat, you will notice the liquid starting to thicken. Continue stirring and let cook for at least 5 minutes.

MAPLE SYRUP: A sweetener made by reducing the clear sap from maple trees into a high-concentration sugar in water. Essentially, it comes in two grades, roughly corresponding to the season in which it was made. Grade A has a mild, more delicate flavor than Grade B, which is darker and has a robust flavor.

MIXED PEEL: This is basically just candied lemon and lime peel or any citrus peel, such as orange and grapefruit. It's used in certain candies and dishes, such as mincemeat, which, despite the name, doesn't necessarily contain meat.

MOLASSES OR TREACLE: A by-product from the processing of sugar cane or sugar beet into sugar, this is a thick syrup that is called blackstrap molasses after the third boiling of the sugars. The latter is very high in such minerals as calcium, potassium, and iron. (Technically, treacle is a generic word in Britain for any syrup made during the process of refining sugar cane.)

NUTS: Having a variety of nuts on hand makes spontaneous baking easy and enjoyable. Of course there are many more varieties of nuts than what I've listed here, but I wanted to include the most popular nuts and those that I recommend for the recipes in this book.

Almonds: Have these on hand to make almond milk, almond butter, or almond meal, or just pop a handful of these raw or toasted nuts into your mouth each day.

Cashews: Because of their high oil content, they're great for making into creams and spreads.

Hazelnuts: Delicious and nutritious, hazelnuts also make a great spread (particularly when combined with chocolate!), and hazelnut milk is also available commercially.

Peanuts: Technically a legume, peanuts go particularly well with chocolate—in any form. They also add great texture to savory dishes, such as stir-fries and Thai-inspired meals.

Pecans: Their rich, buttery flavor make them perfect for caramelizing or using in just about any dessert that calls for nuts.

Walnuts: A great source of omega-3 fatty acids, walnuts are a tasty snack and a great addition to many desserts, especially fruit crisps and crumbles.

OLIVES: The olive tree, native to coastal areas of the Eastern Mediterranean region, is one of the earliest plants cited in recorded literature. Used as a major agricultural product in pre-classical Greece, the fruit of this plant must be treated before it can be eaten by way of fermentation or curing with brine. When unripe olives are processed, green olives are produced. When ripe olives are processed, black olives are the outcome. (See "Cooking oils" for information about olive oil.)

PHYLLO DOUGH: Pronounced FEE-lo, this is a tissue-thin pastry dough cut into sheets that is used in Middle Eastern desserts, such as baklava. You can find it in the freezer section of the grocery store. Look for one made without partially hydrogenated oil and other less wholesome ingredients.

TOFU: A food of Chinese origin, tofu is created by adding a coagulating agent to soymilk, and then pressing the resulting curds into blocks. The process of making tofu from soymilk is similar to the technique of making dairy cheese from cow's milk.

VINEGAR: There are many different types of vinegar, a fermented food that has been used since ancient times and is an important element in cuisines all around the world. The word "vinegar" derives from the Old French vin aigre, which means "sour wine." For baking purposes, white distilled vinegar and apple cider vinegar work equally well as the acid that reacts with baking soda to leaven baked goods. I recommend distilled white in all the recipes that call for vinegar, but apple cider would work equally well.

ZEST: The colored outer portion of the peel of citrus fruits.

Essential Kitchen Tools

BAKING OR CUPCAKE LINER CUPS: These are the little cups that go inside muffin tins and are used for making cupcakes.

BLENDER: A blender is best for liquefying or blending liquid ingredients. Because the blade is all the way at the bottom, it doesn't do as good a job as a food processor. However, I use my blender to make smoothies and shakes, which the food processor isn't meant for.

BUNDT PAN: A decorative pan used for making cakes and breads, it looks like a crimped tube pan, with creased sides and a hole in the center. Available in a variety of designs and sizes, the most common are 9 and 10 inches (23 and 25 cm) around.

CHEF'S KNIVES: A sharp knife is key to safe and effective cutting. A few different sizes and types, including a serrated knife for slicing bread, are best and require periodic sharpening.

COFFEE GRINDER (FOR GRINDING FLAXSEED): I've never had a cup of coffee in my life, but I use this handy-dandy gadget on a regular basis for grinding up the small, nutritious flaxseeds that are good for eating and replacing eggs in baking.

COLANDER: These are made from a variety of materials, including stainless steel, plastic, and wire mesh; I prefer the type that has "legs," so that the food in the colander doesn't touch the sink bottom, which may not be clean.

COOKIE/BAKING SHEET: This is a flat, rigid sheet of metal on which cookies, breads, and biscuits are baked. Shiny aluminum baking sheets are good heat conductors and will produce evenly baked and browned goods. Dark sheets absorb heat and may affect cooking times and final results.

CRÊPE PAN: Nonstick is key when making crêpes; 8-, 9-, or 10-inch (20-, 23-, or 25-cm) sauté pans can be used or those made specifically for crêpes, which have low sides.

CUTTING BOARD: Just one more benefit of vegan cooking and baking is not having to worry about cross-contamination. My favorite cutting board is made of durable, sustainable bamboo.

DRY MEASURING CUPS: These are often sold in a set of various sizes, and I usually have a couple sets on hand at all times. Their straight rim allows for accurate measurements. Stainless steel is best.

ELECTRIC HAND-HELD MIXER: As the name implies, this is a hand-held device, where two stainless steel beaters are immersed in the food (in a mixing bowl) to do the mixing. See also immersion blender (following page).

ELECTRIC STAND MIXER: A stand mixer is essentially the same as a hand mixer but with more powerful motors than their hand-held counterparts. I use my stand mixer for mixing tougher batters and doughs, taking advantage of the various blades, whips, and hooks the machines tend to include.

FOOD PROCESSOR: An essential small appliance, I prefer the KitchenAid brand, as one machine will have two bowls and two blades—large and small—a convenient feature that not all food processors have.

IMMERSION BLENDER: This is also an electric hand-held mixer, but its design enables you to purée soup, for instance, while leaving the food right in the pot. Also called a stick or wand blender.

LIQUID MEASURING CUPS: I really enjoy the flexibility I get from having a few different sizes: 1-cup (235-ml), 2-cup (470-ml), and 4-cup (940-ml). Look for heavy-duty glass that has ounces and cups clearly marked.

LOAF PANS: You can use large (9 × 5 × 3-inch or 23 × 13 × 7.5-cm), medium (8 × 4 × 2-inch or 20 × 10 × 5-cm) or mini (6 × 3 × 2-inch or 15 × 7.5 × 5-cm) loaf pans for any of the quick or yeast bread recipes. The darker the pan, the faster it will absorb heat and may require you to lower the baking temperature.

MEASURING SPOONS: I have several sets of measuring spoons and keep them in a convenient place. Whereas I don't measure too much when I cook, accurate measuring while baking is essential.

METAL SPATULA: With its long, straight blade, this type of spatula is good for leveling the surface of dry ingredients to ensure accuracy.

MICROPLANE: This is a great little kitchen tool that's worth its weight in gold for its ability to zest lemons alone. It's also perfect for grating hard chocolate, nutmeg, and ginger.

MIXING BOWLS: It's helpful to have a variety of sizes. Those with a spout make it easy to pour liquid ingredients into dry.

MUFFIN TIN: Standard muffin tins hold about 3 fluid ounces (90 ml) and 12 muffins. Oversized or jumbo tins hold about ¾ cup (175 ml) of batter in each cup and make 6 muffins. Miniature tins hold 1½ tablespoons (25 ml) of batter and make anywhere from 12 to 24 muffins. Nonstick is best.

NONSTICK WHISK: Never use metal whisks on good cookware or you'll scratch the surface, compromising both safety and quality. Nonstick whisks are good for this purpose.

OFFSET SPATULA: With its raised handle and bend in its blade, this spatula is ideal for spreading batters or frosting a cake. A few different sizes are helpful to have.

PARCHMENT PAPER: Different than waxed paper, which will burn during cooking, parchment paper is great when you want to eliminate the need to grease cookie sheets but still avoid the food sticking to the pan. Choose unbleached.

PIE PLATES: A 9-inch (23-cm) pie plate holds about 5 cups (1175 ml) of filling while an 8-inch (20-cm) pie plate holds about 4 cups (940 ml).

POT HOLDERS: A few good ones for removing pans from the oven include those that have one side treated for fire resistance.

RECTANGULAR BAKING DISHES: One 11 × 7-inch (28 × 18-cm) or 13 × 9-inch (33 × 23-cm) baking dish is good for crisps, cobblers, and crumbles.

ROLLING PIN: This is a necessary tool in any baker's kitchen, and I prefer the type that does not have handles, as it offers the greatest control and flexibility.

ROUND CAKE PANS: The 9- and 10-inch (23- and 25-cm) sizes are usually called for. Nonstick is best.

RUBBER SPATULA: This is the best way to scrape batters out of mixing bowls and for smoothing batters in their pans. Choose pliable rubber or silicone heads.

SAUCEPANS: Every household should have 1½-, 2-, 3-, and 4-quart (1.7-, 2.3-, 3.4-, and 4.5-L) saucepans for cooking and baking. They should all have lids, of course.

SPRINGFORM PANS: The springform pan is a two-piece pan with sides that can be removed and a bottom that comes out too, with the flick of a latch. The pan pieces are assembled for baking, and then, once the contents have cooked and cooled, the band is opened and removed. They are available in a number of sizes; 9- and 10-inch (23- and 25-cm) are the most common and are perfect for cakes, tarts, and cheesecakes.

SQUARE CAKE PANS OR BAKING DISHES: Having one or two 8- and 9-inch (20- and 23-cm) square pans is ideal. I like both glass and metal.

STRAINER: I have a few different sizes of strainers and use them to rinse berries, strain fruit sauces and sorbets, and some to sift confectioners' sugar.

TART PAN: This is a pan with a removable bottom ideal for making elegant tarts and shallow pies. Fluted sides are common, and I prefer nonstick.

TUBE PAN: Similar to the Bundt pan, it is also round with a hollow center. The sides are flat and not creased. They are generally 9 inches (23 cm) in diameter.

VEGETABLE PEELER: A tool in everyone's home, this little gadget removes thin skins, such as those on apples and potatoes.

WIRE COOLING RACK: A staple for every baker, this rack allows air to circulate underneath baked goods for quick, even cooling. Racks with closely spaced wires prevent cookies from slipping through.

WIRE WHISK: A stainless-steel whisk is perfect for whisking up and incorporating ingredients into batter, but I use a nonstick one when whisking something in one of my good metal pots.

WOODEN SPOONS: These are essential for baking and cooking, and I couldn't live without mine. Choose good-quality spoons of varying lengths and sizes, and keep them in a handy location.

WOODEN TOOTHPICKS AND SKEWERS: Short toothpicks and long, thin skewers are helpful to have on hand to test baked goods for doneness.

Resources and Recommendations

Look for the following products at your local grocery store, health or specialty food store, or online. They are also all available in my Amazon store at colleenpatrickgoudreau.com

NONDAIRY MILKS

ALMOND MILK: If you haven't tried almond milk, you're in for a treat. The flavor of fresh homemade almond milk cannot be beat, and you reduce packaging waste—while saving some money. A win-win-win. Check out the easy recipe on page 234. Of course, you can buy a commercial brand, and there are so many these days—including such flavors as original, vanilla, and chocolate; sweetened, and unsweetened. There are also low-fat versions, sugar-free versions, and creamers. Commercial brands are sold in vacuum-packed, aseptic boxes that can sit on the shelf for a long time. (Many brands have changed the materials they use, making these boxes recyclable.) As of this writing, my favorite brand is Califia Farms.

SOYMILK: Whenever I hear people say they don't like soymilk, I ask them if they've tried more than one brand. Usually they say no. There are so many different brands, and each one is different from the other. Try several until you find the one you like. My favorites are Wildwood and Pacific Foods, but try a variety to find your own favorite.

HAZELNUT AND OAT MILKS: Whenever I offer taste tests of different nondairy milks, these two are always a surprise hit. Pacific Foods' oat milk is certified organic, and they also have a multi-grain milk.

NONDAIRY BUTTER

Technically, "margarine" is a nondairy butter, but most margarines don't taste very good, contain trans fat, and don't perform well in baked goods. I highly recommend Earth Balance "buttery spread." You can use it in every way you use dairy butter, and it comes in tubs, sticks, whipped, and shortening—all non-GMO (not genetically modified), non-hydrogenated (no trans fats), and absolutely delicious! There are other nondairy butters on the market as well, so feel free to try others; just make sure they're free of trans fat and animal products. Look for these products in small and large natural food stores.

COMMERCIAL EGG REPLACERS

Though there are many ways to replace eggs in baking, commercial egg replacers are just another option. A powder mixture of vegetable starches (in the case of Ener-G) or microalgae (in the case of the Vegan Egg) that simulates eggs in baking, it can be used in any recipe that calls for eggs. Simply follow instructions on the package to determine the amount of starch to mix with water to obtain one "egg." As of this writing, more vegan eggs are slated for store shelves, so keep your eyes peeled.

Ener-G Egg Replacer: www.ener-g.com

Bob's Red Mill Egg Replacer: www.bobsredmill.com

Follow Your Heart's Vegan Egg: followyourheart.com

NONDAIRY YOGURT, CREAM CHEESE AND SOUR CREAM

There are a so many different brands making nondairy yogurts, cream cheeses, and sour cream these days that this paragraph will be dated by the time you finish reading it if I try to list them all. Just visit the section of the grocery store where dairy yogurts and cream cheeses are, and you'll find a slew of plant-based versions.

EGGLESS MAYONNAISE

Though none of my recipes calls for mayonnaise, it's helpful to know that vegan mayonnaise is available from a few different companies, all of which are fantastic. Wildwood's aioli is by far my favorite. Here are just a few, but check the shelves.

Wildwood's Garlic Aioli: www.wildwoodfoods.com

Hampton Creek's Just Mayo: hamptoncreek.com

Follow Your Heart's Vegenaise: www.followyourheart.com

TOFU

There are so many brands of tofu that it would be difficult to list them all here. I highly recommend purchasing organic, as soybeans are one of the most highly sprayed and genetically modified crops. The recipes in this cookbook that call for tofu refer to silken tofu, and Mori Nu brand is very good and easy to find.

VEGETARIAN GELATIN

Many of the General Vegan Stores listed on page 272 carry a vegetarian gelatin, free of animal products.

VEGETARIAN MARSHMALLOWS

Gelatin-free vegetarian marshmallows are available at most of the General Vegan Stores listed on page 272. The best are made by Sweet & Sara (www.sweetandsara.com).

AGAR-AGAR FLAKES AND KUDZU ROOT

Both of these products may be new to you, but you can find them either in a large natural food store or online.

FLAXSEED

You can find these at any natural food store. I recommend buying whole seeds and then grinding them yourself with a coffee grinder.

VEGAN COOKIES

Here are two specific recommendations based on what's called for in a few of the recipes.

Newman's Own Cookies: For the Cookie Crust recipe (page 222), try Newman's delicious cookie called "Tops and Bottoms," which is essentially their sandwich cookie without the icing in the middle. I find that the entire package is the perfect amount for a 9-inch (23-cm) springform pan.

Graham Crackers: Many brands contain honey. Try a large natural food store for a honey-free version.

GENERAL VEGAN STORES

Food Fight Grocery (Portland): www.foodfightgrocery.com
The Vegan Store (Pangea): www.veganstore.com
Vegan Essentials: www.veganessentials.com
Vegan Store UK: www.veganstore.co.uk

FAIR TRADE ITEMS AND INFORMATION

Equal Exchange: www.equalexchange.com
Global Exchange: www.globalexchange.org

INFORMATION ON VEGANISM

Start at ColleenPatrickGoudreau.com, where you can find everything you need, including links to my favorite resources.

APPENDIX II:
MAKING SENSE OF IT ALL

Glossary of Terms

BAIN MARIE: Pronounced "bane maREE," this hot water bath that is used to keep food warm on the top of a stove is similar to a double boiler. It is also used to cook custards, such as bread pudding, in the oven without burning or curdling.

BEAT: To mix rapidly, smoothing the ingredients and adding air, using a wire whisk, electric hand mixer, or stand mixer.

BLANCH: A preparation method whereby food is briefly cooked in boiling water to aid in the removal of the skin from nuts, fruits, and vegetables.

BLEND: A preparation method that combines ingredients with a spoon, beater, or liquefier to achieve a smooth, uniform mixture.

BLIND BAKING: A technique used for baking an unfilled pastry shell to prevent a liquid filling from making the pie crust too soggy. The pastry shell is first pricked with a fork to prevent puffing, covered with aluminum foil or parchment paper, and then weighted with rice or beans. It is then baked for a short period of time, 10 to 15 minutes.

CARAMELIZE: To bring out the sugar in a fruit or vegetable by browning slowly over heat.

CHOP: To cut food into irregular pieces. The size is specified if it is critical to the outcome of the recipe.

COAT: To cover food completely with a glaze, frosting, or sauce.

COULIS: Pronounced "coo-lee"; a fruit or vegetable puree, used as a sauce.

CREAM: To work one or more foods with a spoon or spatula until smooth.

CRIMP: To create a decorative border on pie crusts by pinching or pressing the dough together using your fingers, a fork, or another utensil.

CURDLE: A process that causes nondairy milk or a sauce to separate into solids and liquids by overheating or by adding an acid, such as in buttermilk.

CUT IN: To blend together cold, solid fat (shortening or nondairy butter) and flour or sugar without creaming (mixing air into) the two. Two knives or a pastry blender may be used to create a mixture that is crumbly or grainy in appearance.

DASH: A measure of dry or liquid ingredient that equals 1/16 teaspoon.

DICE: To cut food into cubes (the shape of dice in a game) that are more or less even. If the recipe doesn't specify the dimension of the dice, then go for a ¼ inch.

DISSOLVE: When a dry substance is stirred into a liquid until solids are no longer remaining, such as dry yeast or sugar dissolving in water.

DOLLOP: A small spoonful of a semiliquid food, such as whipped topping, that is placed on top of another food.

DOT: To scatter bits, such as nondairy butter, over the surface of food.

DOUBLE BOILER: Similar to a bain marie, a double boiler is used to warm or cook heat-sensitive food such as delicate sauces and chocolate without using direct heat. One smaller pot is placed inside a larger pot. The larger pot, which touches the heat directly, holds simmering water, which gently heats the mixture in the smaller pot.

DUSTING: A finishing method whereby flour, sugar, spice, or seasoning is lightly sprinkled on top of the food item.

FOLD (INTO): A gentle mixing process whereby one ingredient or mixture is added to another using a large metal spoon or spatula.

GLAZE: Used to give desserts a smooth and shiny finish; glazes are often made from confectioners' sugar and some kind of liquid.

GRATE: To rub food against a rough, perforated utensil, reducing the food to slivers, chunks, or curls.

GRIND: To cut, crush, or force through a chopper so as to produce small bits.

JULIENNE: To cut vegetables and fruit into long thin strips, usually as small as 1/8 inch wide.

KNEAD: To press, fold, and stretch yeast-based dough until it is elastic and smooth. This can by done with a bread maker, a dough hook in an electric stand mixer, or by hand.

LEAVEN: A process whereby a leavening agent, such as baking soda, baking powder, or yeast, reacts with moisture, heat, acidity, or other triggers to produce gas that becomes trapped as bubbles within the dough. Air and steam are also leavening agents.

MINCE: To cut or chop into very small pieces.

MIX: To stir in circles with a wooden spoon until ingredients are distributed evenly and there aren't any lumps.

MULL(ED): To add spices to a beverage, such as cider or wine, which is usually served hot.

PARCHMENT PAPER: A silicon-based paper that prevents food from sticking to it and that can withstand high heat.

POACH: To cook a food, such as fruit, in a simmering liquid, just below the boiling point.

PURÉE: To reduce the pulp of cooked fruit and vegetables to a smooth and thick liquid by straining or by blending in a food processor or blender.

SAUTÉ: A high-heat cooking method that uses very little fat or oil in the pan.

SCALD: A preparation method whereby non-dairy milk is heated to just below the boiling point.

SCORE: To cut gashes or narrow grooves into the surface of a food, such as on pastry crust or bread dough.

SHRED: To cut or shave food into slivers.

SIEVE: To pass dry and liquid ingredients through a closely meshed metal utensil so as to separate liquid from solid or fine from coarse.

SIFT: To pass dry ingredients through a fine wire mesh so as to produce a uniform consistency and remove any clumps or impurities.

SIMMER: To cook on the stovetop just below the boiling point, usually considered somewhere between 180°F to 190°F (82°C to 88°C).

STEAM: A way of cooking food so as to heat it by the steam of boiling water as opposed to being immersed in the water itself, preserving the color, flavor, and nutrients.

STIR: To move a spoon in a circular motion to incorporate ingredients.

STRAIN: To pass through a strainer, sieve, or cheesecloth to break down or remove solids or impurities.

STREUSEL: A crumbly topping for baked goods, consisting of fat, sugar, and flour rubbed together.

STRUDEL: A baked item consisting of a filling rolled up in layered sheets of phyllo dough.

SYRUP: A viscous, concentrated sugar solution that occurs due to evaporation of a liquid.

WASH: A liquid brushed onto the surface of a product, usually before baking.

WHIP: Preparation method whereby an item is mixed until frothy and creamy in consistency.

WHISK: To beat rapidly using a hand or an electric whisk to introduce air into a mixture or a single ingredient to increase the volume.

Cake Pan Substitutes

Not everyone has a fully equipped kitchen with a variety of cake, pie, bread, and tart pans, but that shouldn't deter an interested baker. Use this helpful chart to determine what to use when a recipe calls for a pan you may not yet own.

If a Recipe Calls For	Use Instead Pan Size (in inches)	Pan Size (in centimeters)
1 (8-inch [20-cm]) round cake pan	1 (8 x 4 x 2-inch) loaf pan	1 (20 x 10 x 5-cm) loaf pan
	1 (9-inch) round cake pan	1 (23-cm) round cake pan
	1 (9-inch) pie plate	1 (23-cm) pie plate
	1 (11 x 7-inch) baking dish	1 (28 x 18-cm) baking dish
2 (8-inch [20-cm]) round cake pans	2 (8 x 4 x 2-inch) loaf pans	2 (20 x 10 x 5-cm) loaf pans
	1 (9-inch) tube pan	1 (23-cm) tube pan
	2 (9-inch) round cake pans	2 (23-cm) round cake pans
	1 (10-inch) Bundt pan	1 (25-cm) Bundt pan
	1 (10-inch) springform pan	1 (25-cm) springform pan
	2 (11 x 7-inch) baking dishes	2 (28 x 18-cm) baking dishes
1 (9-inch [23-cm]) round cake pan	1 (8-inch) round cake pan	1 (20-cm) round cake pan
	1 (8 x 4 x 2-inch) loaf pan	1 (20 x 10 x 5-cm) loaf pan
	1 (11 x 7-inch) baking dish	1 (28 x 18-cm) baking dish
2 (9-inch [23-cm]) round cake pans	2 (8 x 4 x 2-inch) loaf pans	2 (20 x 10 x 5-cm) loaf pans
	2 (8-inch) round cake pans	2 (20-cm) round cake pans
	1 (9-inch) tube pan	1 (23-cm) tube pan
	1 (10-inch) Bundt pan	1 (25-cm) Bundt pan
	1 (10-inch) springform pan	1 (25-cm) springform pan
	2 (11 x 7-inch) baking dishes	2 (28 x 18-cm) baking dishes
1 (10-inch [25-cm]) round cake pan	2 (8-inch) round cake pans	2 (20-cm) round cake pans
	1 (9-inch) tube pan	1 (23-cm) tube pan
	1 (10-inch) springform pan	1 (25-cm) springform pan

If a Recipe Calls For	Use Instead	
	Pan Size (in inches)	Pan Size (in centimeters)
2 (10-inch [25-cm]) round cake pans	4 (8-inch) round cake pans	4 (20-cm) round cake pans
	3 or 4 (9-inch) round cake pans	3 or 4 (23-cm) round cake pans
	2 (10-inch) springform pans	2 (25-cm) springform pans
1 (9-inch [23-cm]) tube pan	2 (8-inch) round cake pans	2 (20-cm) round cake pans
	2 (9-inch) round cake pans	2 (23-cm) round cake pans
	1 (10-inch) Bundt pan	1 (25-cm) Bundt pan
1 (10-inch [25-cm]) tube pan	4 (8-inch) pie plates	4 (20-cm) pie plates
	2 (8-inch) square baking dishes	2 (20-cm) square baking dishes
	2 (9-inch) square baking dishes	2 (23-cm) square baking dishes
	3 (9-inch) round cake pans	3 (23-cm) round cake pans
	2 (10-inch) pie plates	2 (25-cm) pie plates
	2 (9 x 5 x 3-inch) loaf pans	2 (23 x 13 x 7.5-cm) loaf pans
1 (10-inch [25-cm]) Bundt pan	2 (8-inch) round cake pans	2 (20-cm) round cake pans
	2 (9-inch) round cake pans	2 (23-cm) round cake pans
	1 (9-inch) tube pan	1 (23-cm) tube pan
	1 (9 x 13-inch) baking dish	1 (23 x 33-cm) baking dish
	1 (10-inch) springform pan	1 (25-cm) springform pan
	2 (11 x 7-inch) baking dishes	2 (28 x 18-cm) baking dishes
1 (11 x 7 x 2-inch [28 x 18 x 5-cm]) baking dish	1 (8-inch) square baking dish	1 (20-cm) square baking dish
	1 (9-inch) square baking dish	1 (23-cm) square baking dish
	1 (9-inch) round cake pan	1 (23-cm) round cake pan
1 (9 x 13 x 2-inch [23 x 33 x 5-cm]) baking dish	2 (8-inch) round cake pans	2 (20-cm) round cake pans
	2 (9-inch) round cake pans	2 (23-cm) round cake pans
	1 (10-inch) Bundt cake pan	1 (25-cm) Bundt cake pan
	1 (10 x 15-inch) jellyroll pan	1 (25 x 38-cm) jellyroll pan
1 (10 x 15 x 1-inch [25 x 38 x 2.5-cm]) jellyroll pan	2 (8-inch) round cake pans	2 (20-cm) round cake pans
	1 (9-inch) Bundt pan	1 (23-cm) Bundt pan
	2 (9-inch) round cake pans	2 (23-cm) round cake pans
	1 (9 x 13-inch) baking dish	1 (23 x 33-cm) baking dish

If a Recipe Calls For	Use Instead	
	Pan Size (in inches)	Pan Size (in centimeters)
1 (9 x 5 x 3-inch [23 x 13 x 7.5-cm]) loaf pan	1 (8-inch) square baking dish 1 (9-inch) square baking dish 1 (10-inch) pie plate	1 (20-cm) square baking dish 1 (23-cm) square baking dish 1 (25-cm) pie plate
1 (8 x 4 x 2-inch [20 x 10 x 5-cm]) loaf pan	1 (8-inch) round cake pan 1 (11 x 7-inch) baking dish	1 (20-cm) round cake pan 1 (28 x 18-cm) baking dish
1 (8-inch [20-cm]) pie plate	1 (8-inch) round cake pan 1 (8-inch) tart pan	1 (20-cm) round cake pan 1 (20-cm) tart pan
1 (9-inch [23-cm]) pie plate	1 (8-inch) round cake pan 1 (9-inch) round cake pan 1 (9-inch) tart pan	1 (20-cm) round cake pan 1 (23-cm) round cake pan 1 (23-cm) tart pan
1 (9 x 2-inch [23 x 5-cm]) deep dish pie plate	2 (8-inch) pie plates 1 (8-inch) square baking dish 1 (9-inch) square baking dish 1 (9 x 5-inch) loaf pan 1 (10-inch) pie plate	2 (20-cm) pie plates 1 (20-cm) square baking dish 1 (23-cm) square baking dish 1 (23 x 13-cm) loaf pan 1 (25-cm) pie plate
1 (10-inch [25-cm]) pie plate	2 (8-inch) pie plates 1 (8-inch) square baking dish 1 (9-inch) square baking dish 1 (9-inch) deep dish pie plate 1 (9 x 5 x 3-inch) loaf pan	2 (20-cm) pie plates 1 (20-cm) square baking dish 1 (23-cm) square baking dish 1 (23-cm) deep dish pie plate 1 (23 x 13 x 7.5-cm) loaf pan
1 (9-inch [23-cm]) springform pan	2 (8-inch) round cake pans 2 (9-inch) round cake pans 1 (10-inch) round cake pan 1 (10-inch) springform pan	2 (20-cm) round cake pans 2 (23-cm) round cake pans 1 (25-cm) round cake pan 1 (25-cm) springform pan

If a Recipe Calls For	Use Instead	
	Pan Size (in inches)	Pan Size (in centimeters)
1 (10-inch [25-cm]) springform pan	2 (8-inch) round cake pans	2 (20-cm) round cake pans
	2 (8 x 4 x 2-inch) loaf pans	2 (20 x 10 x 5-cm) loaf pans
	1 (9-inch) tube pan	1 (23-cm) tube pan
	2 (9-inch) round cake pans	2 (23-cm) round cake pans
	1 (10-inch) Bundt pan	1 (25-cm) Bundt pan
	2 (11 x 7-inch) baking dishes	2 (28 x 18-cm) baking dishes
1 (8-inch [20-cm]) square baking dish	2 (8-inch) pie plates	2 (20-cm) pie plates
	1 (9-inch) deep dish pie plate	1 (23-cm) deep dish pie plate
	1 (9 x 5 x 3-inch) loaf pan	1 (23 x 13 x 7.5-cm) loaf pan
	1 (11 x 7-inch) baking dish	1 (28 x 18-cm) baking dish
1 (9-inch [23-cm]) square baking dish	2 (8-inch) pie plates	2 (20-cm) pie plates
	1 (9-inch) deep dish pie plate	1 (23-cm) deep dish pie plate
	1 (9 x 5 x 3-inch) loaf pan	1 (23 x 13 x 7.5-cm) loaf pan
	1 (11 x 7-inch) baking dish	1 (28 x 18-cm) baking dish

Common Ingredients: Yields and Equivalents

Knowing how many apples or carrots you may need for a recipe can be difficult, so here's a guide of common ingredients to help you when shopping for groceries and preparing recipes.

FOOD ITEM	IF YOUR RECIPE STATES	YOU WILL NEED APPROXIMATELY
Apples	1 cup (150 g) sliced or chopped	1 medium
	1 pound (455 g)	3 medium
Apricots, dried	1 cup (175 g)	5 ounces (175 g)
Bananas	1 cup (225 g) sliced	1 medium or 2 small
	1 cup (225 g) mashed	2 medium
Bread	12 slices (½-inch [1.3-cm] thick)	1-pound (455-g) loaf
Butter, nondairy	2 cups (450 g)	1 pound (455 g)
	½ cup (112 g)	1 stick
Carrots	1 cup (120 g) shredded	3 medium
Chocolate, baking	1 square or bar	1 ounce (28 g)
Chocolate chips	1 cup (175 g)	6 to 8 ounces (175 g)
Corn	1 medium ear	8 ounces (225 g)
	1 cup (155 g) kernels	2 medium ears
Crumbs, finely crushed		
Chocolate wafer cookie	1½ cups (150 g)	27 cookies
Graham cracker	1½ cups (150 g)	21 squares
Saltine cracker	1 cup (100 g)	29 squares
Vanilla wafer cookie	1½ cups (150 g)	38 cookies

FOOD ITEM	IF YOUR RECIPE STATES	YOU WILL NEED APPROXIMATELY
Flour	3½ cups (440 g)	1 pound (455 g)
Lemons or limes	1½ to 3 teaspoons grated peel (zest)	1 medium
	2 to 3 tablespoons (30 to 45 ml) juice	1 medium
Nuts, shelled		
Chopped, sliced, or slivered	1 cup (100 g)	4 ounces (115 g)
Whole or halves	3 to 4 cups (450 to 600 g)	1 pound (455 g)
Olives		
Pimiento-stuffed	1 cup (175 g) sliced	24 large or 36 small
Ripe, pitted	1 cup (100 g) sliced	32 medium
Oranges	1 to 2 tablespoons (5 to 10 g) grated peel (zest)	1 medium
	⅓ to ½ cup (80 to 120 ml) juice	1 medium
Sugar		
Brown	2¼ cups (500 g) firmly packed	1 pound (455 g)
Granulated	2¼ (450 g) cups	1 pound (455 g)
Powdered	4 cups (400 g)	1 pound (455 g)

Baking Soda and Baking Powder:
What's the Difference?

It's helpful to know what roles these two leaveners play in your baked goods.

BAKING SODA (SODIUM BICARBONATE)

When baking soda, an alkaline substance, is mixed with an acidic substance in a batter, it causes the baked good to rise. Examples of acidic foods are vinegar, citrus juice, chocolate, cocoa (not Dutch-processed), molasses, brown sugar, fruit, and maple syrup. Baking soda starts to react and release carbon dioxide gas as soon as it's added to the batter and moistened, so the batter needs to be baked immediately.

BAKING POWDER

Baking powder is a combination powder, containing baking soda, one or more acid salts (usually cream of tartar), and cornstarch to absorb any moisture. Also a leavening agent, it was developed as a "combination" powder that would help things rise when the batter didn't contain an acidic ingredient. A reaction takes place as soon as liquid is added to the batter, so again, the batter needs to be baked immediately.

SINGLE-ACTING BAKING POWDER

Single-acting baking powder starts to react as soon as liquid is added, so it needs to go into a preheated oven right away or it will lose its efficacy. In other words, the bubbles will begin to disappear. Another drawback is that no matter how dry these combination powders are kept, they lose their potency after a while.

DOUBLE-ACTING BAKING POWDER

When recipes in this cookbook call for baking powder, I recommend double-acting baking powder over single-acting baking powder. Its efficacy is increased because instead of cream of tartar there are two acids (usually calcium acid phosphate and sodium aluminum sulfate), one that reacts to the baking soda as soon as it's wet, and another that reacts when it's heated. This means you can be more leisurely about getting a dough or batter into the oven.

Note: Although calcium aluminum phosphate is also used as one of the acid salts in baking powder, I recommend purchasing the aluminum-free version. There is evidence of links between neurological problems and aluminum, and I just recommend erring on the side of caution.

WHEN TO USE WHICH

There is no situation where you must use baking soda, even when you have an acidic ingredient in your dough or batter. Because baking powder contains both baking soda and an acid, it will create carbon dioxide bubbles even when there's extra acid present.

You can choose to use baking powder alone. If you do, the flavor of the acidic ingredient (vinegar, etc.) will be slightly more pronounced since there is no baking soda to react with or neutralize it. The texture will also be a bit finer than the coarse or "shaggy" texture that is characteristically caused by the baking soda.

You may find you like the flavor and texture of things leavened with baking soda, or you may prefer baking powder. Experiment with both. Just remember that you can't use baking soda in place of baking powder without something acidic to react to it. Without something to neutralize it, it will leave a bitter, salty taste.

WHEN AND HOW TO USE BAKING SODA

Baking soda is used generally when there is an ingredient in a batter that is particularly acidic, such as citrus juice or molasses. Here are some ingredients that will react with ½ teaspoon of baking soda and can replace 2 teaspoons of baking powder. This list is by no means complete, but it may give you a sense of what ingredients can be used.

* 1 cup (235 ml) nondairy milk soured with 1 tablespoon (15 ml) vinegar or lemon juice
* 1 cup (230 g) nondairy yogurt
* 1 cup (235 ml) fruit or vegetable sauces or juice
* ¾ cup (170 g) brown sugar
* ¾ cup (255 g) molasses
* 2 tablespoon (30 ml) vinegar or lemon juice
* ½ cup (65 g) cocoa (not Dutch-processed cocoa, which has been "de-acidified")

WHEN AND HOW TO USE BAKING POWDER

First count the cups of flour your recipe calls for. You want to include at least 1 teaspoon of baking powder per cup. If your recipe contains a cup or more of "additional" ingredients, such as raisins or nuts, add another ½ teaspoon of baking powder per cup (125 g) of flour.

Suggested Reading

All of these books are available at ColleenPatrickGoudreau.com in my Amazon store.

Appetite for Profit: How the Food Industry Undermines Our Health and How to Fight Back by Michele Simon
This is an incredibly important book that finally explains why the answer to our food problems does not lie in the food corporations themselves. With brilliant insight and facts in hand, Simon's book empowers and motivates.

Becoming Vegan: The Complete Guide to Adopting a Healthy Plant-Based Diet by Vesanto Melina, M.S., R.D., and Brenda Davis, R.D.
Two of North America's foremost vegetarian dietitians present the most up-to-date findings on nutrition, disease prevention, and everything you need to know about being vegan or just eating healthfully. A resource for every home.

The China Study: Startling Implications for Diet, Weight Loss, and Long-Term Health by T. Colin Campbell, Ph.D.
This exhaustive presentation of the findings from the China Study conclusively demonstrates the link between nutrition and heart disease, diabetes, and cancer. Referred to as the "Grand Prix of epidemiology" by the New York Times, this study reveals the dramatic effect proper nutrition can have on reducing and reversing these ailments.

Diet for a New America: How Your Food Choices Affect Your Health, Happiness, and the Future of Life on Earth by John Robbins
An extraordinary exposé of the consequences our food choices have on the Earth, animals, and human health. By far the most popular book ever published on the subject matter.

Dominion: The Power of Man, the Suffering of Animals, and the Call to Mercy by Matthew Scully
Dominion is a plea for human benevolence and mercy, a scathing attack on those who would dismiss animal activists as mere sentimentalists, and a demand for reform from the government down to the individual. *Dominion* will appeal to the religious-minded.

Eat to Live: The Revolutionary Formula for Fast and Sustained Weight Loss by Joel Fuhrman, M.D.
With a focus on green leafy vegetables and beans, Dr. Fuhrman's plan is revolutionary in its simplicity. I love his no-nonsense approach to healthful eating.

***Fast Food Nation: The Dark Side of the All-American Meal* by Eric Schlosser**
Frequently using McDonald's as a template, Schlosser, an Atlantic Monthly correspondent, explains how the development of fast-food restaurants has led to the standardization of American culture, widespread obesity, urban sprawl, and more.

***Food Politics: How the Food Industry Influences Nutrition
and Health* by Marion Nestle, chair of nutrition and food studies at NYU**
Nestle offers an exposé of the tactics used by the food industry to protect its economic interests and influence public opinion.

***The Food Revolution: How Your Diet Can Help Save Your Life
and Our World* by John Robbins and Dean Ornish, M.D.**
What can we do to help stop global warming, feed the hungry, prevent cruelty to animals, avoid genetically modified foods, be healthier, and live longer? Eat vegetarian, Robbins argues. He demonstrates that individual dietary choices can be both empowering and have a broader impact.

***For the Prevention of Cruelty: The History and Legacy
of Animal Rights Activism in the United States* by Diane Beers**
I can safely say I think this is one of the most important books to be published—not only for the animal protection movement but also for all social justice causes. Diane is an eloquent writer and has created a fascinating narrative that would interest anyone who's ever adopted a dog or a cat, donated to the local SPCA, or worked on behalf of the voiceless. I highly recommend this book!

***Mad Cowboy: Plain Truth from the Cattle Rancher
Who Won't Eat Meat* by Howard Lyman**
Persuasive, straightforward, and full of down-home good humor and optimism, *Mad Cowboy* is both an inspirational story of personal transformation and a convincing call to action for a plant-based diet.

***Pleasurable Kingdom: Animals and the Nature of Feeling Good* by Jonathan Balcombe**
As a leading animal behavior researcher, Balcombe offers elegant arguments and shares endearing stories in this important book.

***Slaughterhouse: The Shocking Story of Greed, Neglect,
and Inhumane Treatment Inside the U.S. Meat Industry* by Gail Eisnitz**
This book exposes the cruel industry that turns live animals into sterile, cellophane-wrapped food in the meat display case. The testimony of dozens of slaughterhouse workers and USDA inspectors reveals the nightmarish truth as innocent, sentient, and intelligent horses, cows, pigs, and chickens are forced into interminable agony.

Striking at the Roots: A Practical Guide to Animal Activism by Mark Hawthorne
This comprehensive book brings together the most effective tactics for speaking out for animals and gives voice to activists from around the globe, who explain why their models of activism have been successful—and how you can get involved. A fantastic book that's been a long time coming!

An Unnatural Order: Why We Are Destroying the Planet and Each Other by Jim Mason
Mason—attorney, journalist, and coauthor of *Animal Factories*—examines how our nature-alienated culture deprives us of kinship with the rest of the natural world, stifles empathy, and destroys our sense of continuity with other living things.

Why We Love Dogs, Eat Pigs, and Wear Cows: An Introduction to Carnism by Melanie Joy
This groundbreaking work, voted one of the top ten books of 2010 by VegNews Magazine, offers an absorbing look at why and how humans can so wholeheartedly devote ourselves to certain animals and then allow others to suffer needlessly, especially those slaughtered for our consumption.

World Peace Diet: Eating for Spiritual Health and Social Harmony by Will Tuttle, Ph.D.
The author of this eloquently written book challenges our thinking about our relationship to nonhuman animals with respect, sensitivity, and grace. His understanding of the human psyche is deep. His use of language is divine, and his compassion jumps off each and every page.

Suggested Viewing

The Cove
Cowspiracy
Earthlings
Forks Over Knives
Peaceable Kingdom
Sick, Fat, and Nearly Dead
Vegucated
Virunga

FINDING YOUR WAY: THE INDICES

Index I: General

A

agar, 26, 114, 260, 272
    No-Bake Chocolate Pudding
        Tart, 114
agave nectar, 260
    Almond or Cashew Milk, 234
    Baklava, 172
    Fruit Compote, 155
    Ginger Tea, 239
    Panforte, 210–211
    Sautéed Bananas, 150
    Whole Wheat Bread, 179–181
agraz, 215
allspice and allspice berries, 263
    Apple Cake, 78
    Baklava, 172
    Carrot Cake, 82
    Fall Fruit Crisp, 152–153
    Panforte, 210–211
    Rice Pudding, 198–199
    Wassail, 237
Almond or Cashew Milk, 234
almond trees, 234
almonds and almond products, 65,
    162–163, 265
    Almond or Cashew Milk, 234
    Apple Crumble, 141
    Baked Apples, 148
    Baklava, 172
    Berry Smoothie, 218–219
    Chocolate Almond Brittle, 208
    Chocolate Almond Spread,
        257
    Chocolate Cherry Strudel, 164
    Classic Currant Scones, 54–55
    Cranberry Nut Bread, 65
    Date and Almond Butter
        Smoothie, 220
    Mexican Wedding Cookies,
        122–123
    No-Bake Pecan Crust, 226

    Panforte, 210–211
    Royal Icing, 250–251
    Stuffed Dates, 159
amaretto, in Hot Cocoa, 230
anise, 126, 263
    Fall Fruit Crisp, 152–153
    Pine Nut Anise Cookies, 126
Apfelstrudel, 162–163
Apple Cake, 78
apple cider. *See* ciders
Apple Cobbler, 144
Apple Crumble, 141
Apple Pecan Muffins, 44–45
Apple Pie, 108–109
Apple Strudel (*Apfelstrudel*), 162–163
apples and apple products, 148, 157,
    162–163. *See also* applesauce as
    ingredient
    Apple Cake, 78
    Apple Cobbler, 144
    Apple Crumble, 142
    Apple Pecan Muffins, 44–45
    Apple Pie, 108–109
    Applesauce, 156
    Baked Apples, 148
    Chocolate-Dipped Fruit, 160
    Cinnamon Coffee Cake, 90
    Fall Fruit Crisp, 152–153
    Fat-Free Crust, 226
    German Apple Cake, 80–81
    Mulled Cider, 236
    Pancakes, 71
    Party Punch, 240
    Pear Tart, 115
    Waffles II, 74
    Wassail, 237
Applesauce, 156
applesauce as ingredient, 22
Apple Pecan Muffins, 44–45
    Chocolate Brownies, 132
    German Apple Cake, 80–81

    Pumpkin Spice Bread, 68–69
    Zucchini Bread, 64
apricots, dried
    Apple Cake, 78
    Baked Apples, 148
    Dried Fruit and Coconut
        Candies, 212
    Fruit Compote, 155
    Pineapple Walnut Bars, 140
aquafaba, 25
arrowroot, 26, 263
    No-Bake Chocolate Peanut
        Butter Pie, 106

B

bain marie, 191
Baked Apples, 148
Baked Pumpkin Pudding, 202
baking, vegan
    eggs and egg replacers, 20–26
    equipment for, 113, 267–269
    ingredients, 260–266, 280–281
    milk and nondairy milk, 27–31
    pan sizes, 276–279
    recipe use, 34–37
    tips for, 36–38, 39, 57, 75, 79,
        101, 111, 121, 175–177, 183
baking chocolate, 261
baking powder and baking soda,
    20–21, 39, 79, 260, 282–283
Baklava, 172
Banana Chocolate Chip Muffins, 42
Banana Crumble, 143
bananas, 22
    Almond or Cashew Milk, 234
    Banana Chocolate Chip
        Muffins, 42
    Banana Crumble, 143
    Bananas Foster, 151
    Bananas in Sweet Coconut
        Milk, 150

Berry Smoothie, 218–219
Bread Pudding, 200
Chocolate Banana Shake, 216–217
Chocolate Bread Pudding, 201
Chocolate-Dipped Fruit, 160
Chocolate Mousse, 192–193
Date and Almond Butter Smoothie, 220
Fruit Tart, 116
Holiday Nog, 235
Pastry Cream, 256
Sautéed Bananas, 150
Tropical Smoothie, 219
Waffles I, 72–73
Bananas Foster, 151
Bananas in Sweet Coconut Milk, 150
bars. See also cookies, 117
Chocolate Brownies, 132
Date Bars, 138
Lemon Bars, 136–137
Peanut Butter Chocolate Bars, 139
Pineapple Walnut Bars, 140
Raspberry Oatmeal Bars, 133
basic glaze, 241
basil, in Mediterranean Olive Bread, 62–63
Bee Free Honee
Baklava, 172
Fruit Compote, 155
Sautéed Bananas, 150
Whole Wheat Bread, 179–181
berries, 43. See also various berries
Banana Crumble, 143
Berry Smoothie, 218–219
Chocolate Mousse, 192–193
Pancakes, 71
Berry Smoothie, 218–219
beverages, 229
Almond or Cashew Milk, 234
Chai Tea, 238
Chocolate Milk, 233
Ginger Tea, 239
Holiday Nog, 235
Hot Chocolate, 231
Hot Cocoa, 230
Mexican Horchata, 233
Mexican Hot Chocolate I, 231
Mexican Hot Chocolate II, 232
Mulled Cider, 236
Party Punch, 240
Wassail, 237

biscuits, 39
Drop Biscuits, 52
Black Forest Strudel, 164
blintzes, 169
blueberries, 83, 107
Berry Smoothie, 218–219
Blueberry Cake, 83
Blueberry Cobbler, 146–147
Blueberry Cream Cheese Blintzes, 169
Blueberry Lemon Muffins, 43
Blueberry Orange Bundt Cake, 88–89
Blueberry Pie, 107
Cinnamon Coffee Cake, 90
Classic Currant Scones, 54–55
Corn Muffins, 47
Cornbread, 58–59
Fruit Compote, 155
Lemon Bars, 136–137
Pancakes, 71
Blueberry Cake, 83
Blueberry Cobbler, 146–147
Blueberry Cream Cheese Blintzes, 169
Blueberry Lemon Muffins, 43
Blueberry Orange Bundt Cake, 88–89
Blueberry Pie, 107
Bob's Red Mill Egg Replacer, 24
bran, 46, 51. See also oat bran; wheat bran
Bran Muffins with Raisins, 46
brandy
Bananas Foster, 151
Holiday Nog, 235
Hot Cocoa, 230
Wassail, 237
bread as ingredient
Bread Pudding, 200
Chocolate Bread Pudding, 201
Bread Pudding, 200
breads, quick, 57
Brown Bread, 67
Cornbread, 58–59
Cranberry Nut Bread, 65
Fig Date Bread, 70
Irish Soda Bread, 66
Mediterranean Olive Bread, 62–63
Pancakes, 71
Pumpkin Spice Bread, 68–69
Waffles I, 72–73
Waffles II, 74

Zucchini Bread, 64
breads, yeast, 175–177, 183
Chocolate Babka, 188–189
Cinnamon Rolls, 185–187
Focaccia, 182
Leavened North Indian Bread, 178
Soft Pretzels, 184
Whole Wheat Bread, 179–181
Brown Bread, 67
brown rice syrup, 174
Whole Wheat Bread, 179–181
Brown Sugar Syrup, 257
Apple Cake, 78
Blueberry Cream Cheese Blintzes, 169
Pancakes, 71
Waffles II, 74
Brownie Crust, 227
No-Bake Chocolate Peanut Butter Pie, 106
No-Bake Chocolate Pudding Tart, 114
brownies, 117. See also bars
Chocolate Brownies, 132
Buttercream Frosting, 247
Chocolate Cake, 76–77
Strawberry Cupcakes, 93
buttermilk, 30
butter(s), 26, 33–34, 260, 270, 280
Butterscotch Pudding, 195

C
cacao, 77, 261
cakes and cupcakes, 75, 79, 93
Apple Cake, 78
Blueberry Cake, 83
Blueberry Orange Bundt Cake, 88–89
Carrot Cake, 82
Chocolate Cake, 76–77
Chocolate Cheesecake, 97
Chocolate Cream Cheese Cupcakes, 92
Chocolate Peanut Butter Cupcakes, 96
Cinnamon Coffee Cake, 90
decorating, 87
German Apple Cake, 80–81
Lemon Cheesecake, 98–99
Light Lemon Bundt Cake, 86
Pumpkin Cheesecake, 100
Strawberry Cupcakes, 93

Vanilla Cupcakes, 91
calcium, 105
candied fruit
　　Cranberry Nut Bread, 65
　　Panforte, 210–211
candy, 203
　　Caramel Popcorn, 204–205
　　Caramelized Pecans, 207
　　Chocolate Almond Brittle, 208
　　Chocolate Coconut
　　　　Macaroons, 209
　　Chocolate Fudge, 206
　　Dried Fruit and Coconut
　　　　Candies, 212
　　Panforte, 210–211
canola oil, 261
cantaloupe, in Tropical Smoothie, 219
capers, 263
Caramel Popcorn, 204–205
Caramelized Pecans (Pralines), 207
caraway, 31–32, 263
cardamom, 263
　　Chai Tea, 238
　　Cinnamon Coffee Cake, 90
　　Holiday Nog, 235
Carrot Cake, 82
cashew butter, in Chocolate Almond
　　Spread, 257
Cashew Cream, 255
　　Baked Pumpkin Pudding, 202
　　Chocolate Pudding, 194
cashews, 265
　　Almond or Cashew Milk, 234
　　Cashew Cream, 255
cayenne pepper
　　Caramelized Pecans, 207
　　Chocolate Pudding, 194
　　Hot Cocoa, 230
　　Mexican Hot Chocolate I, 231
Chai Tea, 238
Champagne, in Poached Pears, 149
cheesecakes, 98
　　Chocolate Cheesecake, 97
　　Lemon Cheesecake, 98–99
　　Pumpkin Cheesecake, 100
cherries
　　Berry Smoothie, 218–219
　　Cherry Pie, 111
　　Chocolate Cherry Strudel, 164
　　Chocolate-Dipped Fruit, 160
　　Fruit Compote, 155
Cherry Pie, 111
chile peppers, in Drop Biscuits, 52

chili powder, 263
　　Chocolate Cake, 76–77
　　Mexican Hot Chocolate I, 231
chives, in Drop Biscuits, 52
chocolate, 77, 118, 229, 231, 260–261.
　　See also cocoa powder
　　Chocolate Almond Brittle, 208
　　Chocolate Almond Spread,
　　　　257
　　Chocolate Babka, 188–189
　　Chocolate Banana Shake,
　　　　216–217
　　Chocolate Bread Pudding, 201
　　Chocolate Brownies, 132
　　Chocolate Cheesecake, 97
　　Chocolate Cherry Strudel, 164
　　Chocolate Chip Cookies,
　　　　118–119
　　Chocolate Chip Mint Cookies,
　　　　120
　　Chocolate Chip Scones, 53
　　Chocolate Crinkles, 131
　　Chocolate-Dipped Fruit, 160
　　Chocolate Fudge, 206
　　Chocolate Mousse, 192–193
　　Chocolate Pudding, 194
　　Hearty Spiced Cocoa Muffins,
　　　　49
　　Mexican Hot Chocolate I, 231
　　Mexican Hot Chocolate II, 232
　　No-Bake Chocolate Peanut
　　　　Butter Pie, 106
　　No-Bake Chocolate Pudding
　　　　Tart, 114
　　No-Bake Strawberry Pie
　　　　with Chocolate Chunks,
　　　　102–103
　　Pancakes, 71
　　Peanut Butter Chocolate Bars,
　　　　139
　　Peanut Butter Cookies,
　　　　124–125
　　Pumpkin Spice Bread, 68–69
　　Waffles I, 72–73
Chocolate Almond Brittle, 208
Chocolate Almond Spread, 257
Chocolate Babka (Polish Bread),
　　188–189
Chocolate Banana Shake, 216–217
Chocolate Bread Pudding, 201
Chocolate Brownies, 132
Chocolate Cake, 76–77
Chocolate Cheesecake, 97

Chocolate Cherry Strudel (Black
　　Forest Strudel), 164
Chocolate Chip Cookies, 118–119
Chocolate Chip Mint Cookies, 120
Chocolate Chip Scones, 53
Chocolate Coconut Macaroons, 209
Chocolate Cream Cheese Cupcakes,
　　92
Chocolate Crinkles, 131
Chocolate-Dipped Fruit, 160
Chocolate Frosting, 242
　　Chocolate Cake, 76–77
　　Chocolate Peanut Butter
　　　　Cupcakes, 96
　　Vanilla Cupcakes, 91
Chocolate Fudge, 206
Chocolate Fudge Sauce, 252
Chocolate Milk, 233
Chocolate Mousse, 192–193
Chocolate Peanut Butter Cupcakes,
　　96
Chocolate Peanut Butter Frosting,
　　243
　　Chocolate Peanut Butter
　　　　Cupcakes, 96
　　Vanilla Cupcakes, 91
Chocolate Pudding, 194
Chocolate Sauce, 252
　　Chocolate Milk, 233
ciders, 21, 61, 229
　　Applesauce, 156
　　Baked Apples, 148
　　Mulled Cider, 236
　　Poached Pears, 149
　　Wassail, 237
cinnamon, 263
　　Apple Cake, 78
　　Apple Cobbler, 144
　　Apple Crumble, 142
　　Apple Pecan Muffins, 44–45
　　Apple Pie, 108–109
　　Apple Strudel, 162–163
　　Applesauce, 156
　　Baked Apples, 148
　　Baked Pumpkin Pudding, 202
　　Baklava, 172
　　Bananas Foster, 151
　　Bananas in Sweet Coconut
　　　　Milk, 150
　　Blueberry Cake, 83
　　Blueberry Cream Cheese
　　　　Blintzes, 169
　　Blueberry Lemon Muffins, 43

Bread Pudding, 200
Caramelized Pecans, 207
Carrot Cake, 82
Chai Tea, 238
Chocolate Babka, 188–189
Chocolate Cherry Strudel, 164
Chocolate Chip Scones, 53
Chocolate Pudding, 194
Cinnamon Coffee Cake, 90
Cinnamon Rolls, 185–187
Classic Currant Scones, 54–55
Cream Cheese Frosting, 246
Date and Almond Butter
    Smoothie, 220
Date Bars, 138
Fall Fruit Crisp, 152–153
Fruit Compote, 155
German Apple Cake, 80–81
Gingerbread Cookies, 130
Gingerbread Scones, 56
Graham Cracker Crust, 223
Hearty Spiced Cocoa Muffins,
    49
Holiday Nog, 235
Hot Cocoa, 230
Jam-Filled Oat Bran Muffins,
    50–51
Mexican Horchata, 233
Mexican Hot Chocolate I, 231
Mexican Hot Chocolate II, 232
Mulled Cider, 236
Oatmeal Raisin Cookies,
    128–129
Pancakes, 71
Panforte, 210–211
Party Punch, 240
Peach Pie, 110
Pear Tart, 115
Pecan Crust, 223
Poached Pears, 149
Pumpkin Cheesecake, 100
Pumpkin Pie, 112–113
Pumpkin Spice Bread, 68–69
Rice Pudding, 198–199
Rugelach, 170–171
Sautéed Bananas, 150
Waffles II, 74
Wassail, 237
Zucchini Bread, 64
Cinnamon Coffee Cake, 90
Cinnamon Rolls, 185–187
Classic Currant Scones, 54–55
clementines, in Party Punch, 240

cloves, 263
    Apple Cake, 78
    Baklava, 172
    Bananas in Sweet Coconut
        Milk, 150
    Carrot Cake, 82
    Chai Tea, 238
    Gingerbread Cookies, 130
    Gingerbread Scones, 56
    Hearty Spiced Cocoa Muffins,
        49
    Holiday Nog, 235
    Mulled Cider, 236
    Panforte, 210–211
    Party Punch, 240
    Poached Pears, 149
    Pumpkin Cheesecake, 100
    Pumpkin Pie, 112–113
    Pumpkin Spice Bread, 68–69
    Wassail, 237
Cobbler Biscuit Dough
    Apple Cobbler, 144
    Blueberry Cobbler, 146–147
cobblers, 145. See also crisps;
    crumbles
    Apple Cobbler, 144
    Blueberry Cobbler, 146–147
cocoa butter, 77, 261
cocoa powder, 77, 261. See also
    chocolate
    Almond or Cashew Milk, 234
    Brownie Crust, 227
    Chocolate Babka, 188–189
    Chocolate Brownies, 132
    Chocolate Cake, 76–77
    Chocolate Chip Mint Cookies,
        120
    Chocolate Coconut
        Macaroons, 209
    Chocolate Cream Cheese
        Cupcakes, 92
    Chocolate Frosting, 242
    Chocolate Fudge, 206
    Chocolate Fudge Sauce, 252
    Chocolate Peanut Butter
        Cupcakes, 96
    Chocolate Peanut Butter
        Frosting, 243
    Chocolate Pudding, 194
    Chocolate Sauce, 252
    Hearty Spiced Cocoa Muffins,
        49
    Hot Cocoa, 230

No-Bake Chocolate Pudding
    Tart, 114
coconut and coconut products, 261.
    See also milk, coconut
    Banana Crumble, 143
    Blueberry Orange Bundt Cake,
        88–89
    Brownie Crust, 227
    Cashew Cream, 255
    Chocolate Cake, 76–77
    Chocolate Coconut
        Macaroons, 209
    Date Bars, 138
    Dried Fruit and Coconut
        Candies, 212
    Pineapple Walnut Bars, 140
    Tropical Smoothie, 219
Coconut Pudding, 196
coffee
    Chocolate Mousse, 192–193
    Hot Cocoa, 230
cognac, in Holiday Nog, 235
Cointreau, in Crêpes Suzette, 168
confectioners' sugar, 123, 173
confections. See candy
conserves, 133
Cookie Crust, 222
    Chocolate Cheesecake, 97
    No-Bake Chocolate Peanut
        Butter Pie, 106
cookies, 117, 121, 272. See also bars
    Chocolate Chip Cookies,
        118–119
    Chocolate Chip Mint Cookies,
        120
    Chocolate Crinkles, 131
    Gingerbread Cookies, 130
    Mexican Wedding Cookies,
        122–123
    Oatmeal Raisin Cookies,
        128–129
    Peanut Butter Cookies,
        124–125
    Pine Nut Anise Cookies, 126
    Sugar Cookies, 127
cookies, vegan
    Chocolate Cherry Strudel, 164
    Cookie Crust, 222
cooking oils, 261–262
cooking terms, 273–275
coriander, 263
corn and corn products, 26, 47, 59,
    262

Caramel Popcorn, 204–205
Corn Muffins, 47
Cornbread, 58–59
Waffles II, 74
Corn Muffins, 47
Cornbread, 58–59
Coulis, 248
cranberries and cranberry products, 65
Classic Currant Scones, 54–55
Cranberry Nut Bread, 65
Fall Fruit Crisp, 152–153
Party Punch, 240
Wassail, 237
Cranberry Nut Bread, 65
Cream Cheese Frosting, 82, 246
cream cheese, nondairy, 271
Blueberry Cream Cheese Blintzes, 169
Chocolate Cheesecake, 97
Chocolate Cream Cheese Cupcakes, 92
Cream Cheese Frosting, 246
Lemon Cheesecake, 98–99
Pear Tart, 115
Pumpkin Cheesecake, 100
Rugelach, 170–171
cream of tartar, 263
crème de menthe, in Hot Cocoa, 230
crêpes, 161, 167
Blueberry Cream Cheese Blintzes, 169
Crêpes Suzette, 168
Dessert Crêpes, 166–167
Crêpes Suzette, 168
crisps. See also cobblers; crumbles, 145
Fall Fruit Crisp, 152–153
crispy rice cereal, in Peanut Butter Chocolate Bars, 139
croutons, 180
crumbles, 142, 145. See also cobblers; crisps
Apple Crumble, 142
Banana Crumble, 143
crusts, 101, 111, 113, 221, 225
Brownie Crust, 227
Cookie Crust, 222
Fat-Free Crust, 226
Flaky Pie Crust, 224
Graham Cracker Crust, 223
No-Bake Pecan Crust, 226
Pecan Crust, 223

Shortbread Crust, 222
cupcakes. See cakes and cupcakes
currants
Bread Pudding, 200
Classic Currant Scones, 54–55
Drop Biscuits, 52
Gingerbread Scones, 56
curry powder, 263
Custard, 256

D
dairy products, 17, 19, 154
Date and Almond Butter Smoothie, 220
Date Bars, 138
dates, 159, 226, 262
Almond or Cashew Milk, 234
Apple Cake, 78
Baked Apples, 148
Berry Smoothie, 218–219
Date and Almond Butter Smoothie, 220
Date Bars, 138
Dried Fruit and Coconut Candies, 212
Fig Date Bread, 70
Fruit Compote, 155
No-Bake Pecan Crust, 226
No-Bake Strawberry Pie with Chocolate Chunks, 102–103
Stuffed Dates, 159
Dessert Crêpes, 166–167
Blueberry Cream Cheese Blintzes, 169
Crêpes Suzette, 168
desserts, 60–61
Dried Fruit and Coconut Candies, 212
Drop Biscuits, 52
Dutch-processed cocoa, 261

E
eggs and egg replacers, 19–26, 116, 197, 256, 270–271
Ener-G Egg Replacer, 24
Apple Pecan Muffins, 44–45, 46
Chocolate Cheesecake, 97
Chocolate Chip Cookies, 118–119
Dessert Crêpes, 166–167
Japanese Cookie Bread, 190
Lemon Cheesecake, 98–99

Pumpkin Cheesecake, 100
Royal Icing, 250–251
Sugar Cookies, 127
euphemisms, 228

F
Fall Fruit Crisp, 152–153
Fat-Free Crust, 226
fennel, 263
Applesauce, 156
fiber, 51, 69, 70
Fig Date Bread, 70
figs, 70, 262
Fig Date Bread, 70
Flaky Pie Crust, 224
Apple Pie, 108–109
Blueberry Pie, 107
Cherry Pie, 111
Peach Pie, 110
Pumpkin Pie, 112–113
flaxseed, 21, 44, 262, 272
Apple Cake, 78
Apple Pecan Muffins, 44
Berry Smoothie, 218–219
Blueberry Cake, 83
Bran Muffins with Raisins, 46
Carrot Cake, 82
Chocolate Brownies, 132
Chocolate Chip Cookies, 118–119
Chocolate Chip Mint Cookies, 120
Chocolate Chip Scones, 53
Chocolate Cream Cheese Cupcakes, 92
Chocolate Crinkles, 131
Classic Currant Scones, 54–55
Corn Muffins, 47
Cranberry Nut Bread, 65
Fig Date Bread, 70
Ginger Muffins, 48
Gingerbread Cookies, 130
Hearty Spiced Cocoa Muffins, 49
Jam-Filled Oat Bran Muffins, 50–51
Leavened North Indian Bread, 178
Light Lemon Bundt Cake, 86
Mediterranean Olive Bread, 62–63
Oatmeal Raisin Cookies, 128–129

Peanut Butter Cookies, 124–125
Pumpkin Spice Bread, 68–69
Tropical Smoothie, 219
Vanilla Cupcakes, 91
Waffles I, 72–73
Waffles II, 74
Zucchini Bread, 64
flour, 26, 176
Focaccia, 182
frostings and glazes, 91, 241. *See also* sauces
Buttercream Frosting, 247
Chocolate Frosting, 242
Chocolate Peanut Butter Frosting, 243
Cream Cheese Frosting, 246
Maple Glaze, 56
Royal Icing, 250–251
fruit, dried, 212
Chocolate-Dipped Fruit, 160
fruit butter, 133
Fruit Compote, 155
Fruit Tart, 116

G
garlic, in Focaccia, 182
gelatin, 114, 271
German Apple Cake (*Versunkener Apfelkuchen*), 80–81
ginger, 48, 239, 263
Applesauce, 156
Baked Apples, 148
Baked Pumpkin Pudding, 202
Baklava, 172
Blueberry Cream Cheese Blintzes, 169
Chai Tea, 238
Cinnamon Coffee Cake, 90
German Apple Cake, 80–81
Ginger Muffins, 48
Ginger Tea, 239
Gingerbread Cookies, 130
Gingerbread Scones, 56
Pumpkin Cheesecake, 100
Pumpkin Pie, 112–113
Rice Pudding, 198–199
ginger ale, 239
ginger beer, 239
Ginger Muffins, 48
Ginger Tea, 239
Gingerbread Cookies, 130
Gingerbread Scones, 56

glazes. *See* frostings and glazes
Graham Cracker Crust, 223
Lemon Cheesecake, 98–99
No-Bake Chocolate Peanut Butter Pie, 106
Pumpkin Cheesecake, 100
graham crackers
Chocolate Almond Brittle, 208
Chocolate Cherry Strudel, 164
Graham Cracker Crust, 223
Grand Marnier
Crêpes Suzette, 168
Strawberry Sorbet, 214
granita, 215
Grape Nuts Cereal, in Fat-Free Crust, 226
Grenadine syrup, 249
grits, 47

H
hazelnuts and hazelnut products, 265
Chocolate Almond Brittle, 208
Chocolate Almond Spread, 257
Classic Currant Scones, 54–55
Cranberry Nut Bread, 65
Hot Cocoa, 230
Mexican Wedding Cookies, 122–123
Panforte, 210–211
Hearty Spiced Cocoa Muffins, 49
herbs, 263–264
Holiday Nog, 235
hominy, 47
honey, 174
Hot Chocolate, 231
Hot Cocoa, 230

I
ice cream, nondairy
Banana Crumble, 143
Bananas Foster, 151
Blueberry Pie, 107
Peach Melba, 154
Vanilla Shake, 216
icings. *See* frostings and glazes
ingredient yields and equivalents, 280–281
Irish Soda Bread, 66
Irish Whiskey, in Chocolate Mousse, 192–193
Italian herbs, in Focaccia, 182

J
Jam-Filled Oat Bran Muffins, 50–51
jams and jellies, 133, 264
Chocolate Babka, 188–189
Fruit Tart, 116
Jam-Filled Oat Bran Muffins, 50–51
Raspberry Oatmeal Bars, 133
Rugelach, 170–171
Waffles II, 74
Japanese Cookie Bread, 190

K
kitchen tools, 267–269
kiwi, in Fruit Tart, 116
Kow Neuw Mamuang, 158
kudzu root, 25, 264–265, 272
Chocolate Fudge Sauce, 252
Chocolate Pudding, 194
No-Bake Chocolate Peanut Butter Pie, 106

L
Leavened North Indian Bread, 178
lemon and lemon products, 137, 162–163
Apple Pie, 108–109
Blueberry Cobbler, 146–147
Blueberry Cream Cheese Blintzes, 169
Blueberry Lemon Muffins, 43
Blueberry Orange Bundt Cake, 88–89
Blueberry Pie, 107
Cherry Pie, 111
Classic Currant Scones, 54–55
Cranberry Nut Bread, 65
Cream Cheese Frosting, 246
Dried Fruit and Coconut Candies, 212
Fall Fruit Crisp, 152–153
Ginger Muffins, 48
Ginger Tea, 239
Lemon Bars, 136–137
Lemon Cheesecake, 98–99
Lemon Sauce, 248
Light Lemon Bundt Cake, 86
Mulled Cider, 236
No-Bake Strawberry Pie with Chocolate Chunks, 102–103
Party Punch, 240
Pastry Cream, 256

Pineapple Walnut Bars, 140
Raspberry Sorbet, 215
Royal Icing, 250–251
Strawberry Sorbet, 214
Tofu Whipped Topping, 254
Lemon Bars, 136–137
Lemon Cheesecake, 98–99
Lemon Sauce, 248
Light Lemon Bundt Cake, 86
    Light Lemon Bundt Cake, 86
limes, in Blueberry Cobbler, 146–147
liqueurs
    Bananas Foster, 151
    Chocolate Mousse, 192–193
    Cream Cheese Frosting, 246
    Tofu Whipped Topping, 254
    Wassail, 237

M
macaroons, 209
mandarin oranges, in Party Punch, 240
Mango with Sticky Rice (*Kow Neuw Mamuang*) 158
mangoes
    Chocolate-Dipped Fruit, 160
    Coconut Pudding, 196
    Mango with Sticky Rice, 158
    Tropical Smoothie, 219
Maple Glaze, in Gingerbread Scones, 56
maple syrup, 265
    Almond or Cashew Milk, 234
    Blueberry Cream Cheese Blintzes, 169
    Brownie Crust, 227
    Cashew Cream, 255
    Date and Almond Butter Smoothie, 220
    Fall Fruit Crisp, 152–153
    Gingerbread Scones, 56
    Holiday Nog, 235
    Light Lemon Bundt Cake, 86
    Maple Glaze, 56
    Pancakes, 71
    Pecan Crust, 223
    Pine Nut Anise Cookies, 126
    Pumpkin Pie, 112–113
    Tofu Whipped Topping, 254
    Waffles II, 74
    Whole Wheat Bread, 179–181
marjoram, 264
marmalade, 133

marshmallows, vegetarian, 230, 271
    Hot Cocoa, 230
mayonnaise, eggless, 271
Mediterranean Olive Bread, 62–63
Melonpan (Japanese Cookie Bread), 190
Mexican Horchata, 233
Mexican Hot Chocolate I, 231
Mexican Hot Chocolate II, 232
Mexican Wedding Cookies, 122–123
milk, almond, 28, 234, 270
milk, cashew, 29
milk, coconut, 29. *See also* coconut and coconut products
    Bananas in Sweet Coconut Milk, 150
    Chocolate Fudge, 206
    Chocolate Pudding, 194
    Coconut Pudding, 196
    Mango with Sticky Rice, 158
    No-Bake Chocolate Peanut Butter Pie, 106
milk, condensed, 30
milk, cow's, 27, 104–105
milk, hazelnut, 28, 270
milk, nondairy, 270
milk, oat, 28, 270
    Jam-Filled Oat Bran Muffins, 50–51
milk, rice, 28
mint and mint products, 264
    Chocolate Chip Mint Cookies, 120
    Chocolate Frosting, 242
    Chocolate Pudding, 194
    Poached Pears, 149
mixed peel, 265
molasses, 265
    Gingerbread Cookies, 130
    Gingerbread Scones, 56
    Whole Wheat Bread, 179–181
mousses. *See* puddings and mousses
muffins, 39, 93
    Apple Pecan Muffins, 44–45
    Banana Chocolate Chip Muffins, 42
    Blueberry Lemon Muffins, 43
    Bran Muffins with Raisins, 46
    Corn Muffins, 47
    Ginger Muffins, 48
    Hearty Spiced Cocoa Muffins, 49

    Jam-Filled Oat Bran Muffins, 50–51
Mulled Cider, 236

N
Naan (Leavened North Indian Bread), 178
No-Bake Chocolate Peanut Butter Pie, 106
No-Bake Chocolate Pudding Tart, 114
No-Bake Pecan Crust, 226
No-Bake Strawberry Pie with Chocolate Chunks, 102–103
nut butters. *See also* almonds and almond products; butter(s), 26
nutmeg, 264, 265
    Almond or Cashew Milk, 234
    Apple Cake, 78
    Apple Crumble, 142
    Apple Pie, 108–109
    Applesauce, 156
    Baked Apples, 148
    Baked Pumpkin Pudding, 202
    Baklava, 172
    Banana Crumble, 143
    Bananas Foster, 151
    Bananas in Sweet Coconut Milk, 150
    Blueberry Lemon Muffins, 43
    Bread Pudding, 200
    Carrot Cake, 82
    Chocolate Cherry Strudel, 164
    Dessert Crêpes, 166–167
    Fall Fruit Crisp, 152–153
    Gingerbread Cookies, 130
    Holiday Nog, 235
    Oatmeal Raisin Cookies, 128–129
    Panforte, 210–211
    Peach Pie, 110
    Pumpkin Cheesecake, 100
    Pumpkin Pie, 112–113
    Pumpkin Spice Bread, 68–69
    Rice Pudding, 198–199
    Vanilla Shake, 216–217
    Zucchini Bread, 64
nuts. *See also various nuts*
    Blueberry Cream Cheese Blintzes, 169
    Chocolate Babka, 188–189
    Chocolate Chip Cookies, 118–119
    Chocolate-Dipped Fruit, 160

Chocolate Fudge, 206
Irish Soda Bread, 66
No-Bake Chocolate Peanut
Butter Pie, 106

O
oat bran, 51
Jam-Filled Oat Bran Muffins,
50–51
Oatmeal Raisin Cookies,
128–129
Oatmeal Raisin Cookies, 128–129
oats, 129
Banana Crumble, 143
Brown Bread, 67
Chocolate Coconut Maca-
roons, 209
Date Bars, 138
Fall Fruit Crisp, 152–153
Gingerbread Scones, 56
Oatmeal Raisin Cookies,
128–129
Pecan Crust, 223
Raspberry Oatmeal Bars, 133
Waffles II, 74
olive oil, 261–262
Mediterranean Olive Bread,
62–63
olives, 265
Focaccia, 182
Mediterranean Olive Bread,
62–63
onions, Focaccia, 182
oranges and orange products
Berry Smoothie, 218–219
Blueberry Orange Bundt Cake,
88–89
Chocolate-Dipped Fruit, 160
Classic Currant Scones, 54–55
Cranberry Nut Bread, 65
Cream Cheese Frosting, 246
Crêpes Suzette, 168
Dried Fruit and Coconut Can-
dies, 212
Fruit Compote, 155
Pancakes, 71
Poached Pears, 149
Tropical Smoothie, 219
Wassail, 237
oregano, 264
organic food, importance of, 22, 59,
103, 174, 271

P
Pancakes, 71
Panforte, 210–211
papaya
Coconut Pudding, 196
Tropical Smoothie, 219
paprika, 264
parsley, 264
Party Punch, 240
pastries
Apple Strudel, 162–163
Baklava, 172
Blueberry Cream Cheese
Blintzes, 169
Chocolate Cherry Strudel, 164
Crêpes Suzette, 168
Dessert Crêpes, 166–167
Rugelach, 170–171
Pastry Cream (Custard), 256
Fruit Tart, 116
Peach Melba, 154
Peach Pie, 110
peach trees, 110
peaches
Pancakes, 71
Peach Melba, 154
Peach Pie, 110
peanut butter, 139
Chocolate Almond Spread,
257
Chocolate Fudge, 206
Chocolate Peanut Butter Cup-
cakes, 96
Chocolate Peanut Butter
Frosting, 243
No-Bake Chocolate Peanut
Butter Pie, 106
Peanut Butter Chocolate Bars,
139
Peanut Butter Cookies,
124–125
Peanut Butter Chocolate Bars,
139
Peanut Butter Cookies,
124–125
peanuts, 265
Caramel Popcorn, 204–205
Peanut Butter Cookies,
124–125
Pear Tart, 115
pears
Chocolate-Dipped Fruit, 160
Fall Fruit Crisp, 152–153

Pear Tart, 115
Poached Pears, 149
Pecan Crust, 223
Pumpkin Pie, 112–113
pecans, 265
Apple Crumble, 141
Apple Pecan Muffins, 44–45
Baked Apples, 148
Baklava, 172
Bananas Foster, 151
Caramelized Pecans, 207
Chocolate Brownies, 132
Cranberry Nut Bread, 65
Fall Fruit Crisp, 152–153
Hearty Spiced Cocoa Muffins,
49
Mexican Wedding Cookies,
122–123
No-Bake Pecan Crust, 226
Pancakes, 71
Pecan Crust, 223
Pumpkin Pie, 112–113
Rugelach, 170–171
Stuffed Dates, 159
Waffles I, 72–73
pesticide contamination, 103
phyllo dough, 161, 162–163, 266
Baklava, 172
Chocolate Cherry Strudel, 164
pies, 101
Apple Pie, 108–109
Blueberry Pie, 107
Cherry Pie, 111
No-Bake Chocolate Peanut
Butter Pie, 106
No-Bake Strawberry Pie
with Chocolate Chunks,
102–103
Peach Pie, 110
Pumpkin Pie, 112–113
Pine Nut Anise Cookies, 126
pineapple and pineapple juice
Chocolate-Dipped Fruit, 160
Coconut Pudding, 196
Party Punch, 240
Pineapple Walnut Bars, 140
Tropical Smoothie, 219
Pineapple Walnut Bars, 140
pistachios
Applesauce, 156
Baklava, 172
Poached Pears, 149

polenta, 47. *See also* corn and corn products
Polish Bread, 188–189
Pomegranate Sauce, 249
popcorn, in Caramel Popcorn, 204–205
porridge, 129
pralines, 207
preserves. *See* jams and jellies
puddings and mousses, 191
 Baked Pumpkin Pudding, 202
 Bread Pudding, 200
 Butterscotch Pudding, 195
 Chocolate Bread Pudding, 201
 Chocolate Mousse, 192–193
 Chocolate Pudding, 196
 Coconut Pudding, 196
 Rice Pudding, 198–199
Pumpkin Cheesecake, 100
Pumpkin Pie, 112–113
pumpkin puree
 Baked Pumpkin Pudding, 202
 Pumpkin Cheesecake, 100
 Pumpkin Pie, 112–113
 Pumpkin Spice Bread, 68–69
pumpkin seeds, in Drop Biscuits, 52
Pumpkin Spice Bread, 68–69
punches, 240

R
raisins
 Apple Cake, 78
 Apple Pecan Muffins, 46
 Baked Apples, 148
 Bread Pudding, 200
 Brown Bread, 67
 Cinnamon Rolls, 185–187
 Classic Currant Scones, 54–55
 Dried Fruit and Coconut Candies, 212
 Drop Biscuits, 52
 Fall Fruit Crisp, 152–153
 Fruit Compote, 155
 Gingerbread Scones, 56
 Irish Soda Bread, 66
 Oatmeal Raisin Cookies, 128–129
 Pancakes, 71
 Rice Pudding, 198–199
 Rugelach, 170–171
 Waffles I, 72–73
 Zucchini Bread, 64

raspberries and raspberry products
 Chocolate-Dipped Fruit, 160
 Lemon Bars, 136–137
 Raspberry Oatmeal Bars, 133
 Raspberry Sauce, 248
 Raspberry Sorbet, 215
Raspberry Oatmeal Bars, 133
Raspberry Sauce (Coulis), 215, 248
 Blueberry Cream Cheese Blintzes, 169
 Chocolate Mousse, 192–193
 No-Bake Chocolate Pudding Tart, 114
 Peach Melba, 154
 Poached Pears, 149
rhubarb, in Fall Fruit Crisp, 152–153
rice
 Mango with Sticky Rice, 158
 Mexican Horchata, 233
 Rice Pudding, 198–199
Rice Pudding (*Risgrynsgröt*), 198–199
Risgrynsgröt, 198–199
rosemary, 264
 Drop Biscuits, 52
 Focaccia, 182
 Mediterranean Olive Bread, 62–63
Royal Icing, 250–251
 Gingerbread Cookies, 130
 Sugar Cookies, 127
Rugelach, 170–171
rum
 Bananas Foster, 151
 Holiday Nog, 235
 Wassail, 237

S
saffron, 264
sauces, 241
 Applesauce, 156
 Chocolate Fudge Sauce, 252
 Chocolate Sauce, 252
 Lemon Sauce, 248
 Pomegranate Sauce, 249
 Raspberry Sauce, 248
Sautéed Bananas, 150
 Blueberry Cream Cheese Blintzes, 169
scones, 39
 Chocolate Chip Scones, 53
 Classic Currant Scones, 54–55
 Gingerbread Scones, 56

seed butters, 26
sesame, 264
shakes, 213. *See also* smoothies
 Chocolate Banana Shake, 216–217
 Vanilla Shake, 216
Shortbread Crust, 222
 Fruit Tart, 116
 Pear Tart, 115
smoothies, 213. *See also* shakes
 Berry Smoothie, 218–219
 Date and Almond Butter Smoothie, 220
 Tropical Smoothie, 219
Soft Pretzels, 184
sorbets, 213, 215
 Raspberry Sorbet, 215
 Strawberry Sorbet, 214
sour cream, nondairy, 271
 Rugelach, 170–171
soymilk, 29, 270
spreads. *See also* peanut butter
spices, 263–264. *See also various spices*
spreads. *See also* butter(s); also frostings and glazes; jams and jellies, Chocolate Almond Spread, 257
Sprinkles, in Sugar Cookies, 127
strawberries
 Berry Smoothie, 218–219
 Chocolate-Dipped Fruit, 160
 Fruit Tart, 116
 Lemon Cheesecake, 98–99
 No-Bake Strawberry Pie with Chocolate Chunks, 102–103
 Strawberry Cupcakes, 93
 Strawberry Sorbet, 214
Strawberry Cupcakes, 93
Strawberry Sorbet, 214
Stuffed Dates, 159
Sugar Cookies, 127
sugars and sweeteners, 123, 173–174, 227
sunflower seeds, in Drop Biscuits, 52
syrups, 241

T

tarragon, 264
tarts, 101
    Fruit Tart, 116
    No-Bake Chocolate Pudding
        Tart, 114
    Pear Tart, 115
tea, in Chai Tea, 238
thyme, 264
tofu, 23–24, 254, 266, 271
    Blueberry Orange Bundt Cake,
        88–89
    Chocolate Mousse, 192–193
    Ginger Muffins, 48
    Holiday Nog, 235
    Lemon Bars, 136–137
    No-Bake Chocolate Peanut
        Butter Pie, 106
    No-Bake Chocolate Pudding
        Tart, 114
    Pumpkin Pie, 112–113
    Tofu Whipped Topping, 254
Tofu Whipped Topping, 254
    Baked Pumpkin Pudding, 202
    Banana Crumble, 143
    Blueberry Pie, 107
    Chocolate Pudding, 194
tomatoes, sundried
    Drop Biscuits, 52
    Focaccia, 182
    Mediterranean Olive Bread,
        62–63
Tropical Smoothie, 219
turbinado, 173
turmeric, 264

V

vanilla beans
    Almond or Cashew Milk, 234
    Poached Pears, 149
vanilla cookies, in Chocolate Cherry
    Strudel, 164
Vanilla Cupcakes, 91
Vanilla Shake, 216
VeganEgg, 24
veganism, 9–13, 16–18, 165, 253, 272
vegetable oil, 262
Versunkener Apfelkuchen, 80–81

vinegars, 20–21, 90, 266, 283
    Blueberry Lemon Muffins, 43
    Brown Bread, 67
    Chocolate Cake, 76–77
    Cinnamon Coffee Cake, 90
    Cornbread, 58–59
    Focaccia, 182
    Gingerbread Scones, 56
    Irish Soda Bread, 66
    Strawberry Cupcakes, 93
    Zucchini Bread, 64

W

Waffles I, 72–73
Waffles II, 74
walnuts, 265
    Apple Cake, 78
    Apple Crumble, 141
    Baked Apples, 148
    Baklava, 172
    Banana Chocolate Chip Muf-
        fins, 42
    Bananas Foster, 151
    Brown Sugar Syrup, 257
    Carrot Cake, 82
    Chocolate Brownies, 132
    Cinnamon Coffee Cake, 90
    Cinnamon Rolls, 185–187
    Cranberry Nut Bread, 65
    Dried Fruit and Coconut Can-
        dies, 212
    Fall Fruit Crisp, 152–153
    Fig Date Bread, 70
    Hearty Spiced Cocoa Muffins,
        49
    Jam-Filled Oat Bran Muffins,
        50–51
    Mediterranean Olive Bread,
        62–63
    Mexican Wedding Cookies,
        122–123
    Pancakes, 71
    Pineapple Walnut Bars, 140
    Pumpkin Spice Bread, 68–69
    Rugelach, 170–171
    Waffles I, 72–73
    Zucchini Bread, 64
Wassail, 237

watercress, in Drop Biscuits, 52
wheat bran, 51
    Apple Pecan Muffins, 46
whiskey, in Holiday Nog, 235
Whole Wheat Bread, 179–181
wine
    Baked Apples, 148
    Poached Pears, 149
    Wassail, 237

Y

yeast, 175–177, 183
yogurt, nondairy, 271
    Leavened North Indian Bread,
        178

Z

zest, 266
Zucchini Bread, 64

Index II: Seasonal

I encourage people to eat seasonally, locally, and organically as much as possible. When we eat seasonally, we're eating the foods that are supposed to be consumed that time of year. This index is meant to be a guide—not a rigid index written in stone. Some of the desserts listed don't necessarily contain seasonally-grown ingredients as much as they simply correspond to certain seasons, such as a cup of Hot Chocolate in the winter and a cold glass of Mexican Horchata in the summer.

WINTER
Apple Cake, 78
Apple Cobbler, 144
Apple Pie, 108–109
Apple Strudel (*Apfelstrudel*), 162–163
Applesauce, 156
Baked Pumpkin Pudding, 202
Baklava, 172
Banana Crumble, 143
Caramel Popcorn, 204–205
Caramelized Pecans (*Pralines*), 207
Chai Tea, 238
Chocolate Almond Brittle, 208
Chocolate Cake, 76–77
Chocolate Chip Mint Cookies, 120
Chocolate Chip Scones, 53
Chocolate Crinkles, 131
Chocolate-Dipped Fruit, 160
Chocolate Fudge Sauce, 252
Chocolate Sauce, 252
Cinnamon Coffee Cake, 90
Date and Almond Butter Smoothie, 220
Date Bars, 138
Dried Fruit and Coconut Candies, 212
Fall Fruit Crisp, 152–153
German Apple Cake (*Versunkener Apfelkuchen*), 80–81
Ginger Tea, 239
Gingerbread Cookies, 130
Gingerbread Scones, 56
Hearty Spiced Cocoa Muffins, 49
Holiday Nog, 235
Hot Chocolate, 231
Hot Cocoa, 230
Mediterranean Olive Bread, 62–63
Mexican Wedding Cookies, 122–123
Mulled Cider, 236

Panforte, 210–211
Poached Pears, 149
Pomegranate Sauce, 249
Pumpkin Spice Bread, 68–69
Rice Pudding (*Risgrynsgröt*), 198–199
Rugelach, 170–171
Soft Pretzels, 184
Sugar Cookies, 127
Wassail, 237

SPRING
Berry Smoothie, 218–219
Blueberry Cake, 83
Blueberry Cobbler, 146–147
Blueberry Cream Cheese Blintzes, 169
Blueberry Orange Bundt Cake, 88–89
Bran Muffins with Raisins, 46
Chocolate Fudge, 206
Dessert Crêpes, 166–167
Lemon Bars, 136–137
Lemon Sauce, 248
Light Lemon Bundt Cake, 86
Oatmeal Raisin Cookies, 128–129
Raspberry Sorbet, 215
Strawberry Cupcakes, 93
Strawberry Sorbet, 214
Sugar Cookies, 127
Tropical Smoothie, 219
Vanilla Cupcakes, 91

SUMMER

Berry Smoothie, 218–219
Blueberry Cake, 83
Blueberry Lemon Muffins, 43
Blueberry Orange Bundt Cake, 88–89
Chocolate Banana Shake, 216–217
Chocolate Chip Cookies, 118–119
Chocolate-Dipped Fruit, 160
Chocolate Fudge Sauce, 252
Chocolate Mousse, 192–193
Chocolate Pudding, 194
Corn Muffins, 47
Cornbread, 58–59
Lemon Bars, 136–137
Lemon Sauce, 248
Light Lemon Bundt Cake, 86
Mexican Horchata, 233
No-Bake Chocolate Peanut Butter Pie, 106
No-Bake Chocolate Pudding Tart, 114
No-Bake Strawberry Pie with Chocolate Chunks, 102–103
Pineapple Walnut Bars, 140
Raspberry Sauce (Coulis), 248
Raspberry Sorbet, 215
Sautéed Bananas, 150
Strawberry Cupcakes, 93
Strawberry Sorbet, 214
Tofu Whipped Topping, 254
Tropical Smoothie, 219
Vanilla Shake, 216

FALL

Apple Cake, 78
Apple Cobbler, 144
Apple Pecan Muffins, 44–45
Apple Pie, 108–109
Apple Strudel (Apfelstrudel), 162–163
Applesauce, 156
Baked Pumpkin Pudding, 202
Baklava, 172
Banana Chocolate Chip Muffins, 42
Banana Crumble, 143
Carrot Cake, 82
Chai Tea, 238
Chocolate Chip Scones, 53
Cinnamon Coffee Cake, 90
Date and Almond Butter Smoothie, 220
Date Bars, 138
Fall Fruit Crisp, 152–153
Fruit Compote, 155
German Apple Cake (Versunkener Apfelkuchen), 80–81
Gingerbread Cookies, 130
Gingerbread Scones, 56
Hot Chocolate, 231
Hot Cocoa, 230
Jam-Filled Oat Bran Muffins, 50–51
Mediterranean Olive Bread, 62–63
Mulled Cider, 236
No-Bake Pecan Crust, 226
Oatmeal Raisin Cookies, 128–129
Pecan Crust, 223
Pine Nut Anise Cookies, 126
Poached Pears, 149
Pomegranate Sauce, 249
Pumpkin Pie, 112–113
Pumpkin Spice Bread, 68–69
Rice Pudding (Risgrynsgröt), 198–199
Sugar Cookies, 127
Wassail, 237
Whole Wheat Bread, 179–181

Index III: Celebrations and Occasions

Sometimes we need occasion-specific recipes to celebrate an event or to simply entertain a group of friends or colleagues. Here are a few suggestions for some popular celebrations and holidays.

HOLIDAYS
Apple Cake, 78
Apple Strudel (*Apfelstrudel*), 162–163
Baked Apples, 148
Baklava, 172
Caramel Popcorn, 204–205
Caramelized Pecans (*Pralines*), 207
Chai Tea, 238
Chocolate Cherry Strudel (*Black Forest Strudel*), 164
Chocolate Crinkles, 131
Chocolate Fudge, 206
Chocolate Peanut Butter Cupcakes, 96
Dried Fruit and Coconut Candies, 212
Fall Fruit Crisp, 152–153
Gingerbread Cookies, 130
Gingerbread Scones, 56
Holiday Nog, 235
Hot Chocolate, 231
Hot Cocoa, 230
Mexican Hot Chocolate, 231–232
Mexican Wedding Cookies, 122–123
Mulled Cider, 236
Panforte, 210–211
Pine Nut Anise Cookies, 126
Poached Pears, 149
Pumpkin Cheesecake, 100
Pumpkin Pie, 112–113
Pumpkin Spice Bread, 68–69
Rice Pudding (*Risgrynsgröt*), 198–199
Rugelach, 170–171
Sugar Cookies, 127
Wassail, 237

BREAKFAST AND BRUNCH
Berry Smoothie, 218–219
Blueberry Cream Cheese Blintzes, 169
Chai Tea, 238
Chocolate Chip Scones, 53
Classic Currant Scones, 54–55
Dessert Crêpes, 166–167

Ginger Tea, 239
Gingerbread Scones, 56
Pancakes, 71
Tropical Smoothie, 219
Waffles, 72–74

TEA PARTY
Blueberry Cake, 83
Blueberry Orange Bundt Cake, 88–89
Chai Tea, 238
Chocolate Chip Scones, 53
Classic Currant Scones, 54–55
Crêpes Suzette, 168
Gingerbread Scones, 56
Lemon Bars, 136–137
Light Lemon Bundt Cake, 86
Mexican Wedding Cookies, 122–123
Pine Nut Anise Cookies, 126
Raspberry Sorbet, 215
Strawberry Sorbet, 214

CHILDREN'S BIRTHDAY PARTY
Berry Smoothie, 218–219
Chocolate Brownies, 132
Chocolate Cake, 76–77
Chocolate Cream Cheese Cupcakes, 92
Chocolate Fudge, 206
Party Punch, 240
Raspberry Sorbet, 215
Strawberry Cupcakes, 93
Strawberry Sorbet, 214
Vanilla Cupcakes, 91
Vanilla Shake, 216

Acknowledgments

I am so blessed to be surrounded by the most remarkable people on the planet and am grateful to call them my friends, my teachers, my colleagues, and my family. Even if you do not appear here, you are held deep within my heart.

First, I want to thank Kristen Miles, without whose recommendation I would not have been asked to write this book; Wendy Gardner, who tenaciously championed this book; and Michele Simon and Patti Breitman, who guided me throughout the process. Thank you to Cara Connors, William Kiester, Karen Levy, and especially Amanda Waddell at Fair Winds Press, whose input and edits made this a better book than it otherwise would have been.

I'm very grateful to my numerous recipe testers, who so enthusiastically tested recipes in their own kitchens and who so generously provided feedback and suggestions, especially Stephanie Arthur, Christine Cervanek, Shad Clark, Mary Conway, Elizabeth Ferrari, Kathy Gamez, Toni Ann Gestone, Mary Jane Goudreau, Kristi Jackson, John Keathley, Diane Kesty, JoAnn Klassen, Stephen Kling, Connie Leonard, Sharon Lew, Randy Lind, Chris Marco, Bylle Manss, Preeti Mehta, Danielle Puller, Monica Sather, Lauren Schneider, Allison Schwarz, Kristin Schwarz, Kenda Swartz, Mike Stickel, Marybeth Strack, Michael Sugarman, Leigh Wall, and Tami Wall.

Of course, I'm also thankful to everyone who tasted the concoctions I created—not that I ever had to twist anyone's arm! Next to my husband's coworkers, my friend and neighbor Abby Kaster was always there to lend a taste bud or two—along with helpful feedback. And she always came through when I needed to borrow ingredients.

There are so many people who provided moral support through the process of writing this book, including Mom and Dad (aka Arlene and John Patrick), who live too far away to enjoy the sugar love but who constantly sent their best wishes from thousands of miles away. The same can be said of my wonderful in-laws Mary Jane and Paul Goudreau, who provide never-ending support. To Kenda,

Tim, Susie, Kristie, Brighde, Jackie, Cherie, Melanie, Lori, Cathleen, Sky, and Amanda. I can't imagine better friends or brighter beings than the lot of you. A special thank you to my friend and mentor, Diane Miller, an angel to countless souls.

I'm so grateful for the generosity of those who give their time, talents, and resources to make my work possible:

Michelle Cehn and Raitis Stalazs for their incredible love and support; Lori Patotzka and Pam Webb for the cooking class prep and assistance they provided when I was writing this book in 2007; Michele Simon for her wisdom; Mark Hawthorne and Lauren Ornelas for their friendship and tireless devotion to animals; and Danielle Puller for her endless support.

I also want to acknowledge every one of my readers, followers, supporters, and podcast listeners. Their openness and willingness to learn give me reason to hope every day. Thank you for letting me be part of your own journey.

To all the animals of the world, particularly the anonymous victims of our appetites: you are our teachers. We just don't know it yet. Though you are hidden, you will not be forgotten. Though you are nameless, you will be spoken for. Though you are caged and tethered, you will one day be free. That is my promise to you.

In the original edition of *The Joy of Vegan Baking*, I mentioned "my boys," Simon and Schuster—the loveliest, liveliest feline kids a human mother could have. Their vibrancy filled me with joy while they were here. When I lost them, my heart couldn't wait to adopt more kitties into my life, and so now my new beans Charlie and Michiko are daily reminders of the innocent and exquisite nature of non-human animals. I'm so grateful for their presence in my life.

Finally, none of my work would even be possible without the unyielding support of the man I'm blessed to call my best friend and husband, David Goudreau. The world is a better place and I am a better person because of him. His immense patience, kindness, generosity, and love never cease to amaze me, and there is no one with whom I laugh more. *Il mio sol pensier sei tu.*

About the Author

A recognized expert and thought leader on the culinary, social, ethical, and practical aspects of living vegan, Colleen Patrick-Goudreau is an award-winning author of seven books, including the bestselling *The Joy of Vegan Baking, The Vegan Table, Color Me Vegan, Vegan's Daily Companion, On Being Vegan, and The 30-Day Vegan Challenge*. She is an acclaimed speaker and beloved host of the inspiring podcast, *Food for Thought*, which has been voted Favorite Podcast by *VegNews* magazine readers for several years.

Colleen shares her message of compassion and wellness on national and regional television programs, including those broadcast on the Food Network, CBS, PBS, and FOX. Interviews with her have been featured on National Public Radio, The Huffington Post, U.S. News and World Report, and her recipes have been featured on Epicurious.com and Oprah.com. Colleen is a regular contributor to National Public Radio. In her downtime, she can be found obsessively watching films with her husband, running, tending to her organic garden, and cuddling with her cats.

www.colleenpatrickgoudreau.com